Praise for Jean Beauvoir

"I first met Jean Beauvoir in an elevator while I was moving into my first photo studio in New York City, in 1983. With his big smile and great laugh, he welcomed me to the building. We quickly became great friends. A rock star and a rock photographer living in the same building—how lucky is that? I was at the beginning of my career, shooting for *Circus* magazine, and Jean was an accomplished and incredibly talented musician. We began working together, and our friendship grew stronger. Jean welcomed my vision, and I learned from his creativity. He's one of those guys that has an idea and goes the distance with it, never looking back. I cherish our time and our work together—and most of all, our friendship."

—Mark (WEISSGUY) Weiss, photographer

"We—me, Jean, Grace Jones, and artists like Ava Cherry—traveled in the same circles. We stood out. We were Black, children of the night, dressed for onstage, offstage. A spiked-head, chap-wearing ex-Labelle, a drop-dead gorgeous Black man with a huge blond Mohawk, an androgynous Black club diva, and a David Bowie wild child walk into the room, and . . . Jean stood out even in that group! Writing and collaborating on songs with Jean was a musical adventure, creating strong melodies over power pop rock, with thumping bass and blazing guitars!"

—Nona Hendryx, vocalist, producer, actress,
and author, originally from Labelle

"I have known Jean for thirty years now, and he's truly one of the coolest guys I know. Such a great friend, talented musician, and amazing family man—and he keeps getting better!"

—Marcus Schenkenberg, fashion model,
actor, singer, and TV personality

"Jean Beauvoir is the most complete rock star that I ever saw. He's got the talent, the voice, the looks, and the charisma that make him a true and unique rock star icon!"

—Uwe Fahrenkrog-Petersen, producer, composer
and keyboardist for NENA, and TV personality

Diary of a Black Punk Icon

JEAN BEAUVOIR

WITH JOHN OSTROSKY

First edition
Published by Chicago Review Press Incorporated
814 North Franklin Street
Chicago, Illinois 60610
ISBN 978-1-64160-476-5

Library of Congress Control Number: 2021951474

Interior design: Nord Compo

Printed in the United States of America
5 4 3 2 1

In loving memory of my dad, Raoul Beauvoir, and my dear mom, Eddie Beauvoir . . .
Rest in peace, Maman and Papa, I know you're watching me and that your spirits live on . . .

To my amazing family for all their love and support through this roller coaster of a ride . . .

And to all my fans and those who have followed me, appreciated me, respected me, and given me their love . . .

I love you all!

CONTENTS

FOREWORD

I'M KERMIT BLACKWOOD, ghostwriter, lyricist, director, producer, and screenwriter. In 1982, when I was about fourteen years old, I was "discovered" by a professional photographer at Fashion Island in Corona del Mar, California. This led to a few high-profile modeling gigs where I met Robert Gooden Jones, a longtime public relations executive for Motown records.

Bob Jones was more than a public relations master, he was a cultural historian and an "influencer" before the term became synonymous with social media. He was instrumental in not only signing Denise "D.D." Matthews (aka Vanity) to Motown, effectively ending her Prince sidekick era, but also helping her transition from a cutting-edge Motown recording artist to action movie star.

Bob had also been collaborating with Michael Jackson since the superstar was an adolescent. He worked for decades as his primary publicist, and Bob introduced us early on. Michael's cerebral interests in life, separate from entertainment, were not unlike my own, and we jibed from the first day, discussing creativity with pencil on paper. Michael and I shared a common birthday, exactly ten years apart, and we were both avid nature lovers with ever-growing menageries of unusual animals. Michael and I visited zoos and exotic animal breeders throughout southern California. The two of us geeked out on knowledge mostly, and talked about ideas and great artists, masterpieces and icons.

That's how Jean Beauvoir rolled into focus. Beauvoir's "Feel the Heat" video, directed by Mary Lambert—who had also lensed Janet Jackson's "Control" and "Nasty," as well as videos by Sheila E., Madonna, Eurythmics, and Sting—was more than impactful. It pushed the envelope on what was possible for a Black recording artist. Beauvoir broke the mold and kept on pirouetting, axe in hand.

"He's legend!"

That's how Michael described the platinum-mohawked nonconformist burning up the screen during video promotions of Sylvester Stallone's blockbuster, *Cobra*. This genre defying music video was in heavy rotation on MTV back in 1986, and we were so jazzed with Jean's appearance in the video—that perfect mohawk and his power and presence were truly unique. Michael and I must have watched that video twenty times in a row.

It was maddening how mysterious Beauvoir was on the record cover. He wasn't exposing much about himself, and he was an enigma. I think *Drums Along the Mohawk* inspired Michael's "Speed Demon" on *Bad*. There's nothing random about Jackson's apparel on the album cover album either. I'm certain that's a belt Jean wore during his Plasmatics days.

When producer, songwriter, and multi-instrumentalist Bill Bottrell became Michael's primary collaborative partner, it is my understanding that he first floated the idea of the involvement of Jean Beauvoir on Jackson's edgy *Dangerous* album. Bob was also confident that I needed to work with Beauvoir. That was frightening. While I had tremendous respect for Michael Jackson and Prince, they weren't as significant to my creative psyche as Jean Beauvoir had become. He had eclipsed all my idols.

Bob explained to me how Jean had accomplished what Dez Dickerson, Jesse Johnson, and any number of other Prince disciples had failed at. He was not derivative. Jean Beauvoir was, as Prince opined, "on point."

For his *Dangerous* album, Michael wanted to finally enter and dominate the big rock arena. Michael was eager to have Beauvoir join his *Dangerous* promotion junket and basically utilize Jean to Trojan-horse himself into the notoriety sweepstakes necessary for his ascension into the ranks of Mötley Crüe and Guns N' Roses, who were his consistent rivals for rock chart dominance.

Michael knew he could climb still higher in his trajectory if he channeled energies from the right musicians, especially those with their own fan base. He wanted to be associated with Jean's imminent arrival as the ultimate rock deity, and Michael believed Beauvoir would become "as big as Hendrix" after the *Dangerous* tour wrapped up.

I'd just been interviewed on a BET show in Washington, D.C., when I learned that Bob's handler for me, Gordon, had arranged a meeting with Beauvoir, who was recording his Voodoo X *Awakening* opus in a studio in New York City. We were to discuss a possible musical collaboration. I was beyond nervous, but I needn't have been. Jean was working on some guitar lines, and he had that quiet calmness that Michael had in the studio: painters at their canvas, never showboating, no wasting of energy—nothing to prove. He was more imposing in person than I had imagined he would be. He was astonishing to behold, and such was his creativity. He was living his art in its entirety.

I have learned over the years that the authentic stars are generally authentically inclusive, unassuming, and humble. Yeah, real stars are often the nicest ones. They don't seek validation, nor do they look down on anyone. Beauvoir is that kind of guy. We vibed immediately and became fast friends.

Michael was always curious about Jean, and I guess he wanted to know what made him tick. I had a most surreal experience at Winchell's Donuts at 4:00 AM back in 1993. As usual, we were in Mike's Town Car, and we cruised by LA Sound, circling around, waiting for his purported archenemy, Prince, who was recording there. Once he joined us, we ended up at Winchell's in West L.A.

More than once, I recall Jean Beauvoir being a topic of discussion between Michael and Prince. They were basically taunting one another as to who would land Beauvoir in his camp first. We were also discussing Wes Craven's movie, *Shocker*, and Jean's track on the soundtrack. I heard myself asking, a bit too incredulously, why it was that there wasn't a video and promotion elevating Beauvoir? What was going on in his career?

I learned a lot about the politics of the music business and, as usual, a history lesson in Black musicians, managers, lawyers and R&D. I also came to appreciate how significant style is in Black music, and why artists with authentically unique images and sound are pivotal in the progress of civil rights. Pop music mirrors that advancement, but Beauvoir wasn't doing pop music. He was a nonconformist of unparalleled stature if the industry would support his genius.

Both Mike and Prince recognized Beauvoir's fire and decided they needed it to support their respective junkets. Their willful indifference struck me as conceit. Just as they were hypercritical of each other's image and styling, both wanted to be Beauvoir's new stylist.

Michael felt Jean's signature mohawk was perfect in the "Feel the Heat" video, and he put it on guitarist Jennifer Batten during the *Dangerous* tour. Prince wanted Beauvoir to be the sex symbol, and he would make him look so good, the audience would be fainting.

Bob explained to me how big stars operate. Michael and Prince both wanted Jean's iconic rise to support their own brand, Michael boasting about how his machine would "weaponize Beauvoir" in order "to dominate the arena crowd." Apparently, Jean wasn't into it. That was a great deal of money and free publicity to turn down on principle.

This taught me to respect Jean's sense of self and purpose—his confidence in his own vision was reaffirming. Michael was incensed with Jean's rejection. In fact, it was one of the first fits of his temper I ever witnessed.

Someone quipped recently, when asked why Beauvoir declined contributing his genius to Michael's *Dangerous* or *Bad* era offerings, "Name Michael Jackson's bass player."

I tried hard to think of one. I could think of a number of key session players, but not one bassist immediately came to mind.

"Exactly," they said.

Now, with the passing of those iconic luminaries of everything we hold sacred in popular music, I know that Jean Beauvoir will finally attain the level of appreciation that he is due. Not because he is similar to them or was in the wings ready to replace them either. It's just an unfortunate fact that nobody out front in the business lives their art in its entirety anymore.

That's why the very existence of the musical icon, Jean Beauvoir, would inspire me to continue my journey through three decades of oscillating fortunes in the entertainment industry, and I consider my eventful collaboration with Jean Beauvoir one of my greatest accomplishments.

That guy never fails to amaze.

1

GROWING UP

By the time I was fifteen my dad realized I was serious about my music. He was hot and cold, and he couldn't decide if he was proud that I had my own business performing and traveling around the country, or if I was headed down the wrong path of becoming a bum musician.

My father only believed in professional careers like doctor, lawyer, or engineer. Although he truly loved music, he knew of no Haitian who had ever succeeded in the business, and he wasn't confident that I would be the first to do so. He came into my room one day and gave me an ultimatum—either all the music stops, or I leave the house and he'd never want to see me again.

Being the young rebel that I was, I left. My mom stood crying at the door as she watched me leave. I moved into my friend's garage at first, where he set up a little bed for me in the loft. His folks never knew. That was a bad day.

My parents grew up in Haiti. My father was the grandson of a Haitian president, Florville Gelan Hippolyte, and my mother was the daughter of the Haitian ambassador to France as well as the granddaughter of another Haitian president, Franck Sylvain. My father's side practiced Voodoo, and they loved to mix the raw, deep Haitian culture with intellectuality.

My father was a great singer, and he played the accordion well. He had exquisite taste in music, and he had a powerful Marantz stereo system in the living room where he'd blast everything from Isaac Stern to Haitian compas to Joan Baez, Led Zeppelin, ABBA, James Brown, Janis Joplin, Aretha Franklin, and the Beatles. He loved to discover new groups, and I realize now how right on he was about who really mattered. All of these artists have stood the test of time and are now, all these years later, regarded as some of the most important artists of our time.

Although they were both from Haiti, my parents first met in Paris before moving to Chicago, Illinois. After getting married, their plan was that my mom would work two jobs around the clock, even while raising children, to put my father through engineering school, and that would set up their future.

She did just that. Soon, she found herself pregnant with my older brother, Pierre-Marie. A second son, Eddie, was born just two years later, but he unfortunately died at birth. The next child would be me, Jean-Marie Beauvoir, "the rambunctious one," who would climb on every shelf and do everything he was told not to do.

Two years later, my sister, Marie-Louise Beauvoir, was born. She was a little bit more docile and better at following instructions, focusing on school, and keeping her dad happy.

I barely remember anything about Chicago, but my fear of birds originated from there! My mom shared this story with me: "It was a cool, breezy Chicago morning. You were sleeping peacefully in your crib, and I heard a curdling scream. I rushed into the room and saw a pigeon hovering over you, flapping his wings.

"To you, it must have seemed like a monstrous creature. I quickly shooed the bird away and told you, 'It's OK, Jean-Jean, it's just a pigeon—nothing to worry about.'"

It took her a while to calm me down, but those few seconds stayed with me. Anytime we'd walk down the street, if I saw pigeons—or any other bird, for that matter—I'd want to quickly cross or I would freak out. It didn't matter if it was a few or an entire flock. It was mainly the sound and the appearance of their wings that gave me an everlasting fear of birds, up until this day.

Another thing that stayed with me for the rest of my life was a scar from a horrible injury. While cooking one night, my mom had a large skillet filled with sizzling oil atop the stove. The handle must have been facing outwards, as I reached up in curiosity, jarring the pan and causing it to fall on me. The oil covered my entire lower back, and from what my mom told me, I was screaming bloody murder as the ambulance was racing to our home.

I had a strange yet interesting childhood. I would spend part of my summers in Haiti and the other part in France. When in Haiti, I would stay with my uncle, Max Beauvoir, who was my father's brother and a Voodoo priest! He was hailed the supreme chief of Voodoo, the highest title, by the *New York Times* but was, at first, a biochemist. He traveled the world giving speeches and consulted for presidents and other high-powered political figures. He was credited with convincing US President Bill Clinton not to attack Haiti.

Uncle Max was the subject of Wade Davis's bestselling book, *The Serpent and the Rainbow*, and was represented in horror great Wes Craven's Hollywood blockbuster of the same name. When he passed away in 2015, the press credited him with being the founder of the worldwide zombie movement, and the *Daily Mail* in the UK stated that he "proved" that zombies were real.

He had a really funny parrot named Jacko. My sister and I would play chess and checkers in the yard, and Jacko would constantly come and steal the pieces. This bird had a special personality and kept us entertained. His wings were clipped, so he didn't scare me as other birds did. He couldn't get too far, which made it fun to chase him around trying to catch him.

My uncle would have periodic Voodoo ceremonies, and sometimes they would take place while I was there. It was exciting to participate, playing Voodoo drums and dancing while chicken heads were bitten off, goats were sacrificed, and people were being possessed. All kinds of extraordinary things were happening, and for a young kid, it was quite a wild experience.

I also spent time with my grandfather on my mother's side in a small town called Fermathe. It was situated way up in the mountains, and it would sometimes be engulfed in clouds. My grandfather was very strict, as he was a diplomat and the ambassador to France. I loved going up to Fermathe, where I'd meet up with friends and we'd explore, walking through the mountains in search of horses to ride. We'd find horses, usually scruffy old ones, that seemed like strays but were always owned by nearby farmers. We could literally just grab two or three, keep them for a few days, and bring them back. If we found the farmers, we'd give them a few dollars, or they'd just show up at the house to collect the horses. Everyone knew who they belonged to and somehow who took them. Nobody ever worried they'd be stolen.

One of my favorite things to eat while there was *mayi boukannen*, which is a kind of a grilled corn. I'd gather corn in the cornfields, and one of the neighbors would gladly put it on their grill for me, preparing it Haitian-style. It was delicious.

My aunt, Dominique, the daughter of my grandfather by a later marriage, was only a few years older than I was, and her sister, Marie Ange, was just a little bit older. I hung around with Dominique, and we'd go to a local dance clubhouse. It was a little room outside a house with a small DJ booth and held perhaps twenty people.

My grandfather would often be difficult about us going out, and I can remember what an ordeal it was to ask him if we could go to a movie or to the clubhouse. We'd go up to his office, and he would just sit there—a statuesque man, very light skinned, and well over six feet tall—with his glasses on, looking down at his desk.

We'd say, "Grandpère, can we go to a movie tonight?"

He wouldn't look up, and he would say nothing. Sometimes we waited for five minutes, and he would finally just say "Non" or "Oui."

If he would say "Non," we would just turn around, go back downstairs, and mind our business. If he would say "Oui," we would be ecstatic.

There were two sisters who lived down the mountain, and I can still remember their names—Kakin and Tboom. They were cute, and I had a crush on Kakin, so I'd do everything to show off when I was with them.

We'd spend a lot of time combing the hills, going into town together, and messing about. One day, we found ourselves at an abandoned house. I can remember walking in when, all of a sudden, a shitload of bats started flying all around us.

I almost lost my mind! It was the freakiest thing, and my fear of birds did not help. I remember trying to maintain my composure, bluffing that I wasn't scared, but I just wanted to get the hell out of there. Being the little gentleman that I was, I felt obligated to at least give the girls the perception of protecting them, so I pushed them out first but shadowed them within inches. It was a time I will never forget.

After Haiti, I'd go to Paris, France, for another portion of the summer. There, I would stay with my my mother's sister, Tante Raymonde, and her husband, Amadou-Mahtar M'Bow, and sometimes their three children, Farah, Mariami, and Ava. My uncle was an educator and diplomat well known around the world, having begun his career with UNESCO in 1953. In 1974 he became the organization's director-general—and consequently the first Black African to lead a UN agency—a post he would hold until 1987. My aunt, Tante Raymonde, was always by his side, supporting him all the way.

My uncle, like my grandfather, was a strict disciplinarian. When we'd eat dinner, you weren't allowed to speak at the table, proper table manners would be enforced, among other things. We'd at times accompany him by limousine and watch him speak at conferences. This upbringing on my mother's side was very different from that of my father's.

I enjoyed Paris, though, and one of the things I did every morning was head to the local bakery, pick up a nice, fresh baguette, bring it home, slather on some of that delicious French butter, and dip it in some good hot chocolate. Paris was a beautiful city to spend time in, and I did have the opportunity to visit other relatives living there, such as my aunt Mathilda Beauvoir, one of my father's thirteen sisters, who's also a Voodoo priestess. She's lived in Paris for many years and at one point resided in one of Napoleon's homes whose interior was painted by Salvador Dalí. She has consulted for high-level political figures as well. A very eccentric and colorful woman who started as a singer and dancer in Paris, she ran a popular nightclub in the area of Pigalle called Le Vaudou for several years. She had a huge Great Dane named Manfred, who would go everywhere with her. I adored him, and he was probably bigger than I was at the time. We were once driving to her club when I remember her stopping at a small country house, getting out of the car ever so casually, sacrificing a goat, then hopping back in the car and we were on our way. I believe she said something like, "It was for the spirits, *mon amour.*"

After my father finished engineering school, I was about four or five years old, my parents were then off to Providence, Rhode Island, for a couple of years before we moved to Queens, New York.

In Queens we were fish out of water. I spent an awful lot of time fighting, trying to hold on to my lunch money on the way to school.

Haitians are quite different from African Americans, and the fact that we spoke French and Creole and had names like Jean-Marie and Pierre-Marie caused conflict. My father spoke Spanish as well, and my parents were adamant about us not losing our first language, French, so we were not allowed to speak any English in the house, ever!

I was thankful for that later on, as I remained fluent in French. The exposure I had growing up to all these different cultures, languages, and environments helped form my identity and prepared me for situations that would come up later in life, which I could not have imagined at the time. It enabled me to travel and comfortably navigate life in different countries as a traveling recording artist. It taught me to adapt to different cultures, pick up languages on the fly, travel in different circles, and be in my element whether in the woods of Haiti eating a goat hanging from a tree or dining with royalty or high-level political figures.

One thing that sticks out in my mind, however, was that when I started to learn English, it took me a long time to be able to pronounce the word *the*. There was a certain positioning of the tongue that you don't use the same way in French. Of course, the kids in class took every opportunity to tease me about it. After relentless practice, one day, I finally got the gist of it.

My time living in Queens ironically ended up being one of my most creative periods in terms of music discovery. I remember we had a finished basement where I would run down and sing to music all the time. There was a table and chair set that I'd stand on and a turntable down there where I mostly, if not exclusively, played 45s introduced to me once again by my father, such as "Take a Letter Maria," "Sylvia's Mother," Jackson 5, Three Dog Night, "Ride Captain Ride," and other favorites.

I was already into creating my own shows as a frontman, singing to these songs using a broomstick as a microphone, over and over again, probably twenty to thirty times in a row, until I knew them like the back of my hand. I guess I already knew then what I wanted to be.

At one point, my father being fully aware of the incompatibity, vowed to build a house as far out on Long Island as possible. And indeed, he did! One day, he came home and told us that we were taking a trip to see the lot for our new home. It was off exit 60 on the Long Island Expressway, the last exit constructed at the time. It was suburbia to the max and nothing but woods, lakes, and little corner log shops—very different from Queens.

We went out there pretty much every other weekend to watch the progress until construction was completed and we moved in. It was in a middle-class neighborhood with not one African, Haitian, Jamaican, or any other kind of Black person to be seen for miles!

It was wise of my dad to move us out of Queens and to insist on our speaking French, as my cousins who lived nearby remained there and never learned French. One of them, a cute, sweet and innocent little boy, ended up in gangs, shootings, and ultimately in jail.

We'd visit one of my aunts back in Chicago every so often. She was pretty tough when it came to discipline, and she was a true believer that kids should be seen and not heard. I was quite unruly, to be honest—running, climbing, and not sitting still for a second. One day, she got upset, took me by the arm, and threw me in a closet under the stairs. It had a very low slanted ceiling and another entrance on the other side. The other door was slightly open, and you could see the light seeping through.

She told me to sit down and not to move until she came to get me because on the other side of that closet, around a little bend, there was a lion, and if I'd go through, he would eat me for sure, and if I made any noise, he'd hear me and maybe decide to come in and eat me.

I sat in that closet, barely breathing with my heart pounding, for a long time until my aunt finally came to get me. From that day on, I'd always have a problem sleeping if I could see that there was a light on anywhere in the vicinity. I'd have to get up and turn it off, or I wouldn't be able to sleep.

My father worked as an engineer for the Port Authority of New York and helped design the World Trade Center. He would leave every day at 6:00 AM, take the Long Island Railroad into the city, and return home at 7:00 PM every night. My mom was hired as the assistant dean at Stony Brook Medical School.

She loved to take me to the mall on special days—like Easter, when this gigantic Easter bunny stood in the center of the mall. I hated that damn thing, as I was very shy when I was young and didn't like to be singled out or have attention drawn to myself. I dreaded going to the mall because I knew, at one point or another, my mom would end up bringing me over there.

So here we were standing in front of that big bunny, and I knew he was going to see me, sooner than later, because I was the only Black kid there. Sure enough, my efforts to hide were futile and I suddenly heard from that freaky microphone, "Hey, little boy." I was praying he wasn't talking to me, but he was. He called out again, "You, over there."

I looked at him shyly, as if to say, "Don't talk to me." But he carried on and started asking questions. I answered as shortly as I could, hoping he'd stop and move to someone else. Eventually, he did! I grabbed my mom's arm, urging that we leave as quickly as possible! I never understood why she insisted on tormenting me like this, holiday after holiday, year after year.

My parents were very strict, and they didn't go for the ways of the neighborhood kids. They really wanted us to get the most out of living on Long Island, without really having too many friends or getting too close to anyone.

I did get beat with a belt. My father had very good quality leather belts, and if I was bad, I would get whipped. It wasn't a pleasant feeling, as you felt it every time it hit your skin. But no matter how many times my dad would beat my ass, it was to no avail. I'd go right back and do the same thing over again the next day. I was a very mischievous boy.

My mom would also use a belt, but only on my hands. She'd decide whatever the punishment would be, perhaps fifty hits—twenty-five on each hand—and she'd let me go choose the belt. I'd make sure to pick a cheap one that had cardboard inside covered by leather. She would start, and I'd fake some oohs and aahs here and there, but in actuality, it didn't really hurt.

That didn't work with my dad.

Being an engineer, he'd have us building something pretty much every weekend. I'd hear my name being yelled at 8:00 AM on a Saturday to go out and either mow the lawn or build a thirty-by-thirty shed. Everything he built was always twice as big as everybody else's—but well done.

He had us build a fence that surrounded the entire property, and the patio we built was almost the size of a basketball court. The crew was my mother, my sister, him, and me laying all the concrete. My brother had already been thrown out of the house by my dad upon graduation and was making his way in the trenches of Vietnam as an army enlistee. My dad would order a cement truck to come and pour the cement, but the rest was up to us.

Another time, he decided we'd change the engine in the car that he used to drive to the train station, a used Chevy Nova. The next thing we knew, there was a hoist in the garage, and we were summoned to work. There was always something going on.

So, one day, I figured I'd surprise him, and I actually spent the whole day building a tree fort—a big one, and really well constructed. I waited till he came home from work and proudly said, "Papa, Papa, come take a look at what I did!"

He looked in the backyard, saw that tree fort, and had a shit fit! He grabbed me and said, "I want to see that thing down in the next ten minutes."

I was like a monkey climbing up that tree, ripping down pieces of wood, trying to take the thing apart. Afterward, he actually made me get down on my knees on the wood filled with nails, for all my neighbors to witness. He beat the living hell out of me, whipping me on both my butt and back. It was one of the most embarrassing situations I ever encountered. That day, my neighbors and my friends saw that my dad truly "meant business." They had sympathy for me.

Nevertheless, I'd come back a few days later and do something else that would piss him off again. For example, I'd break into his room to borrow his sneakers, as he had the whitest Converse sneakers you could ever imagine. I don't know if he cleaned those things every day or what, but he would wear them for a year, and they would not have so much as a speck of dirt on them. I wanted to wear those sneakers in school, and, of course, it only took an hour of me wearing them for them to have smudges all over them.

Of course, my father would find out, and once again, I'd get punished. I'd be crying throughout with slobber running down my face, thinking, "I'm going to kill him. I hate him!" I still had to walk past him to get to my room, which meant the beatings were not technically over yet. I would try to figure out how I was going to maneuver my way past him without getting another ten, for the road, to the back of the head or any other place that his hand or belt happened to reach when he was swinging wildly!

I'd have to speed through, and, finally, I'd end up back in my room. But sometimes, it still wasn't over. He would start talking to my mom about the whole situation, and I could hear every word.

"I can't believe he did that, that vagabond, that vagabond!" he'd say.

He'd speak loud enough so that even though he was downstairs, I could still hear that he was talking about me. Meanwhile, I wondered if the beatings were really over, or if he'd gotten pissed off again from talking to my mom. Sometimes, he'd get louder and louder, and I'd know I was about to get it again. I would sit in my room in fear, listening quietly by the door.

We had good and bad. He'd promise things, build up your hopes, and then take them away. One that stayed with me for a while was, for an entire year, he'd come home every day and tell me about this Univox Les Paul that he'd seen in the window of a music store in the city. I was playing a crappy homemade type of wood guitar, and that Univox was my dream.

Christmas came, and I was sure I'd get that guitar. I actually looked under his bed a week before, and I saw the shape of a guitar, so I knew I had it. When it was my turn to open my presents, I opened the box, and it was an empty guitar case to put my piece of shit in. I thought I was going to die. I was so upset that it stayed with me till this day.

I never knew what he was thinking. He was set in his ways, but in the end, I learned to understand many things he taught me, and I appreciate him for it.

I was in fourth grade when I started school on Long Island, and it was very different. First, the name Jean just didn't fly. It's a French name, and the proper pronunciation is similar to "Sean," but everyone pronounced it "Jeen," which was, without a doubt, a girl's name. The taunting would have been even worse if anyone caught wind of my full name! Second, the kids were shocked since most of them had never seen a Black person up close. I would ride my bike through the neighborhood only to hear kids yelling out, "Wow, it's chocolate man!" I definitely ran across my share of race issues growing up on Long Island.

One story that stuck with me involved my brother, Pierre. We had some friends in the neighborhood, very close friends of my mother. They'd come over to our house all the time and vice versa. This went on for years. At one point, my brother started liking their daughter. Since she was from a pretty conservative family, he thought it best to ask the parents how they felt about him asking her out.

They blew a gasket! They were really upset about it, and it caused huge problems between our families. They would come to our house, hang out, be great friends, and everything was wonderful, but as soon as he asked to even take her out, that was something they could not accept. This was an example of the hypocritical situations that we had to face growing up as Black kids in an all-White neighborhood.

Despite the prejudice, there were great people there who had a lasting effect on my life. My neighbors from across the street, next door, and many others wanted to be my friend. In a short period, I had a group of great friends.

I spent my first years trying to fit in, not wanting to be different, and then I changed my view. Most kids and their parents had such negative opinions of Black people, but it was just perception. I started to feel that it was my turn to show them the good side, and that Blacks weren't all thieves and criminals like they saw in the movies. At that time, I think the only three Black actors that ever played positive roles were Sidney Poitier, Harry Belafonte, and Sammy Davis Jr.

Being Black, my parents forced me to cut my hair, which was not cool, and some of the kids loved to sing this stupid song, "Fuzzy Wuzzy was a bear. Fuzzy Wuzzy had no hair." Ha, ha, ha! Afros were in style then, and me having short hair—and a girl's name, to boot—made things miserable. I would go to the school in the summer, before the semester started every year, to beg the teachers to change my name on the school's records to "John," so I'd avoid being called in the girls' gym instead of the boys'.

I was, of course, very insecure, and I was always trying to prove myself, which sometimes led to mishaps. One, in particular, was when I had five girls living down the street, about half a mile away, who had a built-in pool. They were all pretty, and about a year apart. I'm trying to remember their names—Leslie, Lynn . . . I think they all started with an *L*. I had crushes on at least two of them.

One day, they invited me to come swim in their pool, which in itself was a major coup! It probably took a year or more of knowing them before this invite was extended. Of course, I enthusiastically accepted and went over there ready to do my thing.

Now, I wasn't a very good swimmer at the time, even though my swimming skills improved from being a Boy Scout patrol leader and having to learn how to swim for survival at Boy Scout camps out in the wild. I most definitely could not stay afloat. You know how some people tread water like it's nothing? It didn't matter whichever way I moved my hands and feet, I went right down like a lead balloon!

Diving boards were a big thing back in those days, and the girls had two of them—a high board and a low board. They asked me, "Can you dive?"

Of course, I blurted out, "Yes!"

A habit I've kept my entire life is, whether I can do it or not, I accept the challenge and figure it out later. In this case, however, it might not have been the smartest answer.

I climbed up the high board, and the truth was, I was not comfortable at all with all five of them standing in line, watching.

I got in position, flexin' and all, saying to myself, "I got this," while the little guy on my shoulder was saying, "You got this?"

I did a couple of fancy hops, and off I went. I landed with half my back hitting the water, which hurt like hell, and then I went straight down to the bottom and didn't come back up! A couple of the girls had to jump in and get me.

I'm laughing now, but this was one of the most embarrassing moments of my childhood. I promptly went home after that and avoided them for at least a month! When we started speaking again, they sure had a field day with me. "Fuzzy Wuzzy was a bear. Fuzzy Wuzzy had no hair. Fuzzy Wuzzy tried to dive, but couldn't swim to save his life!" I eventually got over it.

I was a smart kid, but I frustrated the teachers because they felt I didn't apply myself. My mind was on other things. I was good at several sports. In football, I was a quarterback, but when the next season came, all the guys had gotten much bigger and taller, except me, so I changed position to wide receiver. In baseball I was a pitcher, and I also had college interest as a very good wrestler. That was short lived, unfortunately, as my coach and I were demonstrating a takedown to the class, and a bad move ripped up my knee and ended any future hopes for wrestling. The funny thing is that, since then, my knee would lock up at any given time and could stay that way for weeks, until I accidently put it back in place! It wasn't until one night during a show that I found the secret. When I dropped down to my knees and wiggled left to right, as I usually did as part of my thing, I realized I could lock and unlock my knee. I had played many a Plasmatics gigs with a locked knee that I could not fully straighten—wish I would have known this sooner!

I also excelled at track, where I held the fifty- and hundred-yard dash records as well as the pole-vaulting record, but my father didn't like the idea that the coaches took practice so seriously, out in the rain and on holidays. All that practice made no sense to him. He saw it as a part-time hobby that should not overshadow school, family, and other more important things.

Although sports were important, I loved music from the beginning. From the age of six, I was in every choir as the lead voice and also loved dancing and performing. I was definitely a show-off, but the funny thing was, if I was asked to make a speech, or be singled out to answer a question in class, sing for my mother's few friends who would come over, or other similar situations, I'd feel very uncomfortable—I'd actually freak!—but a big crowd was never a problem. A stadium with a hundred thousand people is a piece of cake, and I feel totally at ease. I'm not sure why this is. Perhaps it came from doing everything possible not to be singled out as a kid due to feeling different and trying to avoid embarrasment. I later learned to own and embrace being different and enjoy using it to my advantage.

I started with the recorder (that little flutelike thing that I think every elementary school kid had to play), then the clarinet, but I really wanted to play the trumpet. When I told the music teacher, he told me that my lips were "wrongly" shaped. I had never heard of that before, and my mom got pretty upset about it. Somehow, he never caved on that and convinced me to play saxophone instead (more appropriate for my lips, I guess). I became a pretty good sax player for my age, and the music teacher came to my house to encourage my mom to really stay on me about continuing. I also played guitar in the jazz band, took all music theory courses, but I wanted something else.

I became an entrepreneur at a very young age. I bought my first minibike, a crappy little frame with a lawnmower engine, and I painted it, fixed it up, and sold it for double what I bought it for. I continued to do this until I was finally able to afford a Honda 50cc at about twelve years old.

When I was finally ready to move up to a full-size dirt bike, my dad said he was going to help me buy it. I found one that I liked, and my father came with me to look at it. He lowballed the guy so much that he basically turned around, walked away, and told us to leave. I was so embarrassed and upset.

When we got home I told my dad I wanted to buy it anyway and that I was willing to spend a bit more to buy it. He told me, "You can, but I'm not chipping in. I don't think it's worth it, but what I will do is buy your Honda from you."

After he bought it, he turned around and gave it to my sister. I was pissed that I had to work years to build up to a Honda 50 and that he'd just decided to give it to her. She didn't even know how to ride! She was all excited, took the bike out of the garage onto our large patio. My dad joined her, she got on it, started it, and took off crashing straight into the wall of the house! I couldn't help but laugh under my breath. The motorcycle was totaled, but she was fine, so that solved that problem.

In my efforts to fit in, I'd often do crazy things. I was always very generous to my friends, and I wanted to have someone to ride motorcycles with. There were five brothers who lived down the street, all a year apart. They all had really blond hair with bangs and they'd blow, or do this side-head movement, to get it out of their eyes. Being around them so much, I was jealous that I couldn't do that with my Brillo pad. My best friend out of the bunch was probably Kevin Baier. One day I told him, "This sucks. You know what? I'll get you a motorcycle, then we can ride together all the time."

"What do you mean?" he asked.

"Don't worry about it. I'll sort it out."

I always felt I needed to prove myself, and of course, my dad felt the way to do that was to set good examples that shed a positive light on Black people. I did, most of the time, but I also wanted to be cool, and I wasn't always a saint.

Now, every little boy must be a boy at some point, and they often do bad things. So one day, without telling him what I was up to, I took Kevin through the woods on my bike, via a back way that I knew, which was close to a local motorcycle dealership.

When we were about fifty yards away, I told him to wait for me.

The gates were open at the back of the dealership, and there were bikes all lined up. I took one that I felt was appropriate and calmly walked it out of the gate. I pushed it all the way to Kevin, started it, and said, "Get on, let's go."

We took off, and rode the rest of the day. Afterward, he brought it home and ended up sharing it with his brother, Karl. As you could imagine, he was pretty grateful, but at the same time he thought I was absolutely out of my mind! We came up with some kind of story for the parents.

He then shared this escapade with the other boys, which at the time made me the coolest kid around—and the one with the biggest balls. We actually kept that bike for months and had a great time, but my conscience finally got the better of me, and believe it or not, I found an opportunity to go back to the dealership and return the bike the same way I had taken it in the first place.

Nobody ever knew what happened, and I'm sure the dealership had no idea what was going on. A bike was stolen, they reported it, and next thing you know, the bike's back some months later. It was a crazy scenario, but sometimes to gain that admiration and respect, there are certain things that you feel you need to do.

I was part of this "clan," a group of friends that all hung out together, including Kevin, his brothers, Karl and Kris Baier, Joe Caccamo, Joe Cassata, and John Romano. I had other friends as well, but these guys were my little posse. We would do everything together. We'd have BB gun fights in the woods, cut out of school to go fishing for catfish, jump off a rope into the lake, and fool around in new home foundations.

There were tons of them out there on Long Island because they were constantly building new neighborhoods. When we moved into our house, it was the last exit on the expressway, exit 60, so they were starting to build farther and farther out.

We had a field day messing about in those foundations, until one day when I didn't quite make the other edge. I landed straight on my face. There was blood gushing all over the place! The other kids helped me to get back home while I was crying hysterically. When I got home my mom saw my face and almost had a heart attack. Thankfully, there was more blood than actual damage.

There was also a fraternity in my area—I believe it was Delta Phi Sigma—and they asked me to join them. I would have never thought of doing this, but some of the guys in the fraternity really liked me. They were older, a few ex-army, ex-marines, bikers, and different types, but in any case, all tough—you had to be—and some were crazier than others! During this time on Long Island, fraternities were more like gangs, unlike typical college fraternities. For some reason, even though there were no Blacks in the fraternity that I knew of, they wanted to recruit me—at a time when some fraternities even had rules forbidding Blacks. It was often said to me, "Oh, you're not Black, you're French. That's different." They felt it was perfectly fine for them to scream vulgarities or say racist things in front of me, without worrying about offending me, since in their minds, I wasn't really Black. Another thing that set me apart from others is the way I spoke. At the time, it was very unusual for a Black boy to speak as I did. On the phone, you couldn't tell if I was Black, White, or something else.

This fraternity was huge, supposedly with thousands of members across the United States, and you felt like you always had protection, because anywhere you'd go, you'd have brothers at other chapters.

Some of my best friends went in other directions. Kevin's brother Karl actually joined a rival fraternity. I remember their colors were yellow and black, and it may have been Omega-Gamma something. My colors were black and gray.

When I got the jacket, I was so stoked! It had a lot of meaning. A black jacket with grey arms in leather and my name embroidered on the front. I hid it in our house, in an attic compartment so that my mom wouldn't see it. But eventually, my teachers called her and told her, "Jean is part of a fraternity, and we would have just never thought that he was the type. He's such a good boy and has so much potential. If he would only apply himself, he'd have no problem in school, but he's just constantly distracted with music, the fraternity, cars, motorcycles, and all these different activities."

I was offered a position as the pledge master for my high school. In other words, if anyone from my school or anyone else they would send through me, wished to join the fraternity, I would be the one to determine what they had to go through to get in. There was a certain amount of pledge time, which I believe was about two weeks, where you'd pretty much say, "That person will be my bitch." I could ask him to do *anything*, including carrying my books around, carrying my jacket in his teeth through the day—usually something stupid and embarrassing.

I was a pretty nice pledge master, though, and I wanted my friends to be in the fraternity, so I tried to go as easy as I could with their pledges. But I had no control over Hell Night, which everyone had to go through, no matter what.

It got to the point where my friend Kevin had passed my pledging and was all good to go, but it was time for him to go through his Hell Night. I spoke to the guys, of course, saying that he was a friend of mine and that I'd like them to please go easy on him, but they didn't really listen to me. As Kevin's Hell Night was approaching, it was something that was well known around the area. It was also pretty mysterious and very scary to a lot of people.

For Kevin's Hell Night we headed up to Lake Ronkonkoma, an enigmatic lake known to take a certain amount of people's lives on an annual basis, with nobody really quite understanding where they'd go. The myth or legend says that there's a hole at the bottom of the lake that sucks people in once they get to a certain point and throws them out somewhere in the ocean.

I actually once had a little wooden motorboat boat that I kept docked at that lake. I had taken boating courses and obtained my boating license at the time, which was required. I wasn't only the only Black kid around, but most definitely the only Black kid with a boat! Unfortunately, someone wasn't thrilled about the idea, and I came one day to find it on the bottom of the lake with the engine stolen. No insurance, of course! So that a put a blunt stop to my nautical life for a bit!

But while I could guess what led to my boat's demise, nobody ever confirmed what caused all the disappearances. It's very spooky at night in the woods that surround the lake. It was definitely a pretty eerie place to be with a bunch of guys who are about to put you through hell! There was also a big campfire where the ceremony would take place, like something you'd see in a movie.

Kevin had two rituals to choose from. One was that all the attending members would line up across from each other, about thirty to forty guys, including certain leaders from the chapter. He would then start at one end and walk slowly through the middle. The guys could choose to use belts, two-by-fours, or their hands to strike him as he passed. The other choice, which he took, was for me to hold him while they all lined up to take a turn at striking him on the ass with two-by-fours.

As things were heating up, I kept asking him, "Are you sure you want to join? It's not that big of a deal. Forget it! You know, why do you want to put yourself through this?" I didn't want to see him get hurt! Things could get violent. On one occasion, Karl was beat up so badly that he ended up in the hospital! As would happen often. His fraternity had left him in the trunk of a car and told us where to retrieve him.

But Kevin insisted. He wanted to be a part of it, and he was ready to take whatever pain was coming his way. He wrapped his arms around me, us being face to face, forehead to forehead, and they put a leather belt in his teeth so that he could squeeze on that, rather than bite his tongue, as he was getting hit. They could choose how hard they could hit him, but these guys showed no mercy. They approached one by one with the two-by-fours, exerting as much energy into the swings as they possibly could. I believe they each had five swings.

He was crying, not screaming, but gritting his teeth and making these moan and groan sounds. He was tough, and I could feel the tears running down my face as he was getting hit over and over. I asked them to chill out, and I pleaded with Kevin, "Let's just stop this," but he just would not, and he kept going for it.

After all thirty or so guys had their turn hitting him repeatedly, it was finally over. After going through hell, he was sworn in and became a member of the fraternity, under me.

The weird thing is that my Hell Night, when I first joined, was very easy for some reason. I was given the line, but most of the guys would not actually hit me hard. They just tapped me with the two-by-fours or whatever they had in hand, but they did little harm. I never really knew why. I guess they just wanted me in and decided to make it as easy as possible.

Pretty much all we would do was hang out at the lake as well as some other different meeting places. They all had different stories from war and whatever they'd gone through and where they came from. Much like a heavy-duty biker gang, they all had pretty crazy backgrounds.

You felt like you were a part of something, and it definitely made you feel safe. If you walked around with that jacket, anywhere in school, down the street, in the mall, or wherever you were, people would move and go to the other side, not to be too close to you or offend you in any way. It was good because you did have a lot of rowdy kids and people who did stupid things back in those days, and if anybody from the fraternity would come in with a complaint of some kind of wrongdoing to one of the members, the fraternity would handle it—no matter what it was, though I never had the opportunity to go back to the mall and get my revenge on that damn talking Easter Bunny for making some of my earlier childhood a living hell!

Back then, I did a lot of other daring things. For example, I would imitate my hero, Evel Knievel, by building ramps in the street and doing stunts while the neighborhood kids watched. I'd lay on top of cars while an older boy driving would try to get me to fall off by making quick turns. I was quite the daredevil and often came home pretty banged up, but I had a reputation for being cool and always pushing the limits.

My dad had a beautiful 1972 Corvette Stingray. It was brand new, orange, and chrome. He loved that car, and so did I! He would only drive it on weekends, usually on Sundays, to take a trip to a nearby city or to take one of us for a ride.

He kept the car keys in his dresser drawer. My parents' bedroom was kept locked, but there was a second door that had a dresser up against it. Somehow, I managed to push the door open, go into the dresser, and grab the keys. I ended up making my own copies. When I think about it now, I was insane!

I even dared to take it to school and give friends rides. My mom always told me, "If your dad ever knew that you did that, you wouldn't be here today." I don't think he would have ever imagined that I would do something that bold.

He didn't realize until one day he came home and noticed the garage was warm from the engine. He called me in and asked me, "Have you started my car?" I hesitated but realized there was no way I'd get out of this. So I said, "Oh, yes, yes, I started it. My friends wanted to hear what it sounded like." I knew I'd get in trouble for that, but not nearly as much as if he knew I actually took it out.

My love of cars dates way back. I had my first car already at thirteen. I called her Auntie Bluebell. She was an old Datsun and ugly as hell, but I sat in that car every day and every night listening to music. We would put-put around the neighborhood with it.

Within two years, I'd go through a Road Runner with a six-pack 440 engine, an Impala, a Nova, an equipment truck, to list but a few. My last car on Long Island was a luxurious blue Cadillac with white leather interior that had taken me a while to save up for. One day, I was coming back home from a late show tired. I fell asleep and smashed it into a tree. It was totaled, and I had no insurance, so my years of work had amounted to almost nothing.

When I discovered rock and roll, at about eleven or twelve years old, it was Led Zeppelin, KISS, Eric Clapton, and Deep Purple that made the most impact on me. After seeing and reading about these bands, rock and roll became my dream! My grandmother didn't share the same enthusiasm. When she'd come to visit, she would refuse to come into my room because of the KISS poster on my wall—she swore that Gene Simmons was the devil.

I wanted to be a rock star, and there was no doubt in my mind! I loved the extravagance, the sound, the adventures, the planes, the glam, and the ability to be whoever you wanted to be. I didn't want to spend my life taking the train every morning to work like my dad did.

I had traded one of my minibikes for a Ludwig drum set and had started playing every day. I would skip school sometimes so I could blast records and practice by playing to them. I'd open the windows so the kids at the bus stops could hear me play. I was a show-off.

I became a pretty good drummer in a short amount of time, but my dad upended that passion one day by opening the front door, taking my drums from my room to the top of the stairs, and kicking them right down the stairs and out the door. He could no longer take the noise and told me to find a quieter instrument. I wasn't happy, but it was what it was.

My brother had a bass and was learning to play. I started borrowing it periodically and found myself learning this very quickly as well. I'd sit in my room, listen to records, and learn the bass parts for every song imaginable: rock, hit singles, Motown, R&B, James Brown, and so on. I heard everything so clearly and knew that God had given me a gift that I needed to pursue.

I became proficient at instruments rapidly, and the teachers would call and remark on the quick progress I was making. I was very focused when I wanted to do something, so although my grades were not great, I kept myself academically above water, despite my other passions.

Meanwhile, I was giving drum lessons to my neighbor and good friend, John Romano, to replace me in the band. My school had a jazz band, which I joined as the guitar player. That's partly where I learned music theory, reading music on the fly, and some other basic tools needed for what I wanted to do, but by and large I was self-taught.

My math teacher, who had caught wind of my abilities, approached me. He was told I was a good drummer. He was also a drummer and had opened for the Who, so I guess he had the bug. He still wanted to play rock 'n' roll, so we decided to form a junior high school rock band.

I was a singing drummer to start, but I moved around to other instruments, depending on what the band needed. I was the leader of the junior high school rock band, which was a lot like the movie *School of Rock*. (I never would have predicted that I would go on to write and produce the main song in the film many years later!)

The concept was that he and I would direct the program. After school, we'd recruit different instrumentalists—two drummers, three guitarists, keys, vocals, and whoever showed promise and was as into the band as we were. Even my hypercritical father loved the idea.

This new school rock band became so popular among the kids that they hired us to play at school functions. We got paid and started taking business away from the band that normally played these dances, a band that included teachers.

This extracurricular pursuit helped me immensely with getting to know the other kids and making friends. Even the girlfriend department became more interesting, as all the girls would come and watch me and my classmates perform. I'd write songs and play them for girls that I liked or that had broken my heart, though it was often their parents who prevented them from seeing me once they found out I was Black.

For a hopelessly romantic yet insecure young boy, rock 'n' roll seemed to be the answer!

2

THE APPRENTICE YEARS

WHEN THE SUMMER ARRIVED, I didn't want to stop playing. I rounded up some older guys and formed a band named Topaz. We started playing clubs on Long Island. To get around venue age restrictions, I'd lie about my age, trusting on my little wisp of a mustache.

An old-time heavy manager, John Apostol, who managed Gary US Bonds (who had a number-one hit in the '60s with "Quarter to Three") at the time, showed up to one of the Topaz gigs. He dug what I was doing and asked me to come meet with Gary at his house. I went and met him; Gary was a handsome, tall, light-skinned Black man. He had a great sense of humor, and we hit it off right away. His wife and daughter, both named Laurie, were also very welcoming, and his wife was a singer in his band.

It was like I was the son he never had. He called me "Boo Boo" and told me, "I don't like to rehearse all that much. Learn these songs, Boo Boo, and meet me in Florida. It's your gig. Whip these guys into shape, hire and fire as you please, and let's rock 'n' roll! All I care about is that you're at the gig."

He made me the musical director, and I was in charge of it all. I always had a really good ear for literally hearing music before it happens, if that makes sense. In other words, I could call out the chords to the musicians before the chord was coming. Even for songs I didn't know. I'd somehow anticipate where he was going.

The first gig was in Sarasota, Florida. We took turns at the wheel, even though I didn't have a license—only one of us did. Of course, I couldn't drive while we went through the southern states. Racism was still full tilt, so the band kept me hidden in the Winnebago when we'd stop for breakfast, dinner, etc.

It was the first time I'd been there, and I just loved the weather and the vibe of the city. We pretty much had the days to ourselves as we performed at night—so we had the opportunity to play tourists or hang by the pool all day. This was the life for me!

It was a great experience playing with Gary. I'd do one set of my songs, covers, some originals, and then we'd do Gary's show.

Then, one day, the truth came out. Gary came to my room and said, "Boo Boo, I just spoke to your mom, and you're going back to school. I know you're gonna be fifteen!"

I kind of felt like I had already made it, as silly as that sounds, so now I thought my life was over. But he promised me I could still work with him and that he'd work it out to get me out of school when he needed me for shows.

At that point, my guys had to go back to school, so Elizabeth Ames came on board on keyboards, Babe on drums, and Tommy Lafferty on guitar, with me on bass and vocals.

The relationship continued, and Gary was as good as his word. Many teachers were fans of his, but in any case, he was well known, so he had pull. They would always agree to let me have off a Thursday, Friday, or Monday. After a short break, he called me a second time out of the blue. He said, "Boo Boo, I got some new boys here with me, but I need you to come and get these guys together. They're great musicians but need some fine-tuning."

I worked with Gary for another year or so touring the United States with a rotating group of band members, including Tommy Lafferty, who had stayed in the band. Gary had also added a very good guitarist, Ronny Drayton, who had played with Nona Hendryx, the Chambers Brothers, the Persuaders, and a female vocalist, Dale, who was Ronny's girlfriend.

We headed down to Bermuda for starters, a very beautiful and mysterious island. The ocean for whatever reason frightened many locals. Being sensitive to spiritual things, I just always felt a strange feeling come over me when I was there. We had a very cool house for the band, big enough for us to also rehearse, and at night we would play at an upscale nightclub called the Forty Thieves that brought in international artists on a regular basis, such as Aretha Franklin, Dionne Warwick, and Tom Jones.

As much fun as it was being there, we had work to do and I was always very serious about that. I called the first rehearsal, and nobody showed. Everyone stayed on the beach, riding mopeds, and completely ignored me. I stood there waiting for hours, getting more and more upset by the minute. *These damn guys have no respect!* I thought Gary was pretty clear when he told everyone I was running the ship. When they finally showed up, I said they would be docked $500 for being late. They freaked out, and I just about got into a fistfight with the keyboard player, Doug, who just hated having to listen to me. Tommy actually defended me and said, "Hey, he's right. We're supposed to be here rehearsing. We have a job to do."

From that point on, Tommy and I became very close. He was a jazz guitarist, a Berkeley graduate, and wore his guitar about five inches from his chin—not very rock 'n' roll, so I got him into a Les Paul and had him lower his guitar about a foot. At that point, I could see he was ready to rock!

We had a really good run in Bermuda, great audiences every night, and it was a lot of fun, especially for a teenage boy from Long Island. What a completely different world!

We went on to join a Dick Clark tour, which featured many of the greats from that era. We played mostly coliseums and the groups included Chuck Berry and Bo Diddley. At any given time, I would be asked to back one of them—when that would happen, there was no notice and no rehearsal. I'd just have to jump on stage and call chords out to the band.

Bo Diddley was a funny man. He wore big glasses, a short black top hat with a wings medallion on it, and played his rectangular guitar unconventionally in open E tuning. He liked me, and I remember once he sat me down and preached that I should always pay my taxes! Another time, Gary and I played a joke on him and hid his guitar right before a big coliseum show. He thought it was stolen and was freaking out. We finally gave it back when he was about to go on. He got pretty mad, but all was good—it was all in fun.

We played Vegas, Reno, and Lake Tahoe; Gary had a wide range of fans and acquaintances, including Mafia guys, who would fly us around in private jets and come to shows. I remember one night, some of these guys stayed at the hotel and hid $10,000 in a room. They gave a couple of the singers a certain amount of time to find it! Neither found it in time, but I believe they still got something for their efforts!

We always had a blast with Gary; he was a fun guy to be around, always joking! Besides that, he is an amazing singer and was really my first school of vocal education. The songs he'd sing apart from his own hits were all beautiful soulful songs filled with harmonies. He always hired top-notch musicians and female background vocalists including his wife, Laurie. In fact, Bruce Springsteen was a huge fan of Gary and for that reason took him into the studio in the '80s, reviving his career with the chart-topping "This Little Girl Is Mine."

After the Dick Clark tour, I had no home to go to, as I had already been thrown out of the house by my dad. I had recently met a guitar player named Bob who I recruited for my band Topaz. He was an interesting long-haired hippie type with a beard who was surprisingly a church caretaker. He let me stay with him, but he didn't really like that he was in my band, since I was so young. This was a constant problem for me—no one wanted to take orders from a teenager. I can still remember him getting drunk and fucking with me mentally about it, but I hung in there.

I kept doing gigs with my band locally until one day I had a stroke of bad luck. I owned a large cargo truck at the time (though I was still too young to drive it) that was really nice—newly painted in bright blue with lots of room. It housed all the equipment I owned, including PA system, lights, amps, and drums. I was doing pretty well for a teenager. Then one day, I woke up to an empty truck. My whole business was out the door. I was extremely distraught and demoralized. It was a very safe neighborhood and all was locked. I never anticipated this happening.

Luckily, shortly after that disaster, I was asked to be a singer for the '50s hit group the Flamingos, of "I Only Have Eyes for You" fame. I met them somewhere out on the road, and they reached out to me. That was a trip, and our first gig was at Nassau Coliseum on Long Island playing for sixteen thousand people. I fit right in and was totally comfortable with the material. Thankfully, I had no problem tackling anything that was thrown at me. No doubt, they had intricate, incredibly beautiful harmonies.

I was asked to wear this Vegas-style suit that was too big for me and shoes that were also two sizes too large. I looked pretty funny, but that suit would actually become an important part of my life further down the line.

We played Las Vegas, the Virgin Islands at a resort called Frenchman's Reef, and all over the United States. I really enjoyed crooning their soulful songs to tables of women and upscale casino types every night. The harmonies that group had were extraordinary, and the original members, Zeke and Jake Carey, were still in the group and just as talented as when they started. I was by far the youngest member they'd ever had, and I learned a lot working with them. It's strange to think that they both passed away more than twenty years ago, in the late '90s. The whole experience was life changing; it was great! To this day, the Flamingos are said to be one of the greatest and most influential vocal groups in Pop and R&B music history, and "I Only Have Eyes For You" has stood the test of time, remaining one of the greatest songs of all time. Being brought in as a lead singer at the age of seventeen was an incredible honor and a solid confirmation of my vocal abilities. It was like being hired by the London Symphony Orchestra before finishing high school.

After the Flamingos, and finishing high school, I decided to try something different and chose to move to New Jersey. I joined a local band for a while and started contemplating going to college. Naive as I was, I felt I had gone through an entire music career! I even tried a very short stint working in a big retail shop, like a Best Buy. That was totally a different experience. I remember a guy who was my superior, not the big boss, and he loved to command me to do this and that. One day, I was downstairs in a stockroom and he yelled something down at me like, "Go get those two boxes. Hurry, now!" in a very arrogant tone. I was already on the brink, but that broke the camel's back, and I just responded, "Why don't you come down and get them yourself." I walked out and never went back to that world again.

Things also began to change with my family. My parents sent my sister to Paris to continue her studies after high school. Unlike me, she enjoyed studying. My brother, Pierre, was still in the army. I remember the letters he sent me when he lost friends and witnessed terrible things in Vietnam. I was really afraid for him, always hoping nothing bad would happen. I also remember that he had a pet boa constrictor that kept him company. Thankfully, he came back safely. He excelled in the army and was in the celebrated 101st Airborne Division. He went on to become an officer.

I stayed in contact with my mom, and she informed me that she and my dad were moving back to Haiti. After many years of working, my father finally decided it was time to sell the house with all their belongings and move down to our property in Haiti. They rented a truck, grabbed our two dogs, Blacky and Husky, and hit the road to Florida. From there, they flew back to their motherland.

My dad later told me that they had encountered racial problems with the police while driving through the South. They were pulled over and detained for no reason, but my father somehow managed to get them out of it. My mom also shared with me the loss of one of our cherished dogs, Blacky. She told me she had somehow gotten out of the truck, and they never found her. This was really tough for me to take.

When they arrived in Haiti my mother was not prepared for what was to come, having lived comfortably on Long Island for so long. My father had partially built a cement structure with a few rooms, but it was still unfinished. She had to use an old-fashioned wooden outhouse to go to the bathroom, and there was no electricity or fresh water! Her baths or showers would be in the river from now on. It wasn't easy to communicate with her since phone service was everything but optimum.

Granted, my mom was Haitian, but she wasn't ready to live this primitively. As you can imagine, she didn't last very long. Neither did our wonderful dog, Husky. He had to fend for himself against Haitian wild dogs, and he was just not prepared, having had a pretty cushy life previously. He didn't live much longer, and my mom was devastated. So were we.

Though the property remained hers equally, she decided to leave and build a house in the Haitian capital, Port-au-Prince. Eventually, my mom and dad divorced.

My life was also about to change drastically as I came home one day to see fire trucks in front of my apartment building. The whole place had burned down, including all my belongings. Now there was really nothing left!

The city gave the tenants 120 bucks as a relief payment. I dropped the college idea, and with that money bought a Schott motorcycle jacket on Canal Street in Manhattan. I'd always been curious about the punk scene, so I decided to venture into that world.

3

THE PLASMATICS

I HAD NO PLACE TO LIVE and really just played it by ear. I spent nights on the street or on cardboard boxes in some seedy spots. The Lower East Side was not what it is today—it was infested with rats, but such is life. I'd find cheap, rundown motels to spend some nights in here and there. I had an arrangement with one cheap motel in East Rutherford; I'd check in at night and check back out in the morning. That way, they could still rent the room out during the day to bosses bringing their secretaries there for a bit of afternoon delight. For that, they gave me a special reduced rate.

There was a diner right across the street on Route 3 that made the tastiest corn muffins. I'd savor those as if they were caviar. That was my lunch and dinner many days. It's funny how you can learn to appreciate and long for something that is usually taken for granted.

I'd pass my days perusing local ads and cards that I'd find on walls in little Lower East Side shops or in the West Village. I was looking to be a part of something. One day, I came across an ad for a band called the New York Niggers who were looking for a lead singer. I went, auditioned, and joined the band. We'd rehearse in some dodgy room downtown, but we were doing music, so it was still cool.

The first gig we did together was opening for the Plasmatics at My Father's Place, a rock 'n' roll club on Long Island. I stuck around after our set to check out what the headliners were doing. It was the beginning of their career, so there were just a few hundred people in attendance.

Within a minute or so, it was obvious that the Plasmatics weren't there just to make music—they were a new kind of visual art, like watching a cartoon or a science fiction movie happening live on stage. It was pretty crazy!

Their lead guitarist, Richie Stotts, stood at least six foot seven and had a blue Mohawk. He bounced around the stage in a nurse's outfit and high-heeled shoes while playing a Flying V guitar. The rhythm guitarist, Wes Beech, ran back and forth in a butcher's coat. The drummer, Stu Deutsch, played only sixteenths the entire night, keeping the beat with his steady right hand, while the bass player, Chosei Funahara, maintained his cool amid the madness. Wendy O. Williams, of course, was the band's frontwoman. She wore white satin panties with a bra and not much else. Her voice blasted out of the speakers like a spray of bullets.

About a week or so after the show at My Father's Place, I spotted an ad in the *Village Voice* announcing that the Plasmatics were looking for a new bass player to replace Chosei. The *Voice* was the go-to paper back in those days. Everybody got it. Anything on its way up in New York City usually came up in that paper. I was NYN's singer, but I'd played bass in Gary US Bonds's touring band, so I thought to myself, *Why not? Let me check this out.*

I dialed the number posted in the ad, and Rod Swenson, the Plasmatics' manager, answered. "Yeah," he said, "I remember you from My Father's Place."

"Great. I'm interested in auditioning," I said, and he gave me a time and date to come in.

En route to the audition, I saw several guys with basses on the subway. "Where's everybody going?" I asked.

"Plasmatics audition," they said.

So, I went to the tryout, and everything went fine. Then I got the first call back. "I just want to let you know that we're interested," said Rod. "We're still checking out people, but we'll get back to you."

"Great," I said.

The next call I got, that was it. "Listen, we've auditioned everybody," Rod said. "We think that you'd be a great fit for the band. Would you be interested in joining us?"

The Plasmatics' style depended too much on imagery, he explained, and the band wanted to get more musicality into the songs. They wanted somebody who could also write and who'd be as involved as possible. And that was me.

Rod explained what the deal would be if I accepted. "Because we're starting out right now, we're reinvesting everything back into the band. There won't be any money for at least the first six months, zero. Can you handle that? We're going to require a full-time commitment from you because we rehearse every day. Being in this band is more like a nine-to-five job. Is that something you'd be comfortable with?"

I had just turned nineteen, and the prospect of not making a lot of money didn't worry me that much, but I wouldn't say it was easy! I also sensed the Plasmatics were about to break big, and I wanted to be around for that, so I said, "Yes."

We started rehearsals right away, which helped me learn the band's material. We ran through all the songs—"Butcher Baby," "Sex Junkie," "Living Dead"—several times a day.

With Richie and Wes trading riffs, my fingers ripping up and down my bass, Stu crushing the drums, and Wendy snarling into the microphone, we created a big, hammering sound that had one foot in heavy metal and the other in hardcore punk.

I can remember the beginning, traveling with some of the gear in an unheated green van. I hated that thing! I think we all did. Our roadies traveled in a Ryder truck, you know, those U-Haul-type moving trucks to carry the gear. That truck looked like a limo in comparison! Especially traveling through the northern states and Canada in below-freezing weather. Being the only one to ever stand up for things, I finally had to insist that the roadies switch with us. Not once, but several times. We were freezing our asses off while they were driving in luxury! With my Carribean blood, those temparatures were not my friend!

Broke as we were, I'd save and buy this sandwich they sold on the corner from the loft during rehearsal breaks. Basically, a grilled pork chop on toast, nothing more! But it seemed heavenly at the time. I still make it now, the same way.

When I'd been with the Flamingos, I was given a white suit to wear on stage that didn't fit well. For the Plasmatics, I decided I'd get something made specifically for me—an all-white tuxedo with tails. I also wore white gloves with the tips snipped off so that my fingers could come through, pre Michael Jackson as someone pointed out to me! I started out with my head shaved, then grew a Mohawk, which I bleached blond with much difficulty. Wendy wore her hair back in a ponytail, which she dyed pink and blonde, later opting for a Mohawk as well.

There was something that the band found interesting and amusing about me: my etiquette and my way of being, especially since I was a punk rocker, and most definitely a rebel. For example, if we'd go to breakfast, Richie would take one egg at a time with his fork and eat the whole thing. Meanwhile, he'd watch me chopping my eggs together with the bacon, putting the bacon together with the egg, and making sure to add a little piece of bread. They would always make fun of me for that. God forbid one of the guys burped or farted at the table, that was it! I couldn't eat anything for the rest of the day! I'd erupt, "You pigs! Don't you have any manners?" Nevertheless, we were pretty close and got along well.

Wendy was amused and liked me, as I did her. She was a bit shy around me. She liked to pronounce my name "Boovwar" because it was exotic. She'd also make little jokes about my manners, with her signature grin I find hard to forget.

A record company hadn't yet signed them when I joined, but Rod had managed to book us in clubs throughout New York, New England, California, and the Rust Belt. We were starting to gather a large following. People dug the energy, the theatrical violence of a Plasmatics show, not knowing what would happen next.

They loved seeing Wendy take the chainsaw to guitars, hoping to get a piece. We each had our own thing, so no matter where you looked, there was punk-rock eye candy. There was the blowing up of Cadillacs on stage, exploding amplifiers—and loud, fast music. No one did drugs, contrary to popular belief. If we did, we wouldn't make it through one night on that stage without getting killed, maimed, shot or some other mishap. We had to be 100 percent on point to deal with timed explosions, smoke all over the place, shotgun shells flying everywhere and car parts galore shooting in all directions. It was totally random. It was also lethal, but what a rush!

The fans were happy to have a home at our shows where they could be themselves and feel totally comfortable being who they wanted to be, whether they were normal folk looking to fantasize or misfits who found some new hope for themselves—hence *New Hope for the Wretched*, the title of our first album.

Plasmatics fans were some of the greatest fans I've ever seen. They would hang patiently outside the venues where we played, waiting hours to meet us. In the fall of 1980, during one of our sold-out runs at the Whisky a Go Go, fans camped out on Sunset Boulevard days before the show. It was like Woodstock—but in the middle of West Hollywood.

We had a regular group of people who came in wheelchairs, too. They'd sit out in front of our hotel or the club. We knew them. They'd be there all the time. The smiles and the excitement that you'd see on their faces as soon as we'd show up made it clear that the Plasmatics were their whole life, their religion. To be able to feel that you can have that kind of an influence as an artist and give people that kind of satisfaction was just amazing!

Wendy had a big heart for the fans because so many of them were emotionally and psychologically vulnerable. She didn't have a great childhood and had been out on her own a lot, and she felt empathy for them. She had a similar affection for mistreated animals. It was one of her ideas to extend the lives of chickens by featuring them in our show.

We went to a slaughterhouse one day, grabbed a bunch of chickens, and took them on the tour bus with us. Wendy gave them names like Gertrude and Linda Ronstadt. She was always making sure they were in good shape, asking things like "How's Gertrude doing today?" and "Did you see Linda this morning?"

When the crew would set up for a show, they'd put the chickens up in the lighting truss, and during the show, they'd drop down on us from the ceiling. Animal rights people objected, but Wendy and the rest of us always thought it was more humane to have the chickens sing backup for the Plasmatics than have their throats slit in a slaughterhouse. Wendy eventually had a change of heart, though, and began to wonder if what we were doing was a little too stressful for them. After that, their performing careers were over, and we kept them simply as pets.

The Plasmatics were never a band driven by a particular ideology. We weren't political punks like the Clash. Our band's mission was philosophical. We wanted people to understand how certain things of perceived value, like appliances and vehicles and even food, lacked true meaning and purpose. Material things shouldn't be life's most important objectives—that was one of the band's key messages. And to emphasize the anticonsumerism theme, we wrecked a lot of technology on stage in spectacular ways.

Wendy would generally come out at the start of each show wrapped up in leather or a faux cheetah-skin outfit. She'd expose more and more of herself as we played, until about midway through she'd be topless, with whipped cream spread all over her and strips of black tape across her nipples. Then, she'd whip out that sledgehammer to smash up radios and TVs, and once she was done doing that, she'd flick her tongue around the head of the sledgehammer and stroke the handle with her fingers. She'd also fire shotgun blanks at the amps, triggering explosions engineered by our pyro guys, Rob Vivona and Petey Cappadocia. The sounds of these explosions would rip through the microphones, the PA, the monitors, and then the speakers. Flames from one of these explosions singed off the back of my Mohawk one night!

For the show's climax, Wendy would throw dynamite into the car that we had on stage, usually a Cadillac. The hood, which was attached by a long chain, would shoot straight up in the air. The amount of explosives used was totally random!

Sometimes, it went twenty feet, sometimes fifty feet, sometimes ten. We never knew where it would land, so we started wearing helmets. I remember one night at the Calderone Theatre in Hempstead, Long Island, the hood went so high that it lit the top curtains on fire! Everyone had to run out of the building. It was mayhem, but that's what drew the crowds.

By the summer of 1980 the underground press was taking notice of the Plasmatics, but commercial radio wouldn't play our songs, and mainstream critics responded to us with hostility. People who didn't like us were against what we represented—our going against the status quo. They looked at us as outcasts, and they were incapable of recognizing and valuing how much it took to play our music and do what we did. We were banned in London. We were set to play to a sold-out crowd at London's premier venue, the Hammersmith Odeon. The Greater London Council heard we were coming and were up in arms! They limited us by saying that there had to be a barricade and fifty feet between us and the audience. That pretty much defeated the purpose of our show and the audience experience, so the show was not to be. The press seized on this, and we were plastered all over the UK in no time. Our fame resonated from there, and we went on to play to soldout crowds all over Europe.

Take a track like "Masterplan," the song we played when Wendy would blow up the cars. It's a loud, angry punk song, but my bass line was like something from Motown played at five times its original speed. Motown-punk! I still play the song in my solo show, and I've had the hardest time finding bass players who can play it correctly. I've had to take it out of the set several times. I really enjoyed working up the bass parts for the Plasmatics. It was a challenge to incorporate my different influences—hard rock, soul, pop, Caribbean—and play in a manner that was very different from what punk bass players normally played. This helped to give the band its own sound.

Out of all the bass playing I've done in my career, which is quite a bit and with top-notch musicians, the Plasmatics parts were probably the most complex. As for Richie's guitar work, he might not have been a Steve Vai or an Yngwie Malmsteen shredder, but the sounds that he got, the kinds of chords he played, the solos, the speed of his down strokes while jumping around in bunny suits, nurse's outfits, and high heels—most people would never be able to do. Wes, too, he was solid as a rock, and after Stu moved on from the band, we never found anyone who could play the sixteenths that he played. We found some amazing drummers, but they all had to play eighths. And all of this was what we did while trying to stay alive on that stage with things blowing up all over the place! It was quite the rush!

Stu was replaced initially by Neal Smith from Alice Cooper's original band. Then by Tony Petri from Twisted Sister. They were both phenomi-nal drummers, and I loved playing with both of them. They were also great guys.

The national attention we'd been waiting for and expecting arrived finally in November 1980. We had secured permission to play a free show at the end of Pier 62 on the West Side of Manhattan along the Hudson River. The city had told us there was space for no more than three-thousand attendees, but almost twenty thousand showed up, with even more lining the rooftops. News channels ABC, NBC, CBS, and others showed up with their trucks, along with a parade of police and fire vehicles.

A helicopter brought us to the pier, and as it hovered above the stage, screaming fans leaped up and down. It was a dangerous landing for me. The band all exited going around the front of the helicopter, but in an adrenaline haze I carelessly went around the back. I could feel the air of the propeller as my brother who happened to be nearby, yelled "Jean-Jean!" I stopped dead in my tracks, realizing that another few feet and I would have been torn into pieces. My heart was pounding out of my chest as I went around and headed to the stage. It was surreal as I looked out into the crowd. Their religion was the Plasmatics, Wendy was their priestess, and they reveled like pilgrims witnessing a sacramental rite. We blasted through our set, playing the songs fast and loud, just as the people wanted.

Then, at the end of the show, Wendy ran fifty yards into the crowd and jumped into a Cadillac, which she drove up a ramp onto the stage! Everything, all the equipment and the car, blew up and went barreling into the Hudson. Wendy got hurt jumping out of the car, and as she was carried on a gurney to an ambulance, the EMTs strapped an oxygen mask on to her face.

"I'm all right!" she shouted to the fans. "I feel fucking great!"

Then the ambulance swept her away. We had a deal with the city that all the debris had to be cleaned out of the river. We had frogmen diving for weeks!

Footage of us playing the pier wound up being a commercial for ABC's *Eyewitness News*. They highlighted the car driving through the stage with everything exploding! Now, people all over the country could see and hear the Plasmatics in their homes, further infusing us into the nation's pysche. The TV coverage, I'm sure, is what helped to sell out the remaining shows of our American tour, which we'd started following the release of *New Hope for the Wretched* in May.

We were increasingly featured on the covers of counterculture publications everywhere, and every time we came to a town, we'd also end up on the front page of the local paper, our photos appearing under headlines like THIS GROUP OF MISFITS IS COMING TO OUR CITY and WHAT ARE WE GOING TO DO ABOUT THE PLASMATICS?

Everybody was a little afraid of what they thought we'd bring—the baggage and the dangerous influence. Nobody wanted their sons looking like Richie, or their daughters wearing tape on their nipples like Wendy. Me, not as much, as there were very few Black fans in the audiences, but there were more and more at every show.

Then we got booked on *Fridays*, a live sketch comedy series ABC had developed to compete against NBC's *Saturday Night Live*. We had just started the midwestern leg of the tour, so we flew out from Minneapolis to Los Angeles to do the show. That was on January 16, 1981. As the featured musical act, we played two songs. During the first one, "Living Dead," Wendy clobbered a TV with her sledgehammer. During the second, "Butcher Baby," she chainsawed a guitar in half after pouring dirt all over her chest. To amplify the weirdness, Wes and I wore black executioner's hoods and Stu donned a gas mask. Richie, who was dressed like a Playboy Club cocktail waitress, sported furry rabbit ears and a cotton tail. The crowd went crazy!

The next night, we played to a full house in Chicago, and then we moved on to Milwaukee to play a club called the Palms. The Palms occupied the ground floor of an enormous red-brick building that had once been a silent movie theater and later a dance hall. At the beginning of the '80s, it was a magnet for bands on the fringe of popularity. The Ramones had played there, the Police and Elvis Costello, too. Now, our name was spelled out across the marquee in black plastic letters next to the words SOLD OUT.

We arrived at the Palms sometime in the afternoon, and fans, some of them who we knew, were already lining up to get in. As we climbed out of the tour bus, we glanced up and down the street, searching for the local safety officials and law enforcement types, who tended to show up to our shows early as well.

These guys would approach us and ask, "Well, what are you guys planning to do here tonight?" They would try to get the specs for the setups and angles of the pyrotechnics, stuff we didn't really know how to answer. A lot was done off the cuff. Most of the time, we'd have to pay these people off to get them to leave us alone. They'd come back and just stand by, watch, make sure everything was cool and then split.

Inside, the Palms was as spacious as it was dingy, with a proscenium stage, a dance floor, and a bar. Our pyro guy, Petey, who'd arrived with the other members of the crew hours before us, waved us over to the stage.

"They've got the paddy wagons out back," he said. "They're here with everything. Police officers, fire marshals. All of it."

The dressing rooms were behind the stage, and we went back to see how everything looked. Each room had a door that opened out to a parking area that stretched behind the building. Sure enough, police cars and emergency vehicles were huddled together just yards away.

We'd arrived in town early enough to run some errands and relax before the show. We'd stop by a hotel to wash up and get some food, and then head back to the venue. Once we got back to the Palms, it was still early evening.

Some detectives from the vice squad approached us immediately and started questioning Rod. They weren't concerned about the measurements of the pyro effects and the safety code. They weren't looking for a bribe, either. They were there to make sure we didn't violate any of the city's prohibitions on public lewdness and indecency. They'd seen the Plasmatics on *Fridays*. We could tell they wanted to shut us down, but they lacked legal grounds to do it, and that was upsetting them.

Planning for a ten o'clock start, we got ourselves ready in our dressing rooms. Already, the club was thick with punks and goths, as well as skaters and the quieter types, the ones who wore jean jackets and Chuck Taylors. Not long before we were supposed to start, though, the electricity cut out in the Palms. Some folks rushed the bar, and they snatched bottles of beer or helped themselves to the tap. When the lights came back on a couple of minutes later, a sense of menace hung in the air. Wendy didn't care. She ran out with her shotgun, blasting rounds toward the ceiling. The stage curtain fell to the floor, and suddenly there we were, the loudest band that night in Wisconsin—the loudest band ever in Wisconsin!

We ripped through our songs, playing nearly everything we had. Tracks from *New Hope for the Wretched* like "Concrete Shoes," "Sex

Junkie," and the Bobby Darin cover "Dream Lover," as well as some unreleased songs like "Pig Is a Pig," which Rod and I wrote together. About two-thirds into the gig, we kicked in with "Butcher Baby," where Wendy smashed a TV with the sledgehammer. Then, just as she had in cities all around the country without incident, she flicked the tip of her tongue at the sledgehammer's head and ran her fingers along the handle, long before Miley Cyrus captured American hearts licking a sledgehammer in her video "Wrecking Ball." She was topless at that point, and she twirled her fingers suggestively in front her vagina, too. The gestures were crass, for sure, but not illegal. At least that's what we thought.

We finished a little before midnight, thanked the crowd, and retreated to our dressing rooms. Our next show was scheduled in Cleveland, and since the drive would take eight hours, we wanted to get out of Milwaukee that night.

In her room, Wendy was getting out of her costume and cleaning herself up. Then two or three detectives walked in and began to menace her, telling her that "her kind" wasn't welcome in Milwaukee. I was nearby and came to the door. Petey came, too. Wendy never took crap, and the cops' insults were pissing her off.

"We're here to arrest you," they said.

"For what?" she said.

"Simulated masturbation with a sledgehammer."

"Huh?"

Then one of the cops reached for her breast. "Are these things real?"

"Don't touch me like that," she said.

"What?"

"You think you can just take liberties and do whatever you want?" she said.

She put her hand up, and once that happened, the detective punched her.

"This isn't fuckin' right!" she yelled.

So, I jumped in, and the cops and some of their reinforcements responded. There were five of them now. They pushed us through the door out into the snowy parking lot. Petey ran to get Rod, who was still inside.

By the time Rod came out, we were all into it on the ground. A photographer sent from one of the local papers to cover the concert fortunately was out there as well, snapping photos.

Wendy was on her belly. She kicked one of the cops in the hand, and for that he slammed her face into the asphalt. Fans threw snowballs and beer bottles at the cops, trying to help us.

Several cops piled on me and took me down to the ground, face in the snow. They locked my arms behind my back and handcuffed me. One guy had his knee on my neck. They shouted at us the whole time, directing racial slurs at me, in particular. You never get used to racism, even though I'd faced quite a bit of it already.

Much of the time I was touring with the Plasmatics, we'd go to truck stops, the ones off the big highways, and I couldn't get out of the bus. The people in these places would watch us walk in, and they would say things like "What the fuck?" and "What the hell is this thing?" and "Who are these niggers and gays?" So, to avoid dealing with trouble at every stop, Richie and the guys were like, "Beauvoir, you better stay on the bus!" They'd bring food out to me.

But back to Milwaukee, the detectives still had Wendy down. They mauled her, grabbed at her private parts, and broke her nose. Rod got into it, too, and they clubbed him with batons and arrested him. Soon enough, the detectives proceeded to shove Petey, Wendy, and me, along with some fans who'd also been arrested, into a police van.

We were driven out to the county jail, where they took our mug shots, fingerprints, and locked us up. In the morning, they charged Petey and me with disorderly conduct, a misdemeanor, but Rod and Wendy were both charged with felonies for resisting arrest and assaulting police officers.

Everybody made bail, and we blew out of Milwaukee as fast as we could. We wanted to get to Cleveland in time for the next show. Demoralized as we were, the show must go on.

We filed a lawsuit against the police officers for $5.95 million, with Wendy O. Williams, Rod Swenson, Jean Beauvoir, and Peter Cappadocia as plaintiffs, and the case went on for three years with one of the main officers dying in the interim! This was always questionable. The deaths and disappearances of the charged officers were always suspicious. But because of that, we lost the case.

We also appeared on the very popular late night talk show *Tomorrow with Tom Snyder*, where we blew up a car! It was one of the highest rated US television shows at the time on NBC and had featured everyone from John Lennon to Charles Manson, Paul McCartney, and U2. Due to the success of our appearance and with the ratings being so high, we were invited yet again to do the show.

I enjoyed my time with the Plasmatics and it was a great experience. The fans were a true inspiration that I'll never forget, but the time came for me to leave. I left for several reasons. One was that I felt the direction the band was about to take was not evident, and I was afraid that this might lead to our demise. Our image and music, blending punk with metal and other genres, were unique, which made us a hard act to follow, even for ourselves! But I felt there were others who were just better at playing metal.

Our present contracts were about to expire, and I had no interest in signing the new one as proposed. It was one-sided, and when I mentioned showing it to a lawyer, I was told, "We don't do lawyers here." So the writing was on the wall. Between the bad contract and some other occurrences, included an evening out with David Lee Roth and some good advice, time was up. After a while, Richie was out of the band as well, revealing that it wasn't a good idea for him to sign that agreement. We were both removed from many of the photos and videos that originally included us, I imagine to try to diminish our importance in the band's history.

I did stay in touch with Richie and Stu and would sometimes hear from Wes. I was extremely saddened when Wendy passed away on April 6, 1998, and was shocked to find out it was from a self-inflicted gunshot wound. She lived for performing and the fans, and I sincerely hope she found the peace and love she was searching for.

4

YEARNING TO BE SOLO

I HAD TAKEN A LEAP OF FAITH making such a move, but I was comfortable and excited about new prospects. I moved into a loft on Thirtieth Street in Manhattan. It was known as the Music Building, and lots of bands would rehearse there. Harry Belafonte was actually right below me. It was a big loft, about three thousand square feet. I built a separate room for my rehearsal studio, and it was always set up with a riser, drum kit, a couple of Marshall amps, an SVT bass rig, and some other gear. Sometimes I'd rent it out to other bands to use, but I used it for all my personal rehearsing and any recording that I needed to do.

I had a Doberman pinscher named Cleopatra. She was my companion and a wonderful dog. We did everything together. She was very smart, very well-trained, and she'd wait for me outside stores or delis, sitting sometimes without a leash and wouldn't move until I came back out.

Once, a friend of mine asked me to take his male Doberman he just couldn't house anymore. Supposedly, he was obedience and protection trained, so I gave it a shot and moved him in with Cleopatra and me. It was rough getting him accustomed to the new environment. For some reason, I could never get him in check. He was always marking his territory, peeing all over the loft, and I just couldn't get him to stop. Yet he fell right into place with Cleopatra, as you could imagine.

When I'd walk with both of them, it was quite the sight. Me, sporting a black leather Schott jacket and Mohawk, walking with two majestic Dobermans right by my side, off leash, through New York.

I eventually had to give him up because I just could not get him to stop soiling the house. Then he almost bit me one day when my then wife and I went to touch each other! He jumped up and took a snap right below my armpit, which would have been a juicy bite if he had hit his target. On top of the soiling, that was the final straw.

During my time in the Plasmatics, I had gotten married, very young, to a woman named Deborah Hoffman. She was very different than I was. She was German, an actress, and she had graduated from Sarah Lawrence College. I always liked things or people who were the opposite of my being a punk in the Plasmatics, so everything was good.

I met her on a New York subway where I saw her, fell in love instantly, and stayed on the train, many exits past mine, to ask her out. Even though I was a Plasmatic, I was extremely shy when it came to girls. I got off when she did at a Brooklyn stop and approached her. Much to my surprise, she was very receptive. She was beautiful, statuesque, and pretty conservative—just what I liked.

It wasn't long before we moved in together on St. Felix Street in Brooklyn, New York. It was a cute ground floor apartment on a pretty street. We then moved to the loft on Thirtieth Street.

Deborah was not a fan of Plasmatics shows. She felt it was just too shocking, crazy, and dangerous. When she did come, she was practically in tears, thinking something was going to happen to me, that I could even get killed on stage. She didn't come to many of the shows.

After I left the Plasmatics, our relationship was unfortunately short lived. I spent a lot of time on the road, she got lonely, got involved with the wrong people in the building, and it led to our demise.

There was never any real money with the Plasmatics, but upon my departure, money was even tighter. I was hoping that I could make it to a solo deal, but that did not come quickly. I played local shows and also put together a project called King Flux with my fellow former Plasmatic Richie Stotts, Tommy Lafferty, Tony Petri, and Andy Hilfiger and Billy Hilfiger, brothers of the clothing designer Tommy Hilfiger. We played around town, and that helped things out a bit.

Things got really rough, to the point where the landlord was about to put padlocks on my door. I ended up making a deal, selling the fixtures in my loft, and getting someone to take over the lease. That made it possible for me to get out amicably and move to my next apartment, which was at Fifty-Eighth Street and Sixth Avenue, one block away from Central Park.

I always liked uptown, as it was a completely different experience of living in New York. It was a great building, and both Bernard Edwards, the bass player for Chic, and Tahnee Welch, Raquel Welch's daughter, lived there. I may have had a bit of a crush on her at the time. It was a studio apartment and so much smaller than my loft, but it was classier.

This was also around the time that Jellybean Benitez introduced me to Madonna at a club where he was spinning. She was spunky, ambitious, talented, hardworking, a great dancer, and a very electric girl. Her career was just starting to take shape. She had released the song "Holiday," which she was shy to share with me, but it was starting to make some noise. The Plasmatics were very well known at that point. We started dating, and she'd come to local shows I was doing around New York after my departure from the Plasmatics. She was also performing around town, so I'd go to watch her perform at dance clubs.

I'd usually head back to the dressing room and we'd sit around together smooching. We'd then walk around the club hand in hand like two teenagers. It was fun, she was fun!

But our romance was short lived, and we soon went our separate ways. I always felt that relationships with female artists would be difficult. Being in the same profession, you'd probably end up competing. Nevertheless, I was kept in the loop by Nile Rodgers, a good friend who was producing her new album. About a year later, she called me and left a message saying that her song "Like a Virgin" had just gone to number one on the *Billboard* charts. She asked if I'd be interested in joining her on the road as her guitarist. I had different plans, so I passed.

My look had left quite an impact in the US, so I always had requests from photographers and film directors for shoots or scripts for me to read, etc. One of the photographers who reached out to me was Annie Leibovitz. She had a unique campaign planned: Polaroid had asked the five most famous photographers in the world to do a campaign, like

Avedon and Nastassja Kinski with the snake, and Annie Leibovitz had chosen me. This was quite an honor.

We did the shoot, but when the photo was sent to me to check out, I really didn't like it. I felt that I just didn't look good. At that stage of my life, I was so picky about how I looked in photos. I was always hard ass and insisted on owning them, so that nothing would get out that I didn't like.

Then I made a big mistake. Despite them not having my approval for the use of the photo, it had already gone to print and was in fashion magazines around the world. I was furious and called my attorney. He of course told me it was an open-and-shut case, so I took legal action.

I was paid off, and the timing couldn't have been better, but it was a move I've always regretted. I dismissed the photograph from my mind, but some years later, I came across it again. It then looked like a beautiful piece of art. It's funny how you look at things sometimes when you're young and realize later you were being an idiot. Rather than gratefully recognize that I had been chosen from all these people to be the subject of such a premier worldwide campaign by one of the world's best-known photographers, my reality was, the more people saw that photo, the more I'd be crushed because I actually thought I looked so bad, that I made this into a monumental problem. This was not the last time this would happen.

I also had the opportunity to shoot many times with Mark Weiss, one of the greatest rock 'n' roll photographers of all time, whom I loved. I was trying out some different looks and he was capturing them all. He photographed me with some really crazy guitars I had designed for me by Guild, leopard and tiger striped. Eventually, Little Steven Van Zandt ended up falling in love with the guitars and buying them all from me. In fact, I introduced Mark to Steven later on and Mark started to shoot us. Little Steven, and Disciples of Soul as well.

I also worked with another well-known photographer, Lynn Goldsmith, among others, and had several requests for shoots from Robert Mapplethorpe. I didn't feel comfortable shooting naked, which was his forte, though he was a fantastic photographer and a great artist. That's another mistake I think I made in my past. I should have accepted, as he went on to become one of history's greats.

Around the same time, an opportunity came along for a role in a film called *The Bronx Warriors*. It was an Italian film being shot in New York. I was always intrigued by acting, and it was something that I wanted to get into, so I decided to go for it.

It was a small role, but it was a start. The director, Enzo Castellari, was Italian, and so was most of the dialogue, but they dubbed it in English. It featured some famed American actors, such as Fred Williamson and Vic Morrow, who was tragically decapitated on set a year later by the blades of a helicopter. It was a fate I had missed by a hair during the Plasmatics pier performance not long before that.

From there, I started looking into acting more seriously, and the next role that came my way was through Amanda Mackey. I don't remember the name of the film, but I do know it was high level, as Amanda Mackey was one of the top casting agents in the US and remained so for many years. She had me come in to read, and I had two callbacks for that role, including being put on tape. She was really sweet to me and took a sudden interest, liking and believing in me as an actor. I ultimately didn't get that role, but it was a good sign that things could have gone very well, especially with somebody like her in my corner. Unfortunately, the next journey in my musical career was about to begin, which put a blunt stop to my acting career.

Because of the Plasmatics' exposure on all those major TV shows, I was easily recognizable—definitely the only Black guy with a blond Mohawk anywhere to be found. Most Blacks I'd come across felt strongly that it was against the roots of our people for me to dye my hair blond. It brought about problems everywhere I went, whether it was getting a taxi or going to a movie. There would always be somebody jumping up and making a comment in theaters, on the street, in shops, no matter where I was.

But this was mostly from Blacks. Whites, apart from a few racists, seemed to love the way my hair looked and always complimented me. So that was crazy, making it more intriguing and making me feel great to see that over the years blond Mohawks, different colored Mohawks, various colors of hair, have become quite the thing among Black people, kids, basketball teams, football players, soccer stars, and many others.

I guess that theory about the blond hair going against the roots was thankfully, eventually, retired! Either that, or I'd like to think that my having that haircut for all that time, suffering and enduring all those hard knocks, empowered many Black people to feel comfortable expressing themselves and trying different haircuts or doing things they might have felt were taboo.

5

DISCIPLES OF SOUL

At this point, I was even more determined to fulfill my dream of being signed as a solo artist. The first offer I got was from Prince's manager, who offered to have me to join his band. I was shocked! I was like, "Prince knows the Plasmatics?"

He said that Prince and his band were huge fans, and that he would make it to any show in the area that he could. I was pleased to hear that, but I told him that my goal was to record a solo album. He said that they had already taken this into consideration, and they'd be willing to put a provision in my contract stating Prince would also produce a solo record for me. They even had a salary offer prepared. I don't remember the exact amount, but nevertheless, I still told him that unfortunately, it would not work for me.

I knew already at that time that radio was segregated and very few Black musicians (if any) who had any kind of rock aspect to them were being played on pop radio, despite Jimi Hendrix's prior success. The few in the running were all light-skinned pretty-boy types, like Prince and myself—Lenny Kravitz wasn't in the mix yet. So I was thinking that Prince was perhaps trying to buy me out of the competition. Later on, it came to mind that I might have made a mistake—not for not joining Prince's band, but for thinking that's why he wanted to work with me.

I was also hanging out with Billy Idol and Steve Stevens. They were good friends, and I was helping them find a bass player. Sometimes they'd say, "Why don't you just do it?" And I'd say, "You know, guys, I really want to do my solo thing. That's really what I want to do."

Even Gene Simmons approached me and said something like, "How would you like to play with Ozzy?" I don't know if it was just a hypothetical or if he had spoken to him, but nevertheless, I just wasn't interested in anything except doing a solo record.

Shortly after that, I signed a deal with John Apostol, who managed Gary US Bonds. He was my first manager, the one who found me at age fourteen on Long Island and put me together with Gary. He was one of the few managers I knew, and I trusted him.

He informed me that he was working with Little Steven Van Zandt and Bruce Springsteen, and they were producing Gary's comeback album. John's idea was to put Steven and me together and move the production rehearsals to my loft. That way, Bruce, Steven, and I would get to know each other better.

He set up a meeting with Steven and me, and I played him some demos I had recorded. I played all the instruments, produced, and wrote everything. I wanted to demonstrate as much of my talent as possible. Meanwhile, I had already gone to every label and had been turned down.

So, Steven tells me, "Listen, Jonny," as he'd call me, "you're not gonna get a deal now. You come from the Plasmatics, and people aren't gonna think you have any musical relevance, so just 'fuggedaboutit' for the moment." Sounding as he did in *The Sopranos*, which is pretty much exactly what the labels would say to me. They said, "If you want to blow up cars, then we're interested, but if you want to sing, forget it!"

Steven went on to say that he was taking a break from Bruce for a while, and he offered to have me come join him. This way I could learn more about the industry and at the same time develop credibility from working with him, Bruce Springsteen's band, and other top-notch musicians. He said, "Then you'll be able to prove what you already know, that you have the talent needed to move forward." So in the end, his was the most convincing out of the offers I had received, and I decided to join him.

When I first joined Steven, it was quite a departure from the Plasmatics. Steven was a great mentor. He didn't seem to have any doubt about my abilities, but of course I was nervous. We immediately went into the Power Station and The Hit Factory, which were the top recording studios in New York at the time, to start recording the album *Men Without Women*. The musicians included a wide range of spectacular talent, such as Dino Danelli, Felix Cavaliere, Clarence Clemons, Danny Federici, Max Weinberg, horn players who had previously worked with Diana Ross, and Bruce Springsteen. The pressure was on.

Steven wanted to get right into it and start cutting the tracks. I had already received the songs and I practiced my ass off. I knew the material—at least as well as I could know it under the circumstances of my being nervous as hell! I was just thrown in the room with me in my own booth and everyone ready to go. After one take or so, I just fell right into the groove and started feeling really comfortable. It felt as if I was meant to be playing this, and I realized that the bass parts that I had played in the Plasmatics were a lot more difficult than people would think.

I was raised on all kinds of music as a bass player, everything from Motown to rock and metal, so I guess I had some things in my mental Rolodex that I could pull from, and I really enjoyed it. Once I got over the initial fright and intimidation, it was smooth sailing. I could relax and concentrate on other things like background vocals and duet parts that Steven and I would do together.

Being in the studio with Jimmy Iovine, Bob Clearmountai, and Shelley Yakus, the world's greatest engineers and producers, was where I learned most of my music production skills. It was a great learning experience. I was already able to make the initial demos that eventually got me signed, but this sharpened my studio skills immensely.

It wasn't long before we did the first video for the song "Forever," the first single from the album. It was actually derived from the film we made called *Men Without Women*. It was about New York City, and we did a lot of filming in Central Park and through the streets of New York. I was riding a small chopper bicycle—similar to what I had as a child. I was wearing a cutoff leather motorcycle vest and riding it through Times Square. It definitely caught people's eyes. The video was well accepted by MTV and played quite a bit.

I think I was probably the first Black guy on MTV. They didn't play any Black artists whatsoever; even Michael Jackson wasn't getting played until the president of Columbia Records gave them an ultimatum that he would remove some of the bigger artists like Bruce Springsteen unless they made a change. MTV finally gave in and started with Michael Jackson.

The time came for this fabulous band to hit the road. Steven pulled out all the stops. He was accustomed to the spoils of touring with Bruce, so even though we were to play smaller venues, the level of touring remained the same. I was in no way complaining. We had a personal trainer available to us and all first-class hotels and travel. We were well taken care of.

I was to him what he was to Bruce Springsteen. I handled a lot of background vocals and different parts and was both the bass player and his second in command.

The shows were great, and the audiences were amazing. We were invited to perform at Rockpalast in Germany, which was the biggest television show in the world. It aired in more countries than any other show. It was incredible and something very special for me beyond the Plasmatics. It was put together by the late Peter Rüchel from WDR, who was just a really wonderful man.

He loved Little Steven and the Disciples of Soul, and we headlined the show. Stevie Ray Vaughan was one of the opening bands, and some other great bands were also on the bill. It was a fantastic festival. We actually did it twice under Peter Rüchel's watch, and it was always as gratifying.

We spent a lot of time in Germany and had a very close relationship with EMI Records over there. They were great guys and definitely some interesting characters. One guy in particular, Lothar Meinerzhagen, would sometimes drive Steven and me in his hot rod BMW to the next town if we needed to get there fast. Every time he was commissioned to drive us, I'd try to fall asleep to avoid this nightmare of an experience. There was no speed limit on the Autobahn in those days, and Lothar would just drive us at ridiculous speeds while telling jokes—which were actually pretty funny, but it's hard to laugh when you're hurtling along at 260 kilometers an hour and just trying to make it out of the car alive! It didn't matter if there was rain, sleet, or snow, it was always the same deal. I like driving fast, but only when I'm driving!

The film we made, *Men Without Women*, was set to air at Cannes Film Festival. The Hells Angels were premiering their film, *Hells Angels Forever*, there at the same time. Steven and I had known the heads of the New York chapter previously and had found that on the road some other Hells Angels branches throughout Europe would give us a hard time for wearing our Little Steven and Disciples of Soul jackets. In certain countries they took it as an offense because the jackets had admittedly very similar patchwork on the back. Steven had clearance when putting it together, but this issue had to be addressed as we were getting threats.

Most of the Hells Angels head guys were flying in for the premiere of their film, so a meeting was set up between Steven and me and the chapter leaders who had flown in. The head of the New York chapter basically told everyone that permission had been granted for us to wear our jackets without interference from anybody, in any country. This was all a pretty wild and amazing happening. Hells Angels have always been really great rock fans, supportive of us, and I still know some of them today, like Chuck Zito, a very cool guy and a friend, who gave me his book and signed it the last time I saw him. He'd do security for high-profile celebs and ultimately went into acting in several films and TV shows. I realized we were both in the 1990 film *The Bronx Warriors*, the first film for both of us, I believe!

While traveling and performing, I got to meet a lot of great people. We opened for the Who on their 1982 comeback tour of the US, which was quite an experience. Immense venues and everything top notch, the audiences were really responsive, and I had a blast.

It was odd to see the relationship between Pete Townshend and Roger Daltrey, since they didn't get along. They would travel separately, and at the shows Pete's bodyguard would bring him to our dressing room before or after the show to hang out a bit, then he'd leave and shortly afterward, Roger's bodyguard would escort him in to hang, or vice versa. Nevertheless, they were out there rockin' it every night. It was a great tour, the guys were wonderful, and we remained friends afterward.

We also played the legendary US Festival that broke U2. Some of the other bands performing were Judas Priest, Ozzy Osbourne, INXS, and many others. The festival was founded by Steve Wozniak of Apple fame and Bill Graham, a well-known US promoter. Another big festival on our horizon was the Reading Festival in England. That was a tough one. I remember being quite acrobatic during that show as I spent most of my time dodging a plethora of UK beer bottles being hurled at us. I guess we weren't their cup of tea!

We continued to tour and had a blast! As with most of the things I do, I learned a lot, and it really prepared me for the times to come.

In our deal, Steven had agreed to record some demos with me for shopping that elusive solo deal I was still desperate to nail. Things were finally starting to look up. I was fairly confident, as Gary Gersh from EMI Records was showing a lot of interest at this point.

He had originally signed Little Steven, and the demos we had recorded were slammin'! Time went by, with me in a constant state of anticipation. You know how it feels when you're waiting for something and the people holding that something know you're waiting for it, yet they opt to procrastinate? Then finally, I got the bad news that EMI wasn't going to sign me, because things were not going as well as he had anticipated. He loved the material, blah, blah, blah, but the bottom line was "fuggedaboutit."

It was extremely disappointing. We had been working a long time recording demos and preparing for this deal that now would never come. It's not like everyone gets what they want in the world. There were and are tons of people dying for deals that never get one, so this does linger in the back of your mind. If it moved to the front, you'd quit!

The label did, no doubt, like the material. Gary Gersh, who I remained friends with, called me and asked if he would be able to use a song of mine, "Dark Side of the Sun," for an upcoming John Waite album.

It wasn't the deal I longed for, but it was definitely a good 100 percent writer credit on John's album. I was a big fan of the Babys, as well as his voice, so I gave it to them to record, and it turned out well. "Missing You," also from that album, became a huge hit. It was great for me, as the album went double platinum, selling over two million copies in the US alone and several millions in the end. It was a nice boost for my songwriting career.

I resumed trying to make things happen in hopes of seeing that solo deal materialize, but it continued to be a rough road, especially after the rejection from EMI. I felt I was starting all over again, back to square one.

Touring with Steven made us pretty tight. He always liked my way of thinking and my foresight in terms of business, so he would often ask me for advice or trust bouncing things off me. I can remember helping to plan his wedding to Maureen Van Zandt. People like Clarence Clemons, Bruce, myself, and all the people involved worked constantly to make it a fantastic event.

Many people are not aware that Little Richard was a minister, so he officiated the couple's ceremony, and Percy Sledge ("When a Man Loves a Woman") was hired to sing. It was a beautiful event, and I truly enjoyed helping to put it together and being one of the groomsmen.

After joining Steven, my personal situation improved. I was able to pay my bills and actually enjoy playing music. I could also work on my image and spend time on my health and fitness. For the Disciples, I wanted to have a completely different style. I didn't want that big bulked-up look, so I went from gladiator mode to a dancer's physique by losing thirty pounds from taking daily ballet, dance, and jazz classes. I wanted to learn how to do pirouettes on stage; I thought that'd be a cool move with a guitar. After a long period of hard work and focus, I built up to be able to do five turns. It was pretty funny to see me hopping around these ballet and turn classes with a Mohawk. It was entertaining for a lot of the students and teachers, and it was a reforming time of my life.

I'd only eat a chef's salad as my main meal, with small snacks throughout the day. I took it very seriously. If you look at pictures of me from the very beginning of my time with the Disciples to the latter part when we did the *Voice of America* record, the difference is astounding.

I upgraded to a trendy one-bedroom apartment at 1 Lincoln Plaza on Manhattan's Upper West Side. They were very strict, and if I even talked in my living room after 10:00 PM the neighbors would be knocking on the walls. That was irritating to have to contend with, but it was a beautiful building (the ASCAP building, right across from the Metropolitan Opera House) with other positive perks, so I lived with it. I wasn't there all that much anyway.

The Upper West Side was filled with artsy types and ballet dancers walking up and down the streets, but most of all, I really loved Central Park. I liked everything about that classiness of uptown, and I felt very much at home. It was so different from the punk world. Nevertheless, I still remained who I was.

New York was a fabulous place because everything was so close and within reach, and there's an energy that's really hard to find anywhere else. I literally had a major recording studio around the corner (Media Sound) and management up the street, with MTV in the same building and my accountant three floors down. You could do all your business within a block or two.

The funny thing about 1 Lincoln Plaza is that it was a different kind of building than I was accustomed to. I had three or four doormen, and they were really great guys. They were always so courteous and respectful that it made me feel somewhat regal. Having people opening doors, helping with packages, and bringing things up to me—it was a completely different life from what I had before. I loved it. The only negative was an incident when I received a curt letter from management saying that they wanted me to move out.

The letter stated that tenants were complaining that I was scaring them in the elevator. I guess that was a possibility. Being a Black man with a blond Mohawk, wearing a leather jacket with spikes, I was quite different from the other residents. I'm pretty sure I was the only Black guy in the entire building.

I called my attorney, advised him of the letter, and sent it over. He laughed and said, "Don't worry about it. I'll handle it."

My attorney at that time was Stu Silfen, a lovely man—relaxed and laid back, but a brilliant attorney. He was very good to me and extremely helpful. He got in touch with the building and told them, "If you would like Mr. Beauvoir to move out, just write us a check for $100,000 and he'll gladly leave."

I had a firm lease, so they couldn't get me out based on the circumstances they shared. The proposal I imagine was a bit rich for their taste, and we never heard anything on this topic again.

I was ready to leave the Disciples after the first tour, but that wasn't a popular decision. EMI Germany called me in a panic, making me offers to stay. Steven also wasn't so keen on my leaving. So I agreed to stay on for another go, but though I played bass on the *Voice of America* album, I chose to play guitar for the second run, which Steven was fine with. I was slowly moving mentally towards what I wanted to be known as: a lead singer and guitarist. I stayed with Little Steven for a while longer, but I still eventually made the decision to leave the band and focus on my main goal. Steven understood. We remained friends and continued to speak often.

6

KISS—"THRILLS IN THE NIGHT"

I FREQUENTLY HIT THE CLUBS IN TOWN, and I always gravitated to the opposite of what a lot of rockers would appreciate. Most would go to a bar or the pub after a show to drink beer, but I always opted for the poshest disco in town, places you wouldn't think would be in my wheelhouse. I guess I always wanted to leave an impression, and you'd make a lot more of one in a disco! I enjoyed the reactions, as I always loved contrast in life in general.

One of these clubs was called Heartbreak. It was a place downtown that welcomed everyone from rock stars to actors, other celebrities, and people from all walks of life. Brooke Shields would be there with her mom; they were always really sweet. Drew Barrymore would be sitting on her parents' shoulders. It was quite the mélange, which made each night different and special.

One night, I walked into the club and a well-dressed guy with long black hair came over and said, "Hey, you're that guy from the Plasmatics?"

"Yeah, that's me, Jean Beauvoir."

"Well, I'm Paul Stanley from KISS. Great to meet you."

I didn't recognize him at first (though he looked vaguely familiar), since KISS was still wearing makeup at the time. We spoke for a bit about this and that before hitting the dance floor. It was an interesting place with a little restaurant that had kind of a diner feel, but there was also a big dance floor and the DJ was blasting great, soulful music. We were dancing like fools with a bunch of girls and having a wild time! We exchanged numbers and started keeping in touch.

The first time we got together, he took me to this place called Serendipity. It was on the Upper East Side, and they had the most amazing desserts you could ever imagine. They were huge, and you could barely finish one. We'd chat on the phone; other times we'd go see a cool movie or go to concerts. Anything fun that was going on, we'd try to get to. It came to a point where it was a weekly thing, and we were really hanging out a lot.

We liked going to a restaurant called Columbus Cafe. It was owned by Paulie Herman, who was also an actor. You see him in many Mafia movies like *Goodfellas* and *Casino*. He had many friends in the industry who would come and hang out at his place, such as Robert de Niro, Sean Penn, and Diane Lane. (I remember once having a late-night dinner with Sean and Diane.) I'd see more of Sean back in those days. Many other well-known or up-and-coming actors, musicians, and rock stars would hang out there. I met quite a lot of people and made some good friends there.

Paul and I had a similar taste in pretty much everything: shoes, clothing, way of life. It was uncanny. We looked like bookends—the Black guy with the blond Mohawk, and a White guy with black hair. We were an interesting pair to see out, the two wingmen.

I remember going to his apartment for the first time, and a beautiful lamp he had caught my eye. I said, "Wow, that's a cool lamp. Where could I get something like that?"

"Well, it's $40,000," I believe he said.

"What! You paid $40,000 for a lamp? What does it do?"

"Yeah, but it's not just any lamp," he said. "These Tiffany lamps are collectibles, and they retain their value. As a matter of fact, it's probably worth close to double what I paid for it at the time."

I exclaimed, "Whoa!"

Another thing that really caught my eye is that he would have all his hi-fi equipment and TVs built into the walls of his apartments. At my place, the wires would be hanging from the back of my equipment in an unsightly tangled mess. I started incorporating this built-in idea into my homes.

There were a lot of little things that we'd talk about and do, and our friendship was a great learning experience. It showed me a completely different way of living as a rocker. It was very comfortable for me, as I came from a pretty posh family of presidents and ambassadors and was brought up and taught to behave a certain way. We had very similar backgrounds, like our fathers not being very supportive of our careers early on and things like that. Paul actually met my family a few times, and I met his dad as their relationship was taking a turn for the better.

Another top-tier hangout spot for many of us was the China Club. We would often go from Columbus, Paulie Herman's place, to the China Club, which was on New York's Upper West Side. It became a very popular hang for musicians, actors, and other celebrities who wanted to sing or play or otherwise listen to great music and have the opportunity to see surprise guests get up to jam on stage—everyone from Elton John to Michael Bolton, Madonna, the Doobie Brothers, Rick James, and Paul and I. Nile Rodgers, Rick James, and I had a great jam one night.

Slash and I jammed another night, or that may have been at another NY club. Then the China Club moved to L.A. probably around the same time that Paul and I moved there. That was very convenient because the same thing started to happen there, and the China Club L.A. got so popular that the fire department came and closed it down one night for exceeding capacity. Beautiful girls, playmates, models, actors, record executives, and just cool people, on top of all the musicians, made this place an integral part of our lives every Monday night.

Paul shared with me once that when KISS had their initial big success, he had made millions of dollars. Before he turned his head, most of it was gone. He was determined to make sure that never happened again, so he tried to teach me some valuable lessons not to make the same mistakes he had made. It was kind of surreal to be such close friends with someone I admired so much. Though I'd had the opportunity to meet a lot of celebrities with Steven and the Plasmatics, KISS was a very special part of my life, so I truly valued my friendship with Paul and the rest of KISS. They treated me like a brother. It was and remains very special.

I admired Paul's way of thinking and how he separated music from his personal life. His places were never filled with music gear; he left that for the studio or for rehearsals. He had a good balance in his life. He urged that keeping it together is what will give you longevity, and he was one hundred percent right. There were no drugs, and no binge drinking. He was so focused on his work and business, it was impressive, and I have to say that I adopted several of his ways in my own life.

He was there as a friend throughout the time I was trying to get a record deal, and he shared with me much of his business acumen and other general advice. He was also a mentor, no doubt, and I believe he cared for me, which made him open up even more. We remained close friends right through when I signed my first solo deal and beyond.

We both loved cool clothing. He might see a jacket I wore and say "Hey! Where did you get that?" He'd always have cool garb and I'd ask the same. We also both had an affinity for fitness and staying in shape. I had just undergone this complete body transformation from the Plasmatics to Little Steven, and I was always training or taking classes. We sometimes would train and do exercises together. I still tease him about the ones I really hated, in particular "peeing dog" and "donkey kick"—like fifty or more times per leg! They were ridiculous looking butt exercises, and I still laugh about it.

We loved to eat, which is not a great attribute for guys that are trying to stay in shape as front men. He introduced me to wontons and peanut sauce, which I still eat to this day, when I can find it! One day, while we were inhaling that glorious Chinese food at his apartment, he pulled out a guitar and started strumming and messing about. I remember going into the bathroom and hearing a melody from what he was playing.

When I came out, I said, "Hey, how about something like this?" We started going back and forth, and from there, we realized that a cool song was being written. That song was "Thrills in the Night" for the KISS *Animalize* album.

Since writing that song together, I became more involved musically and started going to KISS preproduction rehearsals for the recording of the song. Paul and I would initially record demos on a 4-track, Fostex or

Tascam, minirecorder at his apartment. We would bounce and rebounce instruments to make full-fledged demos.

Since we spent so much time together, I would often go into the studio where they would be recording. One day, very casually, nothing planned, Paul said, "Why don't you just pick up the bass and, you know, play to 'Thrills in the Night.' It sounded great on the demo, so we may as well just reproduce that," and so I ended up playing bass on three songs on the album, "Thrills in the Night," "Get All You Can Take," and "Under the Gun."

When *Animalize* was released, it was very well received, spawning the hit singles "Heaven's on Fire" and "Thrills in the Night" and achieving high positions on charts around the world. It was the biggest-selling KISS album since 1977's *Alive II* and was quickly certified platinum in the United States and other territories around the world.

While still enjoying our routine of hanging out, Paul and I were also doing more music together. He started preproduction for the *Asylum* album early, to really fine-tune everything before they'd go into the studio to record. He asked me to do some more writing, so we went back to his apartment (with the Chinese food, of course) and started writing again. Those writing sessions resulted in "Uh! All Night" and "Who Wants to be Lonely," both singles on the KISS *Asylum* album.

Paul was extremely picky about KISS lyrics. You'd think that with songs like "Uh! All Night," where the titles seem so simple, that it was a cinch. In reality, he was so precise as to how he wanted things to be said by KISS that it took a lot more time than you'd imagine. Even though we'd write the melodies and the song very quickly, we'd spend hours on the phone at times working on lyrics. We'd literally be on the phone for hours, me lying in my bed and him on his couch, saying, "Hmmm . . . uh all night, up all night . . . I don't know."

We'd literally go line by line. For some of it, we'd call Desmond Child, who Paul had worked with previously, to do a once-over and see if anything could be improved. A funny coincidence is that Desmond Child, Diane Warren, and myself all started songwriting with KISS. We all then moved on to write on other rock and pop records and have all had successes in different genres. They continued mainly songwriting and producing other artists, while I focused mainly on my artist career.

Similar to the process for *Animalize*, Paul and I would be on the phone and he'd say, "Oh, just come by the studio, Jean. I'll be working from two to six." I'd just pop over there to hang out. He asked, "You want to play a couple of songs on this record? Why don't you play the songs that we recorded together on the demos? You have a good feel for it, so let's just do that."

So I'd just pick up the bass and go for it. I'm a pretty fast learner, so I could listen to the songs for a moment and then lay it down. Gene was around at times, and he never minded. He liked me, and we got along very well. I think he respected me, so he didn't mind me playing the bass parts. He was very supportive, and to him, the end product was most important, so I ended up playing bass on the songs "Uh! All Night" and "Who Wants to Be Lonely" and contributed background vocals.

The album was a major success, and the songs I cowrote and played on were both singles. The album went double platinum in the United States, not to mention all it sold in the rest of the world.

At this stage, I had made a good amount of money, and I was running amok! I had limousines in New York, and I would use them to go everywhere from restaurants to the pharmacy. I literally had one on call twenty-four seven, all year. This thing was so long, he could never find a parking spot. He'd have to drive round and round until I was done. I was also supporting my band, and I had moved to a new apartment nearby, called the Colonnade, on Fifty-Seventh Street.

I also had a personal assistant, Robbie Coleman. He did everything with and for me—a really nice guy, smart and super efficient. He was originally my guitar tech touring with Little Steven, and our relationship evolved from there. He filtered everything and everyone. He kept me up to date, scheduled my time, and practically ran my life.

As I worked so much, my day-to-day life was overwhelming. I don't think people realize what being an artist actually entails. Decisions are constantly being made regarding recordings, photos, artwork, videos, and preparation for all these things, finding clothing or having it made, supporting other artists. The list goes on and on. And not only was I an artist, but I produced and wrote songs with other artists or bands, so there were a hundred things that went with those jobs in addition to maintaining my own artist career. Having an assistant was pretty much imperative.

I remember going out to dinner with Paul and he said, "Jean, you're spending too much money. You're out of control. You're spending more than I am, and I'm in KISS!" I laughed, but I took him seriously, kind of!

He told me, "I promise you that if you keep this up, the bottom will fall out."

7

RICHARD BRANSON—THE VIRGIN DEAL

AROUND THIS TIME, in 1983 and '84, I was traveling back and forth to Sweden and spending a fair amount of time over there. I'd met a girl in Gothenburg during a Disciples tour, Janique Icka Svedberg. She was a talented dancer, singer, and an awesome entertainer. I had gone back to Gothenburg after the Little Steven tour to go spend time with her. We stayed there for a while, enjoyed the city and had a great time. But it came time for me to head back to NY. I asked her to join me, she accepted the invite, and we moved there together. We went out quite a bit in New York and ran into lots of interesting people. Whenever I'd come across talented artists or performers, I'd always do my best to find opportunities for them. It's just something I've always tried to do in life. Now, an opportunity came along for her.

I was very close with Kid Creole and the Coconuts, a very cool and successful musical group. Kid Creole was the leader and front man, percussionist Coati Mundi was a crazy character who added tons of fun to the group, and three beautiful girls—the Coconuts—sang background vocals and danced. One night, we all went to a party together and Adriana, the leader of the Coconuts, approached me and mentioned that they were looking for another girl, urgently!

She asked me if I thought Janique would be interested in joining them. I was excited for her, and I knew that she'd freak out, as performing was her dream. The group was at its peak, so how opportune!

I broke the news to her, and she lost her mind! I remember her trying to conceal the childish grin of excitement on her face. I had brought her over from Sweden, so she was new to the United States. She wasn't very proficient at business or negotiations, but that was my area, and I enjoyed it, so I helped her put the deal together. She was officially in the group. We both knew that with the band's insane touring schedule and me running around the world, our relationship would be in jeopardy. From there, we sort of drifted apart, which was sad, but I was delighted she got that opportunity and the chance to tour around the world.

I continued recording demos, which I'd been doing for some years now, even before Gary US Bonds. I played all the instruments, sang all the vocals, produced and wrote the songs. I did everything to try to show these labels that there was more talent here than met the eye. I had a fancy slap bass and all sorts of other tasty musical bits. It all sounded pretty exciting, at least in my mind. The stand-out song was called "This Year We Live Dangerously," and it was an instrumental with some vocals coming in and out throughout the song. I was hoping that this, in combination with other material, would do it.

It's a tough position to be in when you're basically all alone with this huge belief of yours and oftentimes, only yours. Where does it come from? What puts the air beneath your wings, the resilience, the courage? What makes you believe that people from around the world would want to spend money to see you or to hear you? You need a pretty big ego, lots of confidence, and very tough skin to see that argument through.

My main motivation was actually girls at first, and a record deal would be just one of the vehicles to get me there. Part of me longed to get back at all the ones who wouldn't give me the time of day in junior high and high school, the moms and dads who figured I was a born loser being Black, and that I could never be someone who'd be adequate for their daughters. (Remember, back on Long Island, there were no Black girls anywhere in sight.) Also, all the people who had never believed in me, never supported me, my father who threw me out of the house, and those who had shunned me when I was younger. Sure, I had married a very beautiful woman, Deborah Hoffman, while in the Plasmatics, but that was now over.

I felt MTV, as a "solo artist" and individual success, was the answer to all my woes. I had already been on MTV with Steven, and from that, I could already feel the change. In the Plasmatics, I had had an evil persona. I wore glasses so no one ever saw my eyes. When I joined Steven, I changed quite a bit. I had lost thirty pounds. I was in great shape, and it really helped my stage performances. I could do multiple pirouettes with a guitar, and I really liked where I was going.

I wanted to prove to the world and to myself that I could break barriers by being me. JUST DO YOU has always been my personal slogan. I could not accept the absurd limitations imposed on me because of my skin color. I knew that there were a lot of others who felt as I did, but not everyone has the tough skin to fight this battle and push forward, staying true to themselves against all odds.

There are leaders and followers in the world, and you need both for the world to function. Like fans and bands—if everyone was in a band, we'd have no fans. Some people truly prefer to take a backseat and support the ones out front battling for the cause. It's the same as members of a band. You usually have the star, a couple of other guys in the band who want to be the star, and others who are perfectly happy playing their instruments and going along for the ride.

When someone other than the leader desperately wants to be the leader, too, or several members feel that way, it pretty much always leads to the band breaking up sooner or later. Then they get back together when they run out of money or want more. At that point, they wisely put aside their differences and barrel through it.

I would spend a good amount of time with friends I had in New York, or anywhere in the world, mostly people from other walks of life that I just enjoyed speaking to or bouncing ideas off. They seemed to enjoy my company and views as well. One was a gentleman named Howard Bloom. He was a well-known publicist in New York, a very intelligent man who always had really interesting, insightful, and valuable things to say. I actually don't recall if we had business together, but we were definitely friends. Every once in a while, we would just get together, have a nice lunch, and discuss the industry and world events.

I have always enjoyed doing that, meeting with people from different businesses, different styles of music, different mindsets and different lives—people I could learn from, and as I always say, "More info for my mental Rolodex."

I learned much of what I know from doing this. And I've always felt that there's something to learn from pretty much anybody, regardless of how successful they are or aren't. The fact that they've lived and have had experiences that are different than mine was of value, and made me think of how to incorporate the various input I received into things that I was doing. As a songwriter, I feed off the experiences of others. Their pain, their bliss, their thoughts, and their concerns about anything in life.

But back to the solo deal. I did get one bite after shopping my material everywhere, and it was from Polar Music in Sweden, which was ABBA's label. They liked what they heard, and they offered me a single deal for "This Year We Live Dangerously." I was thrilled, mostly because I loved them as a group, so I was about to head off to Sweden and make this deal.

Well, a couple of days before I was about to take the plane, I had another lunch with Howard Bloom. He told me, "You know, Jean, there's this guy, a manager and promoter named Gary Kurfirst, who worked with very eclectic acts like the Talking Heads, Blondie, the Ramones, the Who, Jimi Hendrix, and the Doors. He likes things that are different, unique, and artists with true talent." Howard had a hunch we'd get along and suggested I meet with him. He said, "Let me make a phone call for you and try to get you in to see him before you leave."

I said, "Great!"

He got back to me quickly and informed me that he set up the meeting. I was excited, but at the same time had little faith. My ass was sore at this point!

I went to Gary's office and was greeted by a short and very thin woman wearing a black motorcycle jacket and tight black pants. She was quite the character; her name was Andrea Starr, Gary's right hand. She was cordial as she guided me into Gary's office. He was sitting in the corner with a view overlooking Columbus Circle. He was charming and very direct, and I liked him right away. He made me feel comfortable, and he had the certain confidence of a man who had truly spent time in the business.

He told me that he had listened to the song, which he liked very much—I had sent it in advance. He basically asked me in so many words, "How much do you want to make for your first contract year?"

I said, "Well, I don't know, I have no idea. As much as possible, but I'm more concerned with getting through the first step, getting signed! What do you think you can make happen? I can't get a deal to save my life."

He said, "Well, the deal is no problem, why don't we say a million dollars? If I don't make you $1 million in the first year, you can leave me. I'll put it in writing."

You have to be pretty confident to believe that you will make an unknown solo artist at least $1 million in the next twelve months, or you've wasted your time. I literally could not believe what I was hearing, and I thought, *He has no idea. I don't think he understands what he's up against, and that he's not the first person to try.*

I also remember him saying that I was a unique artist and that he would set me up so that I could always make a living doing music. He wasn't a "hit"-motivated guy. He felt that many of those would just come and go without gaining credibility. He believed in the long term and building your audience bit by bit until you became an undisputed, highly respected, and valuable artist who could claim his or her place in history.

The problem for the labels was that I didn't fit into a mold. They didn't know if I was rock, funk, R&B, or a combination—they were utterly confused. I wasn't Black enough for the Black label floor nor White enough for the White floor. I was sitting somewhere in the abyss as far as they were concerned.

He told me, "Listen, I will have you a deal within the month."

I did reiterate to Gary that I'd been to every label, and no one, I mean no one, had given me the time of day, unless I was prepared to stick to my old antics of blowing up cars or creating a destructive, visual live performance of some kind.

He said, "You went to the labels. I didn't."

He told me, "Go to Switzerland." (From the beginning, he always confused Sweden with Switzerland.)

I told him, "Sweden, Gary, Sweden!"

He'd say, "Yeah, yeah, you know what I mean, but under no circumstance should you sign anything at this point. Go meet ABBA and the label, enjoy the food, have a little vacation, and I'll call you within the next couple of weeks. If anything comes up while you're there, if you need to reach me for any reason, feel free to give me a call anytime."

I left that meeting flabbergasted! I had finally found a manager, which was already a massive step forward, but my mind was still filled with doubt, expecting to hear the same ole, same ole—that he tried, but just couldn't generate any interest.

I anxiously awaited the agreement. I had my attorney, Stu Silfen, in place. I immediately alerted him that an agreement would be on its way to us. I explained what had happened in the meeting, and he had heard of Gary Kurfirst and his good reputation, so he was very positive about the whole thing.

The agreement arrived promptly. It wasn't very long; it got straight to the point, and yes, indeed, the $1 million provision was included, just as he had said. It was an unusually artist-favorable agreement, something I was definitely not accustomed to seeing. Stuart and I went through everything. There wasn't much to change, so I signed, and we sent it back to Gary.

I went to Sweden as Gary had suggested, met with Polar, and also got to say hello to ABBA. Everyone was very excited to see me and we had good talks, but I didn't sign anything.

Lo and behold, a couple of days later my phone rings, and it's Gary. He greets me and casually goes, "I'm in London right now, and I just sat down with Richard Branson. I played him your music. He loves it and would like to meet you in person as soon as possible. I'm sending you a ticket for tomorrow, and I'll have you picked up at the airport. The driver will take you to the hotel and then off to meet Richard."

I was amazed yet again by this manager. I couldn't believe it—everything was moving forward just as he said. I immediately got it together and headed to London. Richard Branson had his label, Virgin

Records, which I knew all about. I was on my way to London to possibly finally reach my longtime dream—meeting with Richard Branson himself about my career. No one could say they'd "have to speak to this one or that one" or "move it up the ladder" or any of the other expressions I'd so often heard. I jumped on that plane, arrived in London, and a gentleman was waiting for me with a card reading, "Mr. Beauvoir." He helped me with my bags, and we were off to the car. We arrived at the hotel—I believe it was the Royal Garden Hotel, a really nice place. We pulled up to the circular drive, the gentleman took my bags, and I checked in. Virgin had made all the arrangements. Granted, this was not the first time I had seen posh hotels, limos, and nice treatment, but being back on my own, it was nice to see it again, but this time all for *moi*.

I prepared and got ready for the meeting, was picked up by a limo, and arrived at Richard's riverboat. I was escorted on and saw that lunch had been prepared. Richard Branson, a statuesque man with an aristocratic English accent, yet casually hip, greeted me (Gary had just arrived as well), and welcomed us to have a seat. He was polite, nice, and intelligent—all around great—and he loved what he heard.

He started off by complimenting me and telling me what a bright future I'd have and that he was excited to welcome me to Virgin. Gary joked, "If you can afford it!" I sat there and just took it all in—beautiful scenery, sitting on this boat, laughing about the deal that we're going to make, and how great everything's going to be. It was probably the most exciting time of my life. He offered me the deal right there. We even discussed my retaining creative control, and he was fine with everything. From the outset, basic terms were discussed, including tour support, videos, and first-class flights on Virgin were made part of my deal. It was crazy! I was in awe.

We had a great time together. I stayed a few more days in London to try to find some cool clothing at the Kensington Market or on King's Road, then headed back to New York. Upon my return, I went to Gary's office. He asked me, "How would you feel if we made a label deal rather than a straight artist deal?"

I said, "Us with Virgin?"

"Yes," he answered.

I asked him what the benefits were of going this route. "More money and more points for us," he said.

"Oh, is this a question? Of course, I'm in!"

We received the agreement draft from Virgin, which included everything we had discussed—a very big recording advance and budget! We now had our own label with Virgin. I could have hugged and kissed Gary, which I believe I did! Once our business was concluded with Richard, it was time to get to work.

One of my very first phone calls was to my longtime friend Tommy Lafferty, who was the guitar player that I had transformed from a Berkeley jazz guy in Gary US Bonds—a good one at that—to a rock and metal guy. He was dying to rock, and now I'd be able to include him. He was driving a cab at the time, and I surprised him with a call saying, "All right, I got my solo deal! Quit your job, I'm putting you on salary."

It felt so good to do that. I had always told him that I'd be back for him, and he'd be able to do music full-time. We were chomping at the bit, and we knew the journey was about to begin! We got all sorted and started preparing for the next steps. I also called Paul Stanley to give him the good news. They were very happy for me—everyone was happy to see that my hunger was finally being fed.

8

"FEEL THE HEAT"—SLY STALLONE & *COBRA*

There was a well-known studio called Media Sound down the street from where I lived in New York's Upper West Side. The building was on Fifty-Seventh Street and was originally a church. It had beautiful rooms with tall ceilings and great acoustics for cutting live drums and other instruments. At the time, it was a go-to place for many great producers and artists, so it seemed most apropos to start there. I went in with a few song ideas and started laying down tracks. I was playing most of the instruments, but Tommy would come in and play some guitar parts and solos on certain songs while also contributing background vocals and fun company.

I decided to invite some guest musicians into the studio as well, including my brother, Pierre and singers Elizabeth Ames and Malena Belafonte to add background vocals. One day, Mick Jagger and Mick Jones were working in another room. They came by to visit when I was recording a song called "Rockin' in the Street." Of course, I was a big fan of both—I loved the Stones and Foreigner, so it was a real honor to have them in the studio with me.

They were grooving to the track and enjoying themselves, so finally I said to Mick Jones, "Here's a guitar. Why don't you just play along with the track and put in whatever you feel."

He certainly felt it and added some classic Mick Jones guitar, including a tasty solo. I should've asked Mick Jagger to sing!

I continued recording songs, but Gary Kurfirst wasn't very happy with what I sent him. He thought it was good, but he felt it wasn't original enough and that there was something else in me that needed to get out.

I kept working, trying out some different grooves and approaches, and finally recorded the song, "Feel the Heat." I knew there was something there and that it was different. But to be honest, I wasn't sure if he was going to love it or hate it!

He heard the song, jumped on the phone and said, "That's the one. That's what I'm talking about!"

It was an eclectic song with a unique production. I really did what I wanted—huge drums, big bass, powerful guitars, and I played live timbales and other percussion. I followed no rules and just did what came to mind.

I had received a Roland guitar synthesizer that I fell in love with, and I used it religiously for everything. That tends to happen when you get a new toy. On the "Feel the Heat" recording, most of what sounds like keyboards are actually that Roland synth for the string sounds, some of the bell sounds, other melodies, and the slide. Of course, there was also bass and some keyboards playing alongside. My guitar solo was rock, and the rhythm parts I played combined elements of funk, but also rock and pop. I felt "Feel the Heat" was a viable subject, as it was something I'd been feeling for quite a while, so we were on track.

I continued to record until I realized that I was spending a fortune. The studio was thousands a day, plus outboard gear. It was crazy, especially as I would often find myself song writing in the studio as well when an idea sparked, not just recording. Virgin UK was also suggesting I try to do some recording in London. I thought that would be a great experience, so I packed things up and brought over Tommy, Pierre, and my assistant, Robbie.

We moved into a huge apartment in Kensington. Oh, God, we did all kinds of things, and we had a lot of fun during that time. Besides recording in the studio every day, we would hit clubs like the gargantuan Hippodrome in Piccadilly Circus that hosted thousands of people from around the world every night.

It was like paradise to us—and so different from the US, especially for the other guys, who had never experienced something like this before. There's a joy and satisfaction you get when you have the opportunity to show people amazing things.

Over my many trips to London, I had become good friends with a really nice chap named Peter Stringfellow, the owner of the Hippodrome and another popular nightspot called Stringfellows. He took care of me—always had a table waiting and treated me like a superstar. I later learned he owned a club in the '60s where many bands performed, incuding the Who, Pink Floyd, the Yardbirds, the Jimi Hendrix Experience, Stevie Wonder, and many other legendary acts. We would go between Stringfellows and the Hippodrome, and then hit other bars and pubs that were open late. We'd bring people back to the house and get our late-night dose of KFC (which is also popular in the UK, by the way). We'd have cool parties and definitely had fun while making this record.

Richard Branson had assigned me an A&R (artists and repertoire) person named Jeremy, and Gemma was my personal contact at the label. She actually later married Don Was from the group Was Not Was. Jeremy wanted to hear what it would sound like if someone else took the helm, like a well-known engineer or producer, to help me with the track "Feel the Heat."

I wasn't aware that this was what they intended when proposing I'd do some recording in London. This wasn't what I had agreed to originally as I had full creative control of the album, so I was not happy. But I went along with it, just to try something else and not wanting to ruffle any feathers. I got along well enough with the producer and engineer assigned, but I wasn't thrilled about where it was going or the final result.

So I called up Virgin and made a deal with Richard. I told him I'd like to go try another mix of "Feel the Heat" in Sweden. If my mix was superior, I'd be left alone to do whatever I wanted. He agreed.

I had vividly remembered Polar Studios from the time I went to meet the ABBA people about that single deal. I knew the studio was rarely used, and it was state of the art with 3M digital 32-track tape machines, which were not yet being used in the United States to my knowledge. Sweden was always very advanced.

The studio had a complete cutting room where you could cut vinyls and take it to the local clubs to hear the sound and get audience reaction. Literally right upstairs they had a tanning booth, which I really didn't need, so I'd forgo that! The main studio, where I spent most of my time, was an amazing recording room. There was a beautiful grand piano, and you couldn't help but feel the excitement from knowing that the legendary group ABBA wrote and recorded many masterpieces in that very room.

I reached out to the engineer I had met on my last trip to Polar, Anders Oredsson, informed him I was ready to come back, and asked that he'd set up some dates for this test mix I was planning to do. He was a well-known sound engineer in the country who knew the studio very well and was excited to get involved in this project.

We all headed to Stockholm, settled in and got to work. Anders and I moved forward and completed our test mix for "Feel the Heat," which everyone was very happy with. I was falling in love with Sweden and its amazing, open-minded people. So I decided to move to Stockholm to finish the album's recordings and also started looking for more permanent housing.

In New York, I would struggle to get approved for apartments, and people would try to kick me out of my building, but upon my arrival in Sweden, I remember checking out some rental houses where single women would be living with their little children and they'd tell me, "Well, yes, the place won't be available for another month, but you can move in with us if you'd like, until it's ready. It's no problem." There I stood, a Black guy with a blond Mohawk and a leather jacket. The trust that they had in other people was incredible, and I had not experienced this anywhere else. I was intrigued because, bear in mind, the United States still had blatant racial issues compared to Sweden, where nothing like this ever existed. Beautiful girls were dating the guy who worked in the hot dog stand. Race and job status didn't seem to matter.

It wasn't like when you went to a Hollywood nightclub, and you'd see a Black guy sitting at a table with a blonde girl, you'd automatically know that he had to be successful at something. "Oh, he's the world champion boxer," someone would say. And then you'd say to yourself, "Oh, that's why."

That's the way it was in the Hollywood clubs. You would only see people like Rick James, Eddie Murphy, Prince, Russell Simmons, Arsenio Hall, myself, or perhaps a Black guest that one of us would bring in, such as our bodyguards. I became quite friendly with Arsenio, in fact. I loved his show, and he appreciated me as a performer. He told me very seriously one night, "Jean, you better come do my show before there's no show to do." He was right, and his show was canceled not long after that. I should have paid more attention!

This would happen all the time in Hollywood. You'd see everyone almost on a weekly basis, so you found yourself saying, "Yeah, yeah, we'll do that, we'll get together." Then time would go by and the opportunity would be missed. It got to the point where my friends and I started thinking it's better to fly in with a fixed schedule and get everything done rather than actually live there. Otherwise, your presence would be taken for granted.

I remember Jerry Buss, owner of the L.A. Lakers, asked me to sing the national anthem for one their games. But we'd see each other so often, we'd always find ourselves saying, "Yes, we have to do that," but never did.

Back in Sweden, once I decided to bring my entire band there, I did the math. I saw that budget-wise it cost me a lot less to be in Sweden, recording in one of the greatest studios in the world, rather than recording in the United States. Plus, there were the added bonuses of new experiences for everyone, new inspiration, and excitement on every level.

Our next move was finding apartments for all the guys. I was personally involved in this. I always wanted to make sure that the places were nice and would be comfortable for my guys. For a while, I stayed at a place called the Castle Hotel. They had a beautiful two-bedroom suite on the top floor that spanned the hotel, but it wasn't expensive, especially compared to US prices. I loved that hotel, and my suite had these vaulted and arched ceilings, dark wood beams, and just a special feeling when you walked in. I would lie in the bathtub with candles around me and throughout the room, and I wrote most of the lyrics to my first album *Drums Along the Mohawk* in this great place.

The other guys were spread out around the city in different apartments. The girl who was working at Polar even offered up her apartment and moved in with her boyfriend.

I locked out Polar Studios for a year, which swiftly turned into four. I recruited, once again, the engineer Anders Oredson I had met previously and had worked on the test session for "Feel the Heat." But this time, it was for the whole album. He was a nice man and always had a pipe in his mouth. Whenever I made a comment or asked for something, he'd mumble, "Ummm," giving serious thought as to how he'd approach the request. He was a lot of fun, very supportive, and we had a great working relationship. I loved being in Sweden, it was so inspiring.

Living in Sweden was a blast. I met a lot of great press people, musicians, and others from all walks of life who have remained friends til today. When we first got there, it was just crazy! The guys went nuts over the girls. The girls over there were just absolutely beautiful, friendly, self-supportive, intelligent, and witty—a goldmine. I recall the guys sharing some of their weekly experiences that were so different than what they were used to with American girls.

For example, they'd go at night, looking to meet someone to take home. She'd play around with them all night and then finally say, "OK, let's go to my place if you'd like." So of course, being American guys, the thought process was, "Oh, yeah, I'm in now. No problems, this is happening, thank God."

He'd go to her place, have some drinks, and then she'd finally say, "OK, maybe it's time we go to bed." She'd take off all her clothes and then casually say, "You know we're not going to fuck, right?" And the guy would say, "No, I didn't know that!"

This would be an upsetting realization in the wee hours of the night, but since it would be so late at this point, they had no opportunity to go back out and pursue another prospect! However, if they waited a day or two, she might change her mind! I always thought that was a funny story, which seemed to repeat itself often.

These girls in Sweden were very different than American girls, which is why I ended up dating several of them. They just had a completely different attitude. They were more forward than American girls I'd met. A lot of times, I'd never know if the American girls were interested. Swedish girls would let you know without a doubt. I've had some interesting personal experiences myself on that front—to the point where they literally asked me to please take them home!

On the fashion front, I'd go to a store like H&M, which didn't exist in the United States at the time, and I'd find the coolest clothes you could imagine, boots and other accessories. Styles I would never find in the US. They literally had Levis jeans starting at 501 to 515, with all the numbers in between, all varied styles. Levi's Sweden sponsored me for a while and I wore them for some of my press photos.

There was so much originality, and all in a landscape that was pretty unfamiliar. It was rustic European, but it felt like the land of the Vikings—the scenery, the canals were all so beautiful, and the contrast of all these different elements was just mesmerizing. I enjoyed every minute I spent working over there.

On one of my clothing excursions around Stockholm, I met a gentleman who had the most beautiful leather clothing in his little shop in Gamla Stan (Old Town). I don't remember the shop's name, but I went in and spoke to him about wanting a unique look, something with leather, maybe suede, so we came up with a thought for a suit, suede with fringes. We finalized the idea, and he went on to make these beautiful outfits, which became my look for both the *Drums Along the Mohawk* and *Jacknifed* albums. He made me a variety of them in different colors and prints.

In one of our conversations, he told me an interesting but very sad story. He had a longtime girlfriend that he loved very much, and everything was just wonderful with them. One day, a big Black man walked into the store and immediately caught her attention. It turned out to be Clarence Clemons from Bruce Springsteen's E-Street Band. The attraction was mutual, and Clarence whisked her away. The man was almost crying while telling me the story of how the love of his life was taken away from him, and there was nothing he could do about it.

"I just can't compete with the big man, all the fancy hotels, the limos, life in America and being a superstar," he said. "It is what it is." He felt that Clarence being who he was left him no chance. He was so sad about it when we'd speak that it really stayed with me.

The clubs in Stockholm were just amazing; however, drinks were extremely expensive. For that reason, before going out, everybody went to buy alcohol at a place called Systembolaget, which is government run and the only store where you could buy wine and spirits in Sweden. The prices were reasonable in comparison to bars and clubs, where you could pay as much as $20 for a soda! They'd go to a friend's house with a group of people, have a little starter party, and basically get drunk before going out. This way, they wouldn't have to spend as much at the clubs. They'd start fairly early in the evening, and then around ten or so, all the clubs and bars would be packed. Many people actually went to the bars to drink or have dinner as well, but the other method was more common.

Going to clubs, restaurants, and bars in Sweden is much more expensive than it is in the United States, but nowhere near as exorbitant as it is in Norway, which is almost twice as much as Sweden. In both countries they'd measure those drinks right down to the centiliter, so you'd need to order three to make up one American drink!

There were many clubs and bars to choose from, all packed, all happening, as were the streets of Stockholm. For younger people, who were not yet of age, they'd all stand outside in this big square in the center of town and in below-zero temperatures. They'd all be standing around like penguins, just freezing their asses off, but somehow they really enjoyed it. I guess they are Nordic people, after all, so they could handle it! The clubs played the best music. Always the hippest, and the Swedish dance music was fantastic, so I had the opportunity to hear new jams, many of which I liked.

Watching the sunrise in a nightclub at midnight or one o'clock in the morning was a sight to behold. There was one popular hot spot called Café Opera, where I spent a lot of time. It was all glass and really cool to watch the sunrise from there. You'd be dancing day and night!

Inevitably, I met a girl at one of these clubs—Ann-Sofie Lakso, a stunningly beautiful model. At the time, she was the model with the most front covers of any Swedish model to date. To approach her, I devised a little technique where I'd have my friend Tommy stand in front of me, make sure that she was behind me, and then I actually asked him to tell me, by hand signal, every time that she looked at me. One, two, three, four—make a move, which I actually did, and from there we started a relationship.

I eventually moved us into an amazing house, more like a mansion, that I had found in a quaint little town called Djursholm. The house had twenty rooms, a wine cellar downstairs, maid's quarters, maid's kitchens, all kinds of small old rooms to explore. I could literally put the whole band in the living room with a PA for rehearsals, plus I had a studio on the top floor.

I discovered a trap door in a corner of the studio, and inside I found secret documents from the PLO (Palestine Liberation Organization). I later found out that the house had been PLO's headquarters in Sweden. I handed over the paperwork to the authorities, and I'm not sure what ever came of it.

In any case, the house was amazing. Be it day or night, I'd gaze out of my studio window on the top floor to observe deer lying about on a small snow-covered mound in the yard. It was so enchanting. You'd think you were in the Arctic Circle.

My family and other close friends would also come to visit me periodically. My mom loved Sweden and the house, and I'd fly her over every so often. Then I'd take her to London, which was one of her other favorite places.

My lifestyle in Sweden was more than a little extravagant. I had a limo driver named Jerry who drove a beautiful Mercedes limousine in town. KISS and other major bands would always call on him. I was later introduced to another gentleman who had the only American stretch in town, or perhaps the country. That was right up my alley, so I had that car on call constantly. I'd pile my band and friends into that excessive, lavish vehicle and hit the clubs. Somehow, I always ended financing these costly excursions.

I spent a lot of money in those days, and at times, foolishly. My accountant was far from exuberant upon my return from these trips.

Sometime after my solo deal was signed, I bought myself a present—something I'd been lusting after for a long time. I'd been into cars since junior high, and my favorite car was one I had seen in James Bond films, the Lotus Turbo Esprit, made in England. I found out there was one distributor in New Jersey who could get them. I went over there to check things out and created quite the scene upon my entry to the showroom. Of course, they looked at me with that, "What are you doing here? Really?" I was all too familiar with that look, much like the *Pretty Woman* scenario. (Funny enough, Richard Gere was driving a Lotus in that film when he picked up Julia Roberts.)

I told the salesmen that I'd like to purchase a customized Lotus, today! Like a flick of a switch, their level of enthusiasm increased tenfold. They had only one in the showroom, and I was in awe when I saw it live! It was so low, as if you were sitting on the ground! I loved it and took it for a test drive. I wanted a different color, with all the bells and whistles, which included a highly tuned high compression engine (HCI), which the UK had only made a few of. I chose deep black with a red leather Connolly interior, the same as those installed in Rolls-Royces.

Lotus is a well-known UK manufacturer that made its bones racing Formula One. The body design is Italian like Ferrari and Lamborghini. I had vivid dreams of its arrival as I awaited delivery for months, like a kid before Christmas!

Exhausted from holding my breath, I was alerted that it had finally arrived and was ready for pickup! It was every bit as cool as I'd hoped. It arrived in Jersey, so I headed out there to collect it. I took it into New York and parked in my building's garage. I remember not feeling comfortable allowing the valets to drive it, let alone park it!

I used it for quite a while in New York. Paul Stanley had a black Porsche 928, and Nile Rodgers had a black 911 Turbo. We'd speed around the streets of New York making lots of noise like high school boys and then meet up at New York hotspots.

New York was definitely not the place to have this type of vehicle, but that's what made it cool. One day, I decided it would be a good idea to bring it to Sweden, so I shipped it over there. Another waiting period, as it was traveling by ship. It arrived at last, and it was the only one of its kind in the country. There was one other older white Lotus, but it just didn't compare. Mine was a real head-turner and definitely conjured up a fair amount of attention. I'd drive that car everywhere, even in the winter with no snow tires!

My house was up on top of a hill in a cozy upscale neighborhood called Djursholm. Very often, I'd have to leave the car at the bottom of the hill as it was a challenge to make it up to the house with ice covering the streets. When spring and summer arrived, I was definitely recognizable driving around town with that little tee top off and my Mohawk projecting out the top.

Time chugged along as I was living large and thoroughly enjoying the country. I was friends with all the doormen, restaurant owners, and many others in town. I was always cordial and treated everyone with equal respect. Lying in a sea of gorgeous girls who are attracted to me, a beautiful home with a recording studio—it was the epitome of paradise. My girlfriend wasn't very fond of my going out with friends who came to town. Whether it be Paul Stanley, Bon Jovi, or another band passing through Stockholm, they all knew to call me for a good time. It became common knowledge, and as a matter of fact, Scott Greenstein, who heads up Sirius XM Radio, took to calling me "Christopher Columbus."

Stockholm was not a go-to place at that time. Little was known of all the talent, forward thinking, and proficiency that resided here, nor how tech savvy the culture was. When I moved there, though, I knew I had found the motherland, and I became one of Sweden's biggest endorsers to anyone I'd meet. It would later become the epicenter of popular music and the tech world—Spotify, Skype, and many other tech platforms were invented and developed in Sweden. Max Martin, the iconic Swedish music producer, has pretty much nearly surpassed the entire global music industry's producers' achievements in chart successes and hits for years now. Not to mention Roxette, Ace of Base, and the legendary and timeless ABBA.

One time, I received word that Prince was coming to town. Of course, I'm thinking, *What is he coming to do here?* I don't remember who called whom, but in any case, Prince and I were speaking on the phone. I said, "Hey, what's happening? So you're in town? That's great!"

He replied, "Yeah, just got in."

"So what are you doing here?"

"Same thing you are!" he replied.

I thought that was pretty funny. He had decided, as I had, to come to Sweden, set up shop, and prepare for his next tour. Just when you think you have a unique idea, it's ironic how others are sometimes thinking the same.

My girlfriend was standing behind me with that inquisitive look on her face awaiting what I had to say. When I finished the call, I told her, "Prince is in Stockholm!"

She quickly replied, "Good! Now you won't be the only King Shit in town!"

Prince and I got together and ended up jamming in a couple of local clubs. I had the chance to witness a little faux pas that little purple guy made while here. Sweden is one of those places that doesn't accept people thinking too much of themselves. They don't want you thinking that you're better than they are, and if you do, they'll remind you that you're not. They have a social custom throughout Scandinavia called *Janteloven* that basically states that everyone is the same and is to be treated as such.

A good example would be that an investor or the minister of culture would be the funding source for a national radio station. He has a personal interest or even a business initiative and would like the radio station to play a particular song. In the US, this person, the boss, could simply call the person he had employed and placed in that position as the radio programmer and instruct him to add the song. This is very common in the United States and in some other countries where traditionally the programmer would add it. But in Scandinavia, it would be extremely inappropriate for that boss to insult or infringe on the radio programmer's role by suggesting or demanding that he play a song.

As a Swede, when you have more money or you become the biggest model in the world, star in a major American film, or whatever accolades you've attained, when you return to the country, you're treated for the most part as if none of it happened. You'd be expected to jump back into line with everyone else. This also applied to many foreign celebrities. It was a fine line, and your personality also played a big part in how you'd be treated.

So one night, Prince was the recipient of that treatment. It was announced that he was having a party at a club, the Daily News Café. He had his table and area set up, roped off with his personal security and entourage, life-size cardboard cutups of him in the club, and so on. We planned to meet there. Sheila E. was also on the trip, but she told me that Prince would not allow her to see me. I wanted to invite her to play on my record, but under those circumstances, that was obviously out of the question.

The evening of the party, Prince and I were sitting talking on a sofa. I was awaiting the flurry of expected fans. Strangely enough, very few people came. They'd be filtering in throughout the evening, and it was like they were sending a message saying, "Yeah, we love you, but don't think you're soooo big or soooo cool. That just doesn't fly here." The Swedes would do funny things like that.

Another example of this, and a regret of mine, was with Jon Bon Jovi. He had been a fan of my music from the beginning, and he'd told me that when Bon Jovi was touring, the album they were listening to while on tour was *Drums Along the Mohawk*. I was honored, of course. Bon Jovi had not quite really broken yet, but they were getting there.

He had come to Sweden and wanted to write. They were there for a few days, and I didn't really give the writing much attention. We were going out together, to clubs like Café Opera, Daily News, and we went to one other little place that gave us a difficult time about Jon getting in because he had jeans on—or it may have been his shoes. I knew the doorman and everyone working at the place, and still they said, "I'm sorry, Jean, he can't get in. We're not gonna let him in."

I ended up getting the manager and making a big stink about it. I was embarrassed as I was their host, so I was persistent. It finally all worked out.

I was having so much fun going to clubs and enjoying the city that I really wasn't into working that much. Perhaps it was because I had worked so hard on my *Drums Along the Mohawk* record. I felt I needed a break. I had money, so that wasn't a motivation.

I had been going, going, going since I was fourteen years old, non-stop, to try to get to a point. Many people, once they get there, just keep working and don't ever stop. But I kind of felt like I wanted to chill for a moment. I didn't want to be writing and working all the time. Not saying I don't enjoy writing, but everything can get tiresome after a while. You need to recharge your batteries.

To make a long story short, I did not make the effort to write with Bon Jovi for that record. So Jon went to Desmond Child. Next thing you know, boom. Their album *Slippery When Wet* was released and became an instant smash, selling twelve times platinum. I don't know if I expected that!

I did call Jon afterward to speak about the next record. I was like, "Let's write!"

He was very honest with me and rather than just saying, "Fuck you," he told me, "Jean, you know, what can I do? We wrote with Desmond, since I had offered you to write, but you didn't do it. I now have a good working relationship with Desmond, as you can see. I hope you understand."

And that was that. Not a decision I'm proud of, as I've always loved Bon Jovi's music and regret not being a part of their career.

My popularity in Sweden was surreal. Granted, I was easily recognizable and so many knew who I was. Literally it got to the point that when I was single, I could drive by a store or a shop, look inside, and if I saw an attractive girl, I would actually call the store and ask her out. Believe it or not, the answer was mostly yes. The funny thing is that it didn't matter if they had boyfriends or not. The answer was still yes.

This was quite a progression coming from Long Island where I was constantly barraged with derogatory comments, such as the *n*-word, told to "go back to Africa," and arduous racism I had experienced in my past. I guess at this stage, I was truly in rock 'n' roll now, and I was definitely reaping and appreciating the benefits.

Well one day, I did exactly that. I was driving by a store on a main street in Stockholm and a girl through the window working in the shop caught my eye. I decided to try my luck. I picked up my phone and called the establishment. A girl picked up, and I asked her, "Hey, are you the gorgeous girl working behind the counter?" She said yes. I continued, "Well, this is Jean Beauvoir. I know this may seem odd, but I'd like to invite you to dinner tonight." Giggling a bit and seeming quite surprised, she replied exuberantly, "Yes! I would love to! How do you know me?" I said, "I saw you through the window and just couldn't help myself." She was flattered and seemed pretty excited. She gave me her address and I had my assistant book a table at one of my favorite spots. I picked her up around 7:00 PM.

We went out, had a great dinner, and enjoyed each other's company for some hours. She then invited me back to her place, where I spent the night. Fortunately, I managed to circumvent the fate imposed on my bandmates, which I shared earlier, and we shared a quite delightful night together.

Come early morning, I skedaddled out of the apartment still in last night's sparkling evening garb, high-heeled shoes so tight that I could barely walk! My Mohawk was all disheveled and leaning to one side. I could hardly go unnoticed!

As I was leaving the building there was a guy standing there pacing to and fro. It appeared he had been there for quite a while, as I had heard her phone ring a few times throughout the night. He approached me seemingly very upset and with his Irish accent asked me bluntly, "Did you fuck my girlfriend?" Now, I was completely unaware that she had a boyfriend, a fact she had failed to share, so this came as a bit of a surprise, but I could ascertain rather quickly and in all certainty that indeed, he was her boyfriend. I kept my cool thinking—God forbid I'd have to rumble with these damn shoes on and so early in the morning!

I looked him straight in the eye and said, "No, wasn't me." He said, "I just saw you come out of the building, I know you fucked my girlfriend!" Now, why in the world would he assume it was poor, innocent moi? This gent was probably about my height, considering my Mohawk was about five inches tall! He was fairly stocky and looked like one of those Irish pub guys that loved to brawl after getting drunk with his buddies on a Friday night. "Where were you then?" he asked. I told him with full confidence, "Visiting a friend, and I really don't know why you're approaching me, dude, or what you're talking about, but what I do know is I didn't fuck your girlfriend, whoever she is, and I'm offended by the accusation! Gotta go." As if to suggest that he was wasting my time.

I got into my car and said to myself, "Damn! That was close!" Now, if that was me in his shoes, I would've lost my freakin' mind! I got in my car thinking, *I can't believe this girl never mentioned one thing.* I called her and said, "I just spoke to your boyfriend out front, and he's not too happy! He's on his way up! Why the heck didn't you tell me you had a boyfriend?" I believe she said something like, "I didn't think it was important."

So I went along minding my business and carried on. She actually called me to see me again!

Years later, I moved to Key West and had been there for a while, I found myself at an Irish pub one night. For some reason, the bartender looked awfully familiar. So here I am thinking, *Where do I know this guy from?* I just know I've seen him before, but I couldn't place him. He walks over to me to take my order and, of course, instantly recognizes me and says, "You motherfucker! You fucked my girlfriend!"

With not much to do or say, knowing I was guilty as hell, I was prepared to get into it and simply responded, "Yes, I did and I'm sorry about that, I didn't know, she never mentioned having a boyfriend." He paused as we both stood still for a moment in anticipation. Then suddenly, he started to laugh! Prompting me to questionably do the same! He then said, "Well, we're not together anymore, so it doesn't really matter." We continued to talk and ended up casual friends! I saw him at the pub quite often after that.

So, I did, indeed, fall in love with Sweden's Polar Studios and vowed to do any work that I was going to do or was asked to do there. One project I recorded there was for my sister and my girlfriend Ann-Sofie, who wanted to make a record together. We named the project Latin Summer, which notched a Top 10 hit in Norway with the song "Waste My Time."

Now rock 'n' roll is no doubt a roller coaster and it definitely has its ups and downs. I've previously preached how everything was so wonderful and glamorous in Sweden, I did have some bad experiences.

My band and other guys accompanying me were still mesmerized by the girls and everything that was going on in Sweden, particularly Stockholm. Guys, girls, everyone looked great! Well groomed and always dressed to the nines. There was action to be found somewhere every night! One experience I remember vividly. I had arranged so that we'd have our own cars to facilitate getting around. No problem. I had my own car, the band had theirs, and everything was fine. If you can believe this, I was the conservative one. While I'm not saying I was a saint, I didn't do any drugs. I drank a bit of wine, yes, but that was about it. My vice was girls. The never-ending search for true love.

So, we went to an enjoyable dinner, and come the end of our meal, I asked everyone what they wanted to do. The response from the table was "Well, I'm pretty tired, I think I'm gonna turn in early," so we parted ways.

Some of my guys, including Tommy and my brother, decided to take my rental car while I was asleep and headed out to God knows where. I have no idea what possessed them to take my car. It seems that somehow, somewhere, they lost control of the car and crashed. I was awakened by a phone call in the middle of the night.

"We had an accident!" Then they unleash, "Uh, we don't know where the car is. We don't remember, we can't find it."

They then fessed up that there was a girl in the car who had been injured and was in the hospital! I'm thinking to myself, "Oh God, this is the story that never ends!"

I was fuming like you would not believe. I didn't have insurance on the car, at least not the theft and collision insurance option. It was an option I'd rarely forgo, but for some reason I had neglected to opt in. So I'm thinking, *Oh, this is crazy! I'm gonna have to spend $50,000-plus to buy this car!*

This is an absolute conundrum, and nobody's telling me what really happened. I was furious. But there was nothing left to do. I waited for the morning to head over to the rental car company. Upon my arrival, there was a sweet-looking girl working at the desk. As cordially as I could, I approached and told her what had occurred, at least the portion I was privy too. I'm sure she could see that I was really upset and worried.

She looked up and simply said, "OK, don't worry, I'll take care of it."

I said, "Excuse me, really?"

She said, "Yes, Mr. Beauvoir. Don't worry, and have a great day."

I was shocked, but totally stoked! I don't know what she did or what happened, but that was it. I didn't have to pay anything for the car, so I sent her the biggest bouquet of flowers the next day. I was still very concerned about the girl, but they assured me she was in the hospital and being well taken care of. I still didn't know where that car was. Up until today, no one has ever confessed to me where that car actually ended up.

I was back in Sweden a year or so later and out at a club when much to my surprise, this girl enthusiastically ran over to me, and said, "I was hoping I would see you because I wanted you to pass a message along to your friend Tommy. Is he here? I'm the girl who had the accident."

I said, "Oh, I was wondering what happened in the end."

She said, "It was great! I didn't have to go to work for a year, and I still got paid. I love him so much!"

I just couldn't believe my ears. A seemingly grim situation turned out to be a blessing for her. I was really happy to hear that, so I could take that worry out of my mind.

Business continued to move with Virgin Records as we were preparing for the release of my solo album. The album was finished, and I was traveling back and forth from America to Sweden but spending more time in Sweden while everything was getting going. My manager, Gary, had called me just a few months after the Virgin deal had been secured and nonchalantly said, "I'm sitting with Al Teller, the president of Columbia Records. He's the one who signed Michael Jackson. He loves your album and wants to sign you."

That was another pleasant surprise from Gary. He was very intelligent and had some great methods of dealmaking, which helped further educate me in the music biz. The original Virgin label deal was signed for the world, excluding the United States. It was left open to facilitate the signing of a deal for North America. It was just a better way to go and a practice I adopted and used for many years afterward. Just because you had a dedicated country that was really interested in your record didn't mean that they would be able to sell that same enthusiasm to other countries. Many times, an artist would sign a deal in, let's say, Sweden for worldwide rights. When the label would solicit that album around the world, it was a fair bet that the US would not opt in to release. If you separated the deals, you'd have equal excitement on multiple fronts.

I flew back to New York for my meeting with Al Teller, his wife, and Gary. Al's wife was Norwegian, so we had something in common from all my time in Scandinavia. Al was extremely enthusiastic and told me he absolutely loved the record. He went as far as to say, "This is the second album I've listened to as much as I have. First, Michael Jackson, and then yours." He had been on vacation and listened to the album repeatedly. He said, "I think the album is phenomenal and is going to be a huge hit. I will do everything in my power to support it."

He was sincere, and I eagerly watched as he was setting things up. His perseverance, how much attention he gave me, being always there and available to speak with me. Nevertheless, I found that this was not always a great thing. What happens very often is that other executives and A&Rs don't always respond well to that big boss–artist relationship. They feel that because it's the boss who signs it, if the album breaks, then all the credit will go to him. Their jobs depend on the quality and success of their signings. When an A&R person from a label has a hit with an artist he discovered, the success makes him a hero and secures his job.

All in all, Gary had made me some very lucrative deals, with big advances, multiple video budgets, tour support, and just about everything you could ask for. So between the two label deals, we were in the millions. These deals were also for a minimum of two albums firm, with eight options: this was a good situation.

Al Teller, however, was well aware that he would have an extremely difficult time selling me to radio, regardless of how good he felt the song and album were. I was stuck somewhere between the genres, and Columbia as a label was still very segregated. Unlike Europe, in the United States you really had separation: Black/R&B, pop, rock, country, and so on. I fell in between the cracks. "Feel the Heat," the first single, had a heavy dance beat, which worked in clubs; a chorus that sounded like a rock song; guitar synthesizer playing keyboard parts; and I played a blazing rock guitar solo, to boot! It was a combination of various elements that had to find its place. With all that said, I was a Black man with a blond Mohawk to add to the brew. So was I to be promoted on the Black or White floor, as the eventual goal was hit radio?

This put us in an extremely difficult predicament. Nevertheless, I can say firsthand that I witnessed the incredible efforts made by Al. Incentives, bonuses, vacations for his employees around the country to keep them motivated and make things happen. Despite all the pushback Columbia encountered along the way, we still managed to have a reasonable success with the album, much thanks to MTV, VH1, and the other popular video channels in North America that placed the video on heavy rotation for a long time. Mark Goodman, J. J. Jackson, Martha Quinn, Nina Blackwood, and Alan Hunter were a great group of VJs who really supported my record. In the music business, success is relative. Of course, you have the perception by the audience of what is a hit or not. Some artists are massively promoted but in reality are selling very few records, whereas some other artists may have much less visibility, yet are selling much more than you'd think.

Also, the size of the deal plays a big part. Basically, if an artist receives $50,000, all in, to release the record, and they sell a hundred thousand copies, the record company will be very happy. In the case of an artist such as Mariah Carey—who may have received, let's say, $80 million—as great as she may be, if she sells one million copies, the record company may very well drop her.

It wasn't too long before Nancy Brennan approached me from CBS Publishing offering a very lucrative deal to administer my publishing for the album.

When it came time to shoot the video for "Feel the Heat," it was strangely difficult to complete. I was so particular about how I looked at the time that I would not like eighty percent of footage filmed of me. It probably stemmed from some inner insecurity; I would always see a flaw.

Gary Kurfirst thought it would be a great idea to use Mary Lambert to direct the video. They were friends, and I believe had done some work together in the past. No doubt, she was a very talented video and film director. She had made several videos for my former flame Madonna, and throughout her career also worked with Janet Jackson, Lionel Richie, and many others. I had met Mary and felt she was a great lady as well, so I was looking forward to working with her.

For the first shoot, we chose a beautiful house in the Hollywood Hills. As we're preparing for the shoot, I felt the makeup artist had used too much makeup on me, making me look like a girl. Nevertheless, I went with it. Shooting the video was a fun experience, though my nerves were always on edge, hoping that I'd like the outcome.

It then came time for me to go look at footage with Mary. I started choosing shots I didn't like, one by one, and I swear, by the time we had gone through all the footage, we had only one minute of usable material left as far as I was concerned.

Now, Mary was always very sweet to me and wasn't the argumentative type who'd try to strong-arm. She loved me, but at this moment, she may have hated me. But we were still friends. As a matter of fact, she would always bring me little messages from Madonna about our past, as she was often working with her. It was an ongoing joke with Mary as the intermediary.

But for my video, she called Gary, almost in tears, and said, "Jean is making me crazy! We spent all this money shooting what I believe is great stuff, but I had nothing to use for the final edit. Can you please speak with him?"

So Gary gave me a call and, shall I say, voiced her concerns. I was very sincere in my feelings. What I liked, I liked. If I didn't like something, I just didn't like it, and it was very difficult to change my mind. So, Gary, trying to be as accommodating as possible, suggested we'd do a new shoot with Mary to gather some more footage. We agreed, and we went on to rent a soundstage, which we dressed purely black with a couple of risers and some great lighting, where I would perform and dance, a very simple setup. We reshot the entire video, and as it turns out, I loved most of the shots from that shoot. I was finally satisfied, and we combined footage from both shoots, using mainly footage from the new material, which finally gave us our completed video to everyone's satisfaction.

While Mary was editing that final version of "Feel the Heat" at Warner Bros. Studios in Burbank, a new and exciting surprise came to light. It turns out that Sylvester Stallone was also editing his film *Cobra* in the same studio. I was told he happened to go by the studio where Mary was editing and he saw parts of "Feel the Heat," which coincidently included an animated cobra snake. It caught his attention, so he walked in to get more information.

Gary then received a call from Stallone saying that he wanted to use this song for his entire *Cobra* campaign: promotion, trailers, and the film. *Cobra* would be the biggest movie release of all time in American film history. It was released in 2,131 theaters in the US and Canada alone, breaking the previous record, also held by Stallone, for *Rambo*. It more than doubled *Top Gun*! I was paid quite handsomely for this opportunity and even retained ongoing participation in *Cobra* in perpetuity.

I was ecstatic going from some very bad years to finally a really good one. The collaboration began, and "Feel the Heat" trailers were aired all over the world. As *Cobra* was so heavily publicized, it played continuously in all those theaters prior to its release.

Once the single was about to come out (before the album), we had released white label copies to all the clubs. When you'd walk into a club and "Feel the Heat" came on, it sounded so big and just rumbled the dance floor. What a feeling! I remember going to Times Square to watch a film as I would commonly do, since I was an avid moviegoer, and seeing the *Cobra* trailer for the first time. Sitting in a huge theater in Times Square, my heart just jumped. I couldn't believe this was happening, something I had worked for so many years to achieve.

With all that said, the dominant racist atmosphere still had us struggling for radio play, which was extremely frustrating. Spending so much time abroad, where little or none of this existed, gave me a reference and made me more clearly see the injustice. It made me appreciate being accepted with open arms by all people and not putting limitations on the success of my music.

Well, not everyone loved my music abroad, which brings me to another interesting occurrence. While cruising around a club in Stockholm one night with my bodyguard, I had a girl come over to me and ask, "Hey, aren't you Jean Beauvoir?"

I said, "Yeah," all proud.

She looked me right in the eye and said, "I hate your record!" She then turned around and walked away. My ego was most definitely bruised, and it took me a while to get over that one.

Things were now happening with my record, especially in Europe, Japan, and Australia. Gary called me and said, "Jean, you need to get out of Switzerland and come home. There's a lot happening here, and you need to be here to promote your record."

I said, "First of all, Gary, it's Sweden, not Switzerland."

He replied, "Whatever, just get home."

I had a funny philosophy, shared by many in America, and as referenced in the cult film *Scarface*. First you get the money, then you get the power, then you get the woman. Over there, I already had the girl—or girls. So what sense did it make to spend my time in America? Since at that time, that's what it was all about? You could bypass a couple of steps here, which was my reasoning for not wanting to come back! I also didn't want to deal with the racism.

Basically, in Sweden I was living in a twenty-room mansion, where in New York I had a one-bedroom apartment—nice view, but God forbid I'd be sitting with friends talking after 10:00 PM! The neighbors would pound on my wall to get me to simmer down!

Don't get me wrong. I had a lot of wonderful friends in the US, and many would come by the studio to visit. Elizabeth Ames, my dear friend Malena Belafonte, and Randi Michaels came in to record some background vocals. A friend of mine, Kermit Blackwood, also a friend of Michael Jackson's, partially due to a shared affinity for exotic animals, came to visit once with his pet emu! Yes, a real live emu! Now, that was a trip and entertaining for us all! He carried him in a sort of gym bag, safely of course, and would let him out to roam the studio. I guess it was a rock 'n' roll emu, as he seemed to really dig the sounds! Bobby and Ribby (Bobby Cohen and Anthony Ribustello) were so inspirational at the beginning of my *Drums Along the Mohawk* recordings. Bobby was my engineer at Media Sound, and I ultimately referenced them both in the song "Drive You Home," so they'll be a part of my history forever!

When I did head back to New York, I felt it was time to reach out to my father. We'd not had any contact since I'd been shunned from the household in the midst of my adolescence—not even through the Plasmatics era, an exciting portion of my life that he completely missed. I felt the time had come to invite him to spend some time with me in New York. In all honesty, I really wanted to show him how wrong he was and what I had achieved up till then.

He agreed, so I booked him a first-class ticket and sent my bodyguard and assistant to pick him up in a long stretch limo, something I knew he had never been in before, and possibly had never even seen. My well-dressed limo driver greeted him at the gate with a placard penned "Beauvoir" and escorted him to the car, where he met my guys. I called the car while they were en route to make sure his arrival was safe and pleasurable. He was driven to my apartment at Lincoln Plaza on the Upper West side of New York. The building's lobby was ultraluxurious, and upon his arrival, he was greeted by suited doormen and myself. I may have even been wearing a robe with fluffy slippers! Now, mind you, he had never seen me with a Mohawk—the ripped jeans I'd wear while still at home were already a sacrilege!

They took his bags and escorted us upstairs. My apartment was on a high floor with breathtaking views of Central Park. I could tell he was flabbergasted and impressed by the whole situation, which was precisely what I had intended. Ironically, as I started opening my mail while hanging about the dining room table with him by my side, one of the envelopes contained a pleasant surprise. I said, "Oh! Good news." Lo and behold, the envelope contained a check for $100,000 and some change. I guess my spirits were playing along that day.

He saw it and gasped! He went on to say that he couldn't believe what he was seeing and that he had never seen that amount of money in one place at one time. He proceeded to make a confession and actually apologized, "Jean-Jean, listen, I'm so sorry for not believing in you. It seemed all just so far-fetched. We have just never had any Haitian music or rock stars in the history of the country, so for me to believe that you would break that mold was hard to conceive. Not to mention that you were a young Black kid in a racist country, living way out on Long Island away from all possibilities, yet standing there trying to convince me that you wanted to pursue becoming an internationally known recording artist. My common sense from my years and experience, living as long as I have, was that I just couldn't see this as reality. As a matter of fact, I thought that from all those motocross falls, some brain cells may have been dislodged causing you to fantasize as you were doing! I feared that you would end up playing for coins in the subway, on the streets, or worse. And that's definitely not the future I envisioned for my son."

He wasn't that far off! I did spend my share of time living on the streets.

He continued, "I have to say that I was wrong and that I misjudged you. I should have believed in you and your vision, but you were so young! Bravo, and I'm sorry. I hope we can move forward from here."

I was profoundly grateful for that apology. I guess it's true that appreciation, belief, admiration, and support from our fathers are sentiments often longed for, no matter what you tell yourself. It made me feel really good inside, whole and complete. From there, we were able to resume once again, as father and son. During this reunion, I realized that music was indeed a bond between us.

9

SELF-EXPRESSING—MOHAWK & BLUE EYES

When I joined Little Steven, I wanted to do something a little bit different with my Mohawk. I felt it needed a little extra oomph, so I had my hair braided in a certain way. It was my dear friend Gittan Gooding who did the braiding for me. It gave me a different look, and I was happy with it. It fit the outfits I had with Little Steven, and I still felt unique.

You see, the Mohawk, when I first integrated it, was meant to show racelessness. That's not a real word, but it's one I often use. I had worked my whole life trying to integrate with other cultures, and I always believed everyone was equal and should be able to do whatever they wanted to do in life. I kind of felt that the blond hair represented, "I'm Black, but I can have blond hair, blue or green eyes. I can dress like this or like that and express myself in whatever manner I see fit." I was hoping that my example would lead others to follow suit.

After leaving Steven, I yet again felt the Mohawk needed to go to a different place. I found another hairdresser at the time who started helping me develop my new look, which would be extensions connected to the Mohawk I already had. This was around the time I started working on *Drums Along the Mohawk*. I had also ordered a pair of custom-made blue contact lenses in 1984. Soft-colored lenses to turn brown eyes to blue did not exist at the time and were not introduced until a couple of years later by a Chicago contact lens company, Wesley-Jessen, and FDA approved in November 1986. (Their sales for these lenses amounted to over $100 million the first half-year on the market, selling predominantly to Black customers.) You could find colored lenses to change light-colored eyes, but from brown to light was impossible to obtain. Yet again I was striving to be the first to break down another barrier in the way of self-expression.

I found one special doctor in London, after an endless search around the world, who assured me he could make these blue soft contact lenses for me, as I knew how painful hard lenses were! I was excited about this prospect, paid him a lot of money and waited over a year. When asking him again, he started adding "semipermeable" into our conversation. I'd say, "You mean soft, as we discussed, right?"

He was just dismissive and said, "Yes, what you asked for."

Finally, I flew to London and went to his home office to pick them up. When I arrived, he handed me the case, which actually contained what seemed to be two hard lenses! They were in fact semipermeable. I freaked—I was so upset! I immediately told him I wanted my money back and I couldn't believe he made me wait all this time under false pretenses.

He refused. I had friends with me, and we started taking things out of his apartment. I went a bit crazy and everything was going, lamps, paintings, other objects, one thing after another, and told him we would keep going until he wrote me a check. He was freaking out saying, "I'm going to call the police."

"Go ahead. Call the police," I told him, as we were taking more things out to the street. I guess I was pretty reckless. Maybe my Plasmatics days left me with an attitude. Eventually, the police showed up and listened to the story. Surprisingly they took my side and ordered the gentleman to write me a check right there on the spot. On top of it, I ended up with the lenses anyways, because he had no use for them. Despite all the trouble, keeping them did make me the first Black person who changed their brown eyes to blue publicly as previewed in the video "Feel the Heat," on MTV, other video channels, TV shows, and many of my photographs. This was before Whoopi Goldberg made a splash on the cover of a national magazine a year or so later for doing the same. After the police left the house, I met them downstairs on the street and thanked them for their assistance. They said, "No worries. Just get us tickets for your next show."

We shook hands, and we went our separate ways.

As for my Mohawk, it continued to evolve. Over the years, it got shorter, combed back, flatter, taller, but still remained a blond Mohawk. I did take a break for a moment, when I moved to Germany, where I shaved the Mohawk off completely. I tried a Chinese tail, shaved head, hats, but nothing made me feel as whole and as natural as I did with my Mohawk. I eventually opted to go back, and that's where I am to this day. I still feel it represents the same thing for me, and it's become such an identifiable part of who I am that I even feel more comfortable now than I did back then.

10

THE GIFT

SINCE I WAS A LITTLE BOY, I realized that I had been given a gift.

I felt I had a purpose and that doing music was a plan from above. I heard music in more detail than many other people I knew, and it became more obvious as I started working with more and more talented people. They'd make comments and asked to use my skills repeatedly.

I could hear vocal parts and harmonies instantly, with no doubt in my mind. I could write a song in my head, hear all the instrumentation, arrangement, vocal parts, and so on, in a matter of minutes, as if it just flowed through me.

Perfect pitch, one example was when a song would play in my head, it would stop abruptly and change keys automatically to the correct recorded key. It would be and still is difficult—at times, painful—to listen to music or instruments that are out of tune. I have read that only about ten thousand people are known to have this ability. Even other skills, which seemed unimportant to me, such as being able to play just about any drumbeat using my teeth or mouth, including incredibly intricate fills, came with ease. Things I never practiced and didn't know where they came from! Listening to a simple beat with chord changes, I could instantly hear many different bass lines and sing them throughout an entire song, without one mistake or wrong note.

While recording drums in the Hit Factory or Power Station, Little Steven would call me in at times to redo parts played by my drummer or someone else, because of my ability to play in time to a click, which I had rarely practiced. I could sing lead simultaneously, which seemed very difficult for other musicians I knew. These various abilities made me feel in my heart that I was blessed with tools with a specific purpose, which I humbly accepted. The whole situation felt bigger than me.

I had many indicators, which kept me believing and gave me the strength to follow the road. Whenever I'd think it was over, the spirits would mysteriously come down and lend a hand, even in my deepest despair.

I'd imitate guitars and play just about any solo with my voice. Some nights, I would get what felt like musical attacks where hundreds of notes would start going through my head, scaling up and down in minutes, changing from minor to major, to augmented and diminished, like the notes were toying in my head. My brain would seem engulfed for a certain period of time, sometimes for hours, a few days, and sometimes nothing at all.

Songs would come the same way. Most songs that I've written myself were written in my head in one pass, with nothing changed afterward. The melodies remained the same as when they first came to mind, with all the musical parts present. The song would play in my head from intro to verse, to chorus, middle eight or solo, all inclusive until the end. So in a few quick recordings on my phone or tape recorder, everything would be there, precise with guides, instrument ideas and all vocal parts ready to be recorded. The whole process can literally take five minutes or less.

Now, whether it's always a great song is yet to be determined. Possessing these abilities has no bearing on whether you'll be successful or not!

I had a desperate urge to be original and different, as if it was ordained. When you think about it, someone was the original creator for everything. That's why we have all that exists. So you need people in the world, who I believe are chosen and given a certain set of skills to be original. Not everyone wants to be original.

Be it Beethoven, Thomas Edison, or the guy who invented Tupperware, they all had people say, "Nahhh, what are you gonna do with that? It'll never work. It looks or sounds terrible!" Yet they persevered and saw their vision through.

Well, I went through exactly that when I chose a look that no one else had and went against the beliefs of an entire race.

I'm sure I'm not the only one who's been fortunate enough or chosen to experience these musical infusions, sensations, moments of musical revelations and enlightenments, if you will. To those others who have been given what I call "the Gift," I'm sure you know exactly what I'm talking about.

I believe that people who have been granted a particular gift can recognize it in others. Think of Michael Jackson and Prince. In my life, I've had an eclectic group of people who have gravitated to me, and many of them, I believe, have a gift, whatever it may be. They were not necessarily on the same level as I was—oftentimes, they may have been at a higher level—but yet they would still be attracted to me.

Now, gifts come in all different shapes and sizes. I spoke of musical gifts, but there are people gifted with all sorts of abilities. A dancer who from birth happens to be far more limber than others. Or someone who deals with numbers extraordinarily well. Richard Branson and Jimmy Iovine may have gifts for business, and athletes such as Simone Biles and Michael Phelps have been granted their gifts of athleticism.

I shared this with you in the effort to enlighten you as to who I am and what makes me tick, why I became who I am today, and how I create what you ultimately hear. I'm so thankful for this gift and always vowed to use it to the best of my ability. Perhaps I have occasionally veered off course, but I try my best.

Do you feel there's something in your life that comes to you effortlessly without you having to really work at it? As if you already have the basis for it within you before you start, and beyond others who have been working at it for a long time? Well, that may be your gift.

11

DRUMS ALONG THE MOHAWK—ON TOUR

I RECEIVED A CALL FROM GARY with an offer to tour the United States with the Eurythmics, which was an incredible opportunity. I now had to decide who to take with me. Sweden is full of fantastic musicians. Mats Olausson, in particular, was one I had used as a keyboard player. This was before he joined Yngwie Malmsteen's band. He was one of Sweden's premier keyboardists and played with many greats. He was full of energy, a lot of fun, and a wonderful musician, so I decided to bring him on the US tour. Later in life, I was deeply saddened to hear he was found dead in a hotel room in Thailand.

I also invited Tommy, who played on parts of the album, Garry Nutt on bass, and Peter Clemente on drums. I also decided to bring over my engineer, Anders Oredsson, to do live sound for the tour. In addition to engineering *Drums Along the Mohawk*, he later engineered *Jacknifed*. He was also very excited about doing a US tour, which was a new situation for him.

I also wanted to bring Rebecca and Vivian, two girls I used in the studio to sing background vocals. Although I was pitched the best options for female background vocalists when I was about to start recording at Polar in Stockholm, I've always enjoyed discovery. I remember walking through town one day when I entered a little shop, where the girl behind the counter recognized me and blurted out, "I can sing!"

That really impressed me as I've always been drawn to musicians who are go-getters. So I said, "OK, why don't you come to the studio tomorrow."

Her name was Rebecca de Ruvo. She was a cute, teenage Swedish girl with blonde hair and blue eyes, very perky, full of energy. I was anxious to hear what she could do. The next day, she came by the studio, and I put her out in the room and sang a part for her to try. She sounded great, and I was like, *Whoa, this girl's got the voice!*

From that day on, I started using her for background parts, which there were quite a few of, and she nailed it every time. I'd found an undiscovered artist that I could hopefully help to achieve her goals. I also added another great singer named Vivian Cardinal, and they both worked out very nicely.

With Rebecca being only sixteen years old, bringing her on tour posed a challenge. I had to first convince her mother. I expressed to her that Rebecca had a wonderful talent and that I wanted to bring her on my US tour, which I felt would be beneficial to her. I assured her mother that I'd watch over her and make sure she'd stay safe.

Her mom finally agreed and all was good. I personally loved this type of situation, as discovering talent has always been one of my favorite things to do—giving opportunities and new experiences to people, hoping to bring them to a place they may have never thought they'd get to before. Thankfully, there are a lot of people I've managed to do that for.

Finding alternative solutions to challenges is a passion of mine, and now it was time to find the right rehearsal space. I didn't want to go to a run-of-the-mill rehearsal studio where the band is crowded into a ten-by-fifteen room, like everyone does in New York, or rent some insanely expensive soundstage for thousands of dollars a day. I wanted to spend my budget wisely, and I was set on rehearsing in Stockholm. I decided to personally search for the space and started by looking up old theaters that were not currently in use. I ended up getting an entire beautiful vacant old theater in the middle of Stockholm. I called and went to meet the owner. He gave me the key and was ecstatic to have me rehearse there. It was wonderful, and a ridiculous deal for only a few hundred dollars a month!

As rehearsals got off the ground, I would usually watch and listen from the board in the middle of the room. It was all coming together, and the band was starting to rock!

I was very strict and had rules about drugs and alcohol on the road. If I found out that things were happening that I didn't approve of, whoever it was—band, crew, whoever—they would be replaced immediately with plane tickets home awaiting at the front desk of the hotel.

The tour was a success! We had wild times, fun times, rockin' audiences, and a great feeling of accomplishment, as this was my first major tour with me as the focus and a hit climbing the charts! The Eurythmics were great to us as we toured across the USA! We played some outstanding venues, and Annie was really sweet to me. She taught me some great vocal warm-up techniques, which I still use today. And Rebecca gained Dave Stuart's attention, which opened doors for her.

But there were some disturbing situations that would crop up over the course of the tour. A couple of members of my band had some differences that caused some drama. Husbands would bring their wives to the show, tell me how crazy they were about me, and literally ask me to sleep with their wives! I thought it was utterly ridiculous when they would say something like, "It would make her so happy. I love her so much and just want to give her what makes her happy." Insanity! But I've also been victim to quite different sentiments where husbands or boyfriends would lunge in an attempt to rip my Mohawk off my head! Or wanting to kill me for my very existence! Luckily, my bodyguards were always alert to save the day!

When the tour made its way to Utah, we made jokes about how all the Mormon women were so conservative. I had a Black football player security guy, Larry, working with me at the time. He was a big, fairly soft-spoken guy who had a different philosophy than I did. He shied away from going to places he felt uncomfortable or that he thought he didn't belong.

By working with me, he learned things were not as they seemed. For example, I would take him to clubs I would frequent or clubs on the road, and he would say, "No, we can't go in there. It's not right for us, and it'll probably be uncomfortable. Let me find a Black club where we can go." I'd insist he follow my lead, "You'll see. It's going to be fine, and we'll have a great time." When we were in L.A., I took him to a place called Roxbury, one of the top Hollywood hot spots at the time, which was predominantly White. He had the time of his life.

As we were leaving, he said to me, "Thank you. I really had a great time! I'm actually surprised. Because of my upbringing, I would never go to places like this." It was interesting to learn of his mindset, and that of many of his friends, that automatically assumed segregation as the norm. This is the same thing that happened at the beginning of the Plasmatics, when Black fans didn't feel comfortable coming to the shows until I was in the band.

Back in Utah, we arrived at the hotel and it was packed with girls! It was just insane, like I'd never seen before, and 90 percent of the girls were White. They were all trying to get in the hotel to see me, meet me, and some wanted more than that!

After rockin' our asses off at Park West, we drove back to the hotel and soon realized the situation had escalated and gotten completely out of control. There were hundreds of girls pushing the car and banging on the windows. It was like the movie *The Birds*. I was shocked! I just couldn't believe it. The worst of it was that some of these girls were so young—sixteen- and seventeen-year-old high school girls.

Larry was really upset about it all, as his job was to protect me—from everything! He said, "We're getting out of here right now."

I said, "What do you mean? We're supposed to stay here overnight." I was kind of soaking it all in, and I liked it.

Larry was so persistent and worried, he told me, "Jean, listen, you're gonna end up in jail if we stay here. Something's gonna happen. I can feel it." He had me pack, took my bags, and forced me to get in a car that same night and leave town.

We proceeded to a fantastic venue in Colorado called Red Rocks, which is one of the most scenic venues we played on our American tour. A beautiful amphitheater nestled amidst breathtaking natural red rocks, as the name suggests. Performing in those surroundings was just awesome!

As the tour started to wind down, I was offered the Eurythmics European tour, but by then the band drama had escalated, despite my rules and efforts to contain it. I had just about had it. I'd have to change members and so on, with very little time to prepare for the next leg, so I stupidly declined. That was something I also regretted for a long time. In retrospect, I might have blown things out of proportion, since band drama is one of the most common problems and people just get through it. I had also had plenty of experience in that department from my earlier years as a musical director, so I'm not sure what I was thinking.

After the tour, Dave Stewart invited Rebecca to London. From then on, her career was well on its way. She was introduced to Mick Jagger, she recorded an album, and she went on to become one of the most successful VJs on MTV UK and Europe. It was a fairytale story, and I was so proud of her.

We are still in touch now. She married a man named Andreas Åkerlund, who is the brother of a good friend and well-known video/film director, Jonas Åkerlund. Jonas once invited me to a get-together in Miami and surprisingly informed me that Rebecca was married to his brother, so we had the chance to meet again!

In the meantime, "Feel the Heat" was charting around the world and really cooking in France where Virgin and the promotion team were supporting the record full tilt.

When I signed with my manager, he asked me, "What do you want to call yourself?"

I said, "Jean Beauvoir," my real name.

"Jean, there are two things in this world that never work: French and Japanese." He was saying that the two things that don't sell in music on an international basis are French and Japanese. So according to him, keeping a French name was suicide. But I stuck to my guns and kept my French name. And I'll tell you, when the success came in France, the way they reacted and the pride that the country had was extraordinary. They put me on a pedestal and treated me like a god.

I believe that because my name was French, and I spoke French fluently, I was someone they felt they could adopt as their own. As far as they were concerned, I was a product of France, yet also American, as well as being partnered with the superstar Sylvester Stallone.

I remember when I did one of the most popular TV shows in France, called *Cocoricocoboy*. They designed a wonderful set around my look. They had beautiful girls all dressed up in American Indian fringed outfits very much like mine. Teepees were scattered around, and though I don't remember the dialogue, it was a really funny skit somewhat like *Saturday Night Live*. The viewership was amazing, and the day after that I received a call from my radio and press promoters saying, "We are selling thirty thousand records a day!" They're flying off the shelves!" I did all of the French top TV shows, one after the other, and after all was said and done, they called to say, "You've broken the record for the biggest-selling American single in France to date!" Be it right or wrong, it was great to hear!

I'd head out to nightclubs, which Paris was full of, and great ones at that, very luxurious, many with bottle service and always tables and tables of celebrities and models. As soon as I'd walk in, you'd hear my track "Feel the Heat" come on. The dance floor would be packed, and it was exhilarating! I also remember going to a very popular shopping area called Les Halles. There were gigantic screens that had my video playing over and over in a loop for hours on end. I don't remember seeing any other videos, which was also incredible.

One of the clubs I visited often was called Les Bains Douches, which actually means the Baths-Showers in English. It was a very popular club, and people from all over the world would go there—musicians, actors, models, sports stars, and the like. One time, I'd see Steven Segal, another time, Björn Borg, and the DJ that was slammin' there at the time playing my track was none other than David Guetta, who later went on to have a huge success with his own album.

I continued doing whatever I could to promote my album around the world. "Feel the Heat" has continued to gain momentum up until today. It was on the soundtrack album for *Cobra*, on all videocassettes, DVDs, in addition to all the digital platforms and has actually been included on over ninety compilations in France and Belgium alone in the past several years. All in all, this converts to millions and millions of sales of that song.

Another rare attribute, which Céline Dion and I share, is that we were able to exist on all the major label compilations (Sony BMG, Warner, etc.), whether they be French or English, meaning that "Feel the Heat" appeared on compilations with international artists, such as Michael Jackson, Whitney Houston, Prince, the Pointer Sisters, George Michael, James Brown, Santana, Rick Astley, and Earth, Wind & Fire. At the same time, the song appeared on other compilations that featured only top French artists, such as Johnny Hallyday, Caroline Loeb, Début de Soirée, and many others. Uniquely, the song was included on French rock compilations with artists such as ZZ Top, Scorpions, Van Halen, Europe, Joe Cocker, Billy Idol, and Toto. Inclusion in all these different compilations is pretty much unheard of. I imagine it is partially due to my French name. In any case, it tripled the exposure.

12

ROCKIN' WITH ROYALTY

In 1986 my career had significantly progressed and my celebrity hightened. I had more and more opportunities to mix and mingle with all kinds of people, from paupers to high society. Invitations to countless celebrities' homes around the world. Private exclusive parties in the Carribean, the South of France, Paris, London, Milan, and other exotic locales. Exclusive day- and nightclubs nestled in the mountains of little French towns, the Monaco Grand Prix, or championship tennis matches in the Swedish summer paradise Båstad. It was all in abundance, including personal invites from Royalty.

It was interesting to meet Princess Stéphanie of Monaco, who with the royal family had cordially invited me to perform for them. I was very familiar with the royal family, their rich history, and of course, her mother, Grace Kelly.

We both had hits in the French charts and had been recently featured on the cover of *Top 50*, the official French magazine for singles sales charts, with giant posters on the inside of each of us. The front cover featured three photos: Princess Stéphanie, Sylvester Stallone, and myself.

I accepted the invitation and flew over with my band. When I arrived, I was treated like royalty. All was set up ideally for the show. The concert went well and a dinner had been arranged for us at night. Princess Stéphanie had a table with a place set for me with her. A separate table was prepared for the band. It was my guitarist's birthday, so I asked if she'd mind me sitting a while with the boys to celebrate his birthday.

I stayed there for a quite a while, to the point where she suddenly appeared not particularly pleased with me. We actually found ourselves in somewhat of a "boy-meets-girl" unexpected tiff! But where I was not afforded much to say! It made her seem even cooler as she chastised me for not giving her the attention she believed she deserved. I couldn't remember the last time I had been reprimanded like that by a beautiful princess—and in perfect English, no less, though we did speak French to each other as well.

I retreated and had my security guard escort me back to my room, where I received another call from Her Highness reiterating her previous thoughts. I had obviously upset her, and I admit it was a bit rude of me when I reflect back on it.

Granted, I had a huge hit over there at the time—and along with that, perhaps some attitude. She had invited me and paid quite a bit to have me there, so certainly my company was expected. I said goodbye cordially, and we hung up. That was the end of our contact for that trip.

In the morning, as I was leaving the hotel to get to the limo, I was surrounded by a mob of fans going crazy! They surrounded the limousine and literally started rocking it so hard that it was lifting off the ground as we were trying to leave for the airport. We finally got away, raced to the airport, and I caught my flight back to the US.

Some months went by, and one night I was having dinner with a friend at a West Hollywood hotspot I frequented called Le Dome on Sunset Boulevard. A waiter came over and handed me a sweet note from a mystery person. The note said something like, "This is a friend of yours. I'm sorry for my behavior when we last met, and I'd like to say hi." I looked up in shock as Her Highness stood up and started walking towards me! We laughed, gave a kiss, and spent a little time together.

Aside from her being a princess, she was a wonderful and fun girl.

A few years later, I was invited to the World Music Awards in Monaco. When I arrived, we saw each other from across the room. We both got up, ran over, and gave each other a big hug. Everyone seemed surprised.

From then on, we hung out throughout the evening having a great time. We and some other friends were then invited to an after-party on a yacht. The port of Monaco is gorgeous, and some of the world's most beautiful yachts are kept there. I led her by the hand to the limo as we scurried through all the people causing quite the scene. To be expected from a Black guy with a blond Mohawk and a princess. Photographers and press were flashing away as we got into the limo. We drove off to the party and hung out together.

The next day, the press reported in French and other European magazines stories and photos of us from the evening. They also wrote that my Mohawk was spotted sneaking out of the palace.

13

THE RAMONES—PICKING UP THE PIECES

I HAD KNOWN THE RAMONES for a long time, going way back to the Plasmatics days. We were all punks hanging out downtown at CBGB and Max's Kansas City, so we would always bump into each other. We had the same management, Gary Kurfirst of Overland Productions. One day, Gary, who was always pretty innovative, said, "Jean, what do you think about producing the Ramones?"

I was like, "You know what, that could be interesting."

He had a vision and felt that with my musical style and everything I knew, it could be a great collaboration. I also understood punk and that punks lived a particular way and had a certain way of thinking. They were a class of their own, so not everyone would just be able to get in there and be comfortable. I liked the idea.

"Well, have you mentioned it to the band?" I asked.

"Yeah, they're in," he answered.

We decided to move forward, and I went to meet Seymour Stein, who was the head of their label, Sire, at the time. He was a very interesting and colorful character. We discussed what was going to happen, but he gave me no real direction. He just said, "Keep the guys in line. We want a record that's gonna be commercially successful, and it'll be really interesting to see what you guys come up with."

So the band and I started spending time together, and Joey, Dee Dee, and I began writing. They'd come over to my apartment, one or the other, and we'd write things fairly quickly.

Dee Dee was a great lyricist and always had something interesting to bring to the table. I really liked his thought process and how witty he was. Joey was also a great guy and a lot of fun—a tall, gawky-looking guy, soft-spoken yet very emotional at times. He exerted a certain kind of charm, which made him easily likable. His hair would cover his eyes most of the time as he stood there talking to you in his worn jeans, leather motorcycle jacket, and glasses, like a caricature of himself. He'd warm up to record his vocals by sucking on a lemon to open up his throat, and it worked for him.

Joey was very musical and liked beautiful sounds—piano, orchestration, and tasteful melodies. Dee Dee did as well, but he didn't gravitate to it as much, but if I'd play something on the piano or sang something melodic that worked nicely over a very heavy punk thing, he'd go, "Wow, Jean, that's beautiful. I love that."

I was always moved by contrast and things that were different, so the combination of adding musical melodies to something that, at its base, was so out of control was exciting. It became our recipe for the album.

Johnny, on the other hand, was more of a purist, and he believed the Ramones were a punk band and that nothing else should be introduced. He wanted it to be guitar-based, and as soon as he heard any word of piano or strings, he was usually dead against it. But in my case, they had a certain amount of trust, which allowed me to try different things that were, at times, out of their comfort zone.

My whole approach to producing was trying to get the most out of the band and create the best version of who they were. I would add certain elements—the melodies, background vocals, piano, and orchestration—that they hadn't done much of in the past, but that lay dormant within some of them. I had to find a balance to keep everyone happy. I considered myself a fifth member while working with them, trying to really understand what they liked, what they were trying to get across, and how far in any direction they'd be willing to go. In the end, I wanted them to remain true and sound like the Ramones. This is the same approach that I take across the board when producing.

Our working relationship was unusually harmonious. I can't even remember one actual argument of any kind, though I would get a little frustrated with Joey sometimes. He was extremely picky about his vocals. At times, we'd have numerous takes and would be choosing words from each of them because he liked the way this or that word sounded, where technically, and for me, they mostly sounded great. He would always ask my opinion in that sad puppy voice of his, and I just couldn't say no. I'd cave and pretty much did whatever he asked. I always wanted everyone to be 100 percent satisfied with their performances. Perhaps you can imagine working on those old mixing desks, with forty-eight channels, and you're sitting with your engineer, four hands, as the track is running, and punching in different words on track thirty-one, then two, then nine, four, three—it could be quite grueling.

Being that Joey liked strings and piano, we wrote this beautiful song called "She Belongs to Me." It was a really sad song, and I think that Joey delivered it wonderfully. I made an effort to make sure that everyone was represented in one way or another on the album. For example, Richie had a song called "Somebody Put Something in My Drink." No one really cared much about doing that song, but I spent time on it with Richie. I liked the song and supported him in wanting to record and sing it. It turned out great—as a matter of fact, he ended up using it as a platform to further his career after the Ramones.

It's unfortunate, then, that though I've always felt good about my work on the album over the years, I did read a disparaging comment that Richie made later. I was expecting some praise for supporting him and that song, but instead he said something like, "Oh, we got Jean because he was cheap," as I was told by a journalist, which was definitely not the case, nor was he privy to this information.

But to focus on the good memories, I do recall a funny incident with Dee Dee. At the time, I was in Sweden working on the album at Polar Studios, and he was in the United States. We had already recorded the vocals for "Animal Boy," one of the punkier, faster songs, and he had a lyric in there that was offensive to someone. It was a friend of his, but also a fairly well-known artist. I guess his conscience got to him.

He called me one night and said, "Jean, I have a problem. I wanna change that lyric because I think he's gonna get mad at me." Of course,

I wanted to help him out. I said, "OK, this is what you're going to do. Put the song on in the background across the room, but make sure it's really, really low in volume. Bring the cassette recorder right next to your mouth and record the new vocal part, singing along with the track." That's exactly what he did, and he sent it over to me. It worked brilliantly.

I loved challenges in the studio, and in this instance, I had to match a vocal recorded on a cheap cassette player—with background noise—to a vocal that was recorded with a Neumann U87 microphone in a professional recording studio. It worked seamlessly, and nobody would ever know that this happened or what line had been replaced. Dee Dee was ecstatic about the results, and we moved on.

I really loved the guys and working on the album, but it was a bit stressful for me at times. Although I had been recording nonstop for the past couple of years and I was very comfortable in the studio, this was one of my first big productions for someone other than myself. The eclectic personalities made the whole thing even more interesting. I'm not gonna lie, there were times when I felt I was going to lose my Mohawk—or pull it out of my head! At the end of the day, I had to make sure *everyone* was happy, which included the record company, Seymour Stein, Gary Kurfirst, the band, the band's girlfriends, and everyone else involved. This was quite a feat.

We did have a situation with one of the song titles on a track that was written by myself, Dee Dee, and Joey called "My Brain Is Hanging Upside Down." It was originally titled "Bonzo Goes to Bitburg," and it was the definitive story of Ronald Reagan going to Germany to visit the Nazi SS graves. Johnny didn't like the idea of that somewhat derogatory title, being a Reagan supporter, and he wanted to change it to "My Brain Is Hanging Upside Down." We finally all agreed.

I wrote 50 percent of that song, with Joey and Dee Dee each writing 25 percent. I wrote all the music and melodies, plus a portion of the lyrics. I'm saying this because I've seen the song being credited differently in so many places by people who could not actually know, as they were not present during the writing process. I also contributed much of the background vocals and played most of the guitars, as Johnny refused to play minor or suspended chords.

I really liked the song and fought for its release in the United States to no avail. The record company was against it. They felt it was too controversial and too much of a departure for the Ramones. Warner Bros. / Sire gave differing reasons for not releasing it, ranging from financial to political to it just wasn't a good enough record. The original jacket of the single included a photo of Reagan speaking at the site of the Bergen-Belsen concentration camp just hours before his trip to Bitburg, but this image was removed in future pressings.

We moved on and released it in the UK on Beggars Banquet Records. The song came out, charted in the Top 100, but the US was still not prepared to release it. But I felt I had good instincts, and I'd been pretty lucky with sometimes foreseeing the future—perhaps owing to my Voodoo heritage! It started to get very heavy play as an import at college radio in the US, and it went on to win Best Independent Single at the New York Music Awards, and *Animal Boy* won Best Album. It finally got to the point where the record company had to cave and release the song in the US. The single was a major critical success.

John Leland wrote for the October 1985 issue of *Spin* magazine: "Just listen to Johnny's freight cars of guitar chords, Dee Dee's 'ahh, naa naa naa' surf harmonies, and Joey's down-to-earth irritation at watching our commander in chief on TV. The Ramones are so brilliant because they perceive the world the way regular people do—through television."

In the annual Pazz & Jop critics poll conducted by the *Village Voice*, "Bonzo Goes to Bitburg" was ranked the fifth best single of 1985, where the editor wrote that it was "a pleasure to see the Ramones place so high after the intrepid Seymour Stein refused to release their most overt political act." In his review of *Animal Boy*, *Rolling Stone*'s David Fricke called the song "brilliant." He wrote that it "vividly captures the sense of helplessness and confusion felt by rock youth in the Age of Reagan." In his book *Music: What Happened?* Scott Miller includes it among his list of best songs from 1986, while *Salon*'s Bill Wyman retrospectively describes it as "the group's greatest song and greatest vocal performance." This song is considered the most important song ever released by the Ramones, and I was happy to see that my instincts were on point and that the song did get its just due.

It also became the song most used in the film *School of Rock* and has been used in other films as well. It was even referenced during the Trump/Putin situation on NBC and Fox, so it's a song I'm very proud of.

The first single off the album was "Something to Believe In," and written by Dee Dee and myself. There was also a great video filmed called "Ramones Aid," which was on heavy rotation at MTV. It was a parody of "Hands Across America" with a number of special guests, such as Afrika Bambaataa, the B-52s, Berlin, Fishbone, Ted Nugent, Spinal Tap, Gary US Bonds, and Weird Al Yankovic. There were also Michael Jackson, Lionel Richie, and Cyndi Lauper look-alikes from the 1985 "We Are the World" video. It was nominated for the New York City Music Awards Best Video Clip, and it was only surpassed by Peter Gabriel's "Sledgehammer," but both the *Animal Boy* album and "Animal Boy" single did win. Ironically, as one of his last accomplishments before his death, Johnny Ramone produced a version of "Something to Believe In" for the Pretenders, which was included on the album *We're a Happy Family: A Tribute to Ramones.*

Speaking of the Pretenders, I love them and always have. Chrissie Hynde's voice is mesmerizing, and her performance on "I'll Stand by You" puts the song at the top of my list of beautiful ballads of our time. Coincidentally, I heard through someone that she had been speaking of me, and it turns out we had mutual admiration. I got her number and rang her up. We had a great chat; she was sweet, and we ended with "we must get together sometime!" At one point, she was going to play in Paris, and my sister was living there at the time. I couldn't make it, so I set up a meeting between them so Chrissie could meet her and maybe get shown around Paris by a native. I thought my sister would enjoy that.

To this day, Chrissie and I have never met face-to-face, but she is someone I'd love to write with. I believe we could produce another beautiful, timeless ballad. Perhaps a duet. Time will tell, but in any case, I remain a fan.

All in all, the *Animal Boy* album was well received and accomplished something I strive for. Songs becoming increasingly important as time goes by. People now understand its value—sometimes it takes longer than you'd like.

Not long after we did the album, I was called in to produce the song "Pet Sematary" for the Stephen King film. Stephen King wanted to include a Ramones song as the title track, and the band had a basic idea that needed to become reality, but quickly! Mary Lambert, who had produced my "Feel the Heat" video, was the director of the film. We all got together to discuss the plan and get to work.

I chose to record at Sigma Sound in New York and called Fernando Kral, a talented young engineer whom I had worked with before. We were doing preproduction rehearsals at SIR, a professional rehearsal studio in New York, so I brought him along to get a feel for the song.

When we got to the studio around noon, Fernando set up everything as I liked it. Marky Ramone, an accomplished drummer, played on this track, and everything was mic'd up and ready to rock. The band showed up some hours later. Unfortunately, Dee Dee didn't show up for the session even though he had been there for the rehearsals, so I played a guide bass part, which was ultimately used for the record. Dee Dee may have had his mind on other things, as he would soon quit the band to pursue a career as a rap artist under the name Dee Dee King.

It was pretty straightforward, and within a few hours we had a master take—no cutting pieces together and no edits, just a good, straight take. In a March 2008 interview for *Sound on Sound*, Fernando said, "It's not like we were dumping things into Pro Tools and moving them around, and there also wasn't any punching-in on the basic track. Don't forget, Jean Beauvoir is a pretty darn good musician himself, he's got some great music chops, and he knew what he wanted to get out of these guys. What's more, having rehearsed with them beforehand, he also knew what they needed and expected, and whatever coaching needed to be done. In other words, he knew what the headphones needed to sound like for Johnny to play along, and what Marky needed in that regard. He was the fifth Ramone that day."

Joey came in that same night to lay down a rough vocal, and he returned the next day to finish. Fernando and I worked through the night into the following day on recording overdubs and background vocals. Finally, by the next day we had everything ready to mix, which went pretty fast.

The mix was sent to the record and production companies, and they loved it. A couple of months later they got back to me saying they needed another mix with louder lead and background vocals. This time I brought them to the Hit Factory, where I had often worked. The production of this song was higher end than what the Ramones were accustomed to. The session began at midnight, and we were trying to beat the clock—my Lotus was parked on Fifty-Fourth Street. As it turned out, my car was towed, but the mix sounded great!

The band commented that we ended up spending more than twice the cost of the first album, on this one song: a week at SIR Rehearsal Studio, three days at Sigma, and a day at the Hit Factory—in addition to my fee! The good news was that the film company was paying for everything.

At one point, later down the road, another producer was brought in to try a remix, but in the end, only my mix was used for the film and major releases. The song charted at number four on the *Billboard* charts in the US, making it the highest charting Ramones song of their career. It's strange to think that out of all the songs that the Ramones had released throughout the years, nothing ever charted above eighty, from what I read. I was happy to break that mold for the band, and it still holds that record in terms of commercial success.

For the Ramones song "Merry Christmas," I was called in yet again, I guess for the same reason—looking for that sound! Joey came in with a very, very rough idea, literally just a vocal and a guitar. I added quite a bit to that song, and probably should have been credited as a writer as well. I must have been feeling generous at the time. We recorded the song, and I loved the way it turned out. Again, more contrast combining punk rock with a cool melody. That song ended up in the films *Why Him?* and *Christmas with the Kranks*, which became the thirteenth-highest-grossing film at the box office of all time. It's become a very popular song for the band, and I recently watched a video of Miley Cyrus dancing to it as only she can!

It was really funny to be listening to Sirius XM Radio many years later and hear the song on the main pop Christmas channel. It was such a strange feeling to hear that song playing alongside Mariah Carey, George Michael, and all these popular Christmas songs. I just found it so amazing that a song that was produced and recorded thirty-five years ago would be able to live next to these very pop, huge hit songs, and it still sounded great!

I wish the Ramones were around to see what's been happening and how much fame and accolades came after the original members passed.

It's such a shame that sometimes people have to die before their genius is realized. That was precisely the case with the Ramones. In my mind, at least, it was eventually recognized, but so many never are. The Ramones were innovators, and with their simplicity they turned their limitations into assets. I always found a real genius to that. I've seen so many artists who didn't have as much perceived talent that others may have had, but they used it to their advantage. They worked twice as hard and stayed within a framework that they either created or had been created for them, eventually leading to success.

Dee Dee and I remained friends for a long time, up until his passing, and we'd get together on a regular basis. He always spoke to me about his various projects or any ideas he had in mind. I enjoyed spending time with him. It felt like he was a younger brother I'd mentor, but he was older than me!

Punkers are funny—especially Dee Dee, who just had such an exciting personality, eccentric and almost a cartoon character of what you would expect somebody in the Ramones to be. He was still filled with so much fuel when he passed. His girlfriend was a big deal in his life at that time. Any time there was a decision to be made, he'd say, "OK, Jean, I like this, but I don't know if she's gonna like it. Let me find out." That was the big test.

Other times, he'd say, "Oh, no, she's not gonna like it, she's never gonna let me do that. She's not gonna like that." There were times I'd have to get on the phone with her and talk about certain things, explaining what was needed. She was always really nice to me, and I could relate to her. I'd explain things to her truthfully and tell her why I felt that a certain something was valid. She'd say, "OK, Jean, all right, if you think it's good"—meaning, if it wasn't good, it was my ass!

Then Dee Dee would call me, all excited, saying, "She likes it! She likes it!" My ass was put on the chopping block many a time, with very little left of it when all was said and done!

One day, Pat Lucas, the film and TV head at SBK Records in L.A. (who I knew very well), called me and asked about doing a song for a movie called *Rock 'n' Roll High School Forever*, which was starring Corey Feldman. She, of course, knew of my punk history. I then thought to call Dee Dee, as he was then out of the Ramones and doing his own thing. There was a decent budget as well that I was sure he'd welcome, and it was probably the first time he would be commissioned to write a song for a film.

He loved the idea, so we got together and wrote the song "Cut Me to Pieces" in my house. We decided to record it as a duet. It turned out pretty good, so Pat and the film company were content. It was used in part and featured in the film, but it was never released in its entirety.

Tons of people have asked me over the years "When will the full song be released?" I respond, "Let's see what the future holds." As of this writing, no one has ever heard the entire song.

After Dee Dee formed his hip-hop project, he came to Berlin, Germany, where I was living at the time. I was happy to get a call from him and stoked to see him. He was just so diverse in his thinking and extremely creative, very smart and exactly as crazy as people would imagine him to be—including drugs and whatever else he was into. Nevertheless, he was a really talented guy. I respected him, loved him, and miss him!

Around this time, I had the opportunity to cowrite with some legendary artists. Debbie Harry came over to my place, and we wrote a song called "Do It Yourself." It was a poppy punk-type song that was later released with Palmyra Delran on an album called *Kinder Angst*, which addressed the growing pains of childhood from a kid's perspective. It was a blast working with her! She always had funny and witty things to say! What a talent! She's done it all. I spent a fair amount of time with her and Chris Stein. We all came from the same era and the days of CBGB. Years later, Hartwig Masuch, head of BMG worldwide, told me on a call that he'd love to sign her if he could, so I called her while she was on a trip, I believe in South America. I knew she didn't have a label at the time, and I felt BMG would be perfect for Blondie. I made the introduction and they ultimately signed with BMG. This deal lead to more hits and reignited their touring opportunities around the world, which was well deserved. I was happy to see that happen.

I also worked several times with another great artist, Nona Hendryx, from the group Labelle. She was working on a solo album and we cowrote "I Need Love," which was the single and was featured heavily on MTV.

The song was produced by the famed producer Arthur Baker. She is a passionate artist, with so much to say. We worked well together and I always embraced her morals, talent, and personality.

I played lead guitar on the track, helped with background vocal arrangements, and also sang backgrounds on the record. Prince wrote the single on her following album, "Baby Go-Go."

Nona and I later went on to cowrite several more songs, including "In Praise of Older Men (Father, Brother, Lover, Son)" and "When Love Goes to War."

Another legendary rock artist I worked with was Glenn Hughes from Deep Purple and Black Sabbath, who was then solo. He is a great vocalist and bassist. We wrote the song "The Liar" in my studio in Malibu, which was featured on his album *From Now On . . .* He was introduced to me by a good friend of mine, Scott Rabin, and we were excited to work together. I also did a session with George Brown from Kool and the Gang. It wasn't specifically for the band, as they were not recording a new album at the time. We just got together to create. I once received a call from a gentleman named Larry Blackmon, the lead singer and founder of the funk and R&B band Cameo. He was making the album *Machismo*, and he asked me to come play some rhythm and lead guitar. He liked my solo guitar work from hearing "Feel the Heat" and wanted some rock guitar on his forthcoming album.

The album reached #10 on the Billboard Soul Album Charts and also charted well around the world. That was a lot of fun and a nice surprise. It was a great album with amazing contributions—Miles Davis also played on it! The album was certified gold in the US, so yet another gold album for me! I had accrued quite a number of these gold and platinum awards around the world at this point!

After Joey Ramone's passing I was told of a posthumous album that the estate wanted to release. That was exciting news to me, as I loved working with those guys. Ed Stasium, who I had worked with previously in the Plasmatics, and I were sent vocals recorded by Joey and Daniel Ray on a 4-track. We individually produced songs for the album released by BMG entitled *Ya Know?* The album received great reviews from *Rolling Stone* and other major publications, and I'd like to think that Joey would be happy to see how well his work was received.

14

JACKNIFED & VOODOO X

Drums Along the Mohawk had run its course, and it was time to move on to my next album. At this stage of the game, I had been very spoiled. While Gary Kurfirst was a blessing to me, at times he could say some awful things. He spoke his mind; he was honest but blunt. I remember sending him a demo idea I had recorded from Sweden, and we spoke after he listened to it.

"You know, Jean, this sounds like everything I hate," he said. I remember sitting in a corner of my studio distraught, but he was just telling me his true feelings. He had made me a lot of money, millions at this point in a very short time. But when it came time to record my second album, *Jacknifed*, I was a different person.

For an artist's first album, you have your entire life's worth of anguish, love, sadness, every kind of emotion you can imagine, rolled up and tightly wound, to pour into the album. I was also determined to prove to myself and to others by getting out there in the world, and I saw no limits.

For the second album, you don't have the same motivation. You've accomplished half of what you set out to do, so you just don't have that dire need for recognition or other things you desired in the past. You've used up a lot of your inspiration and need to find something new to fuel the fire. You've just lived a couple of years with all the girls you'd want, money, traveling, everything first class. I had a mansion in Sweden, an apartment in New York, another one in Los Angeles, and the Lotus I always wanted. I was also able to help out my family, so there wasn't much to cry about.

Columbia appointed me a new A&R rep for the second album, and from the beginning, we were not seeing eye to eye. He was really concerned about the Black floor / White floor situation at the label, and he just didn't see where I'd fit in. He attributed the success of the first album to the cooperation with Sylvester Stallone and the *Cobra* film, so that was swept aside.

I didn't agree with him, but his words messed with my head. I started feeling that I needed to lean more toward an R&B direction. Radio had been very difficult for the *Drums* album, and we all wanted to improve that situation. But I didn't feel that trying to conform and reign in my creativity was the answer.

It got to the point where I wasn't clear on what I was doing. I started writing, experimenting, and trying different things, but it wasn't feeling right. I had started working at Polar Studios in Stockholm again, but I said to myself, "Maybe I need a different vibe." I started looking at other places around Europe.

There were beautiful French studios in old castles and a fair number of options, but one that stood out to me was a studio called Puk in Denmark. It was a beautiful compound boasting the largest speakers in the world, a swimming pool, chefs, and other great amenities. George Michael was recording there at the time.

We worked there for weeks, but even with such a state-of-the-art studio we couldn't get a proper vocal sound. I had to order special microphone preamps from England, which took several days to arrive while we were still paying the expensive daily studio rate. You also had to import women, as there were absolutely none out there. The saying went, "Where men are men and sheep are nervous!"

The smart guys actually took their advances from the labels and built their own studios, like Pat Regan, a producer I often worked with in L.A. I remember when he got an advance for a deal, he told me, "We're buying a studio with the cash." I thought, *Wow, what a brilliant idea!* But did I do it? No. I just kept giving away money to all the major studios in the world. I actually did have my own studio up on top of the house in Sweden, but at the time it was only a demo studio. I felt I needed to go to a professional one to get the real sound.

It's funny when I realize that today I can get an excellent vocal sound with my laptop. What the hell was I thinking? What were we all thinking? Was it our hearing, or are those new cheap $40 microphone preamps really that good?

I started leaning toward R&B in my writing, which I could do. That music was a major part of my roots. But I just couldn't get things to click like I wanted them to. While the album did have some solid songs on it and performed fairly well, it was a difficult record for me to make.

Thinking about it in retrospect, I was hanging out a lot with Nile Rodgers, for example, and we were talking about doing something. I was still hung up on producing myself. I should have given up control for a moment and let him, or someone else of that caliber, produce an album for me—someone who understood the mélange that I was about. They would have probably gotten the very best out of me. It is hard to have the same perspective when you produce yourself. Sometimes an outside opinion is good. So many artists make the same mistake.

I did, however, have the chance to work with Nile, who was producing a very talented actress and recording artist, Carole Davis. I contributed some lead vocals and cowrote the song "Love to Make Love to You" on her Warner Bros. album *I'm No Angel.* Carole was a wonderful singer and had previously cowritten Prince's single "Slow Love," featured on his Grammy award–nominated album *Sign o' the Times.* She has been featured in many films and TV shows, became an animal activist, and we've remained friends ever since.

On *Jacknifed* we did bring in one producer, Shep Pettibone, to produce one song. He was a well-known club remixer who had done mixes for Madonna, Janet Jackson, the Bee Gees, David Bowie, Cyndi Lauper, and a long list of other well-known artists. I was apprehensive of someone taking the reins of one of my recordings. It made me extremely nervous, but Gary spent a good amount of time trying to get me to relax.

I went into Sigma Sound in New York to meet him. Upon my arrival, they were eating Chinese food and had already started to work on the mix. I left and paced around Times Square in anticipation. I called Gary again, and he basically told me to chill out and let him do his work. I was surprised at some things he had let slide, specifically tuning, where the engineer felt the same. The song "If Love Could Only" came out sounding good in the end.

When it came to the release of the album, the song "Jimmy" had been chosen as the first single. It was a very cool midtempo song, and I had a great concept for it. I wanted to create an alter ego, a Lil' Jimmy, who was a cute animated character that I would perform with in the video as my costar. There would be some sort of interaction between myself and this character, showing the emotions he felt from bad things that kept happening to him. I would be showing support. I was thinking along the lines of Disney, and that perhaps I'd be singing about him, as his narrator, about how everybody's always picking on Jimmy.

My A&R rep begged to differ, however, and he saw it as everybody's always picking on Jimmy Carter! WTF! In the context of my album, I personally didn't have any connection or thought of why I would possibly be singing about how everyone's always picking on Jimmy Carter!

Creatively, we were not on the same page. The video was made as he wanted. I knew that this was the beginning of the end. As I anticipated, the song came out with the video, and it did OK, but it didn't have the same impact that I had on the first run. We got to the point where I said, "Listen, Gary, I'm not happy here. I don't get this guy, and he doesn't get me. I don't anticipate having any more hits here, and I'd like to get off the label."

He said, "Well, if you were to make some less than satisfactory demos, I'll get you out of the deal." I did just that, and, as he said, I got out of the deal.

So here I was after two records with Columbia and Virgin, at a point where I needed to get a new deal. Whenever that happens, your income flow from the label stops suddenly but your expenses don't. You're still living the same lifestyle. You still have the houses, the car, the limos, payroll, and everything else you had previously, so you need to do your next thing for financial as much as creative reasons!

For some reason, I felt lonely making *Jacknifed*, even though I had a couple of guys along with me. Making all the decisions, always fighting for your position, and being the boss is great. But you're alone, and you always have to keep your guard up. I decided I wanted to give a band concept a shot.

I had recently visited my Voodoo priest uncle, Max Beauvoir, and as my brain was always turning, I was thinking of a new concept. I wanted to do something bigger than life, extraordinary, and something that would showcase the magical Haitian Voodoo culture to the world. My uncle was the supreme chief of Voodoo, as written by the *New York Times*, and had already been the subject of the book and film *The Serpent and the Rainbow* by Wes Craven. But he was always open to anything that would further promote the Voodoo culture.

We were always very close, and he just understood me right from the beginning. He called me the gambler—and yes, that I was. He was a positive man and was into curing and helping to find solutions for problems. Not all Voodoo practitioners follow this route. I thought this to be a perfect subject to promote, and combining Voodoo with rock and metal was the kind of contrast I was looking for. This led to Voodoo X.

I was at a party in New York City at the Hard Rock Cafe around the time of the New Music Seminar, and someone introduced me to a colorful and eccentric guy named Uwe Fahrenkrog-Petersen. We were both wearing unique long rock 'n' roll coats and had over-the-top hair, and somehow, there was a definite connection. It turns out that he was the keyboard player for the group Nena, who had the massive hit, "99 Luftballons," which he cowrote and played on. They were then one of Germany's top three exports. We really hit it off. Before the night was over, we decided that I would fly to Berlin to spend some time with him in his studio and basically just vibe.

I told him that I wasn't really in the head to do another solo record. I was looking to do something new. At the time, we were actually discussing a totally different project with just the two of us that we would call The Boys. I flew to Berlin to further discuss putting it together. Berlin was fantastic, and Uwe controlled that city. He knew all the spots and all the best clubs. We'd hit one that was open until 1:00 AM, then we'd be off to the next one that closed at 6:00 AM, and then another club would start at 7:00 AM and go throughout the day. It was ultimate craziness but loads of fun.

Uwe had a cool red Ferrari that he would park in front of any club, even up on the curb near the front door, and nobody said anything. He could go back after two or three crazy nights and pick it up unscathed.

We went to great restaurants like Borchardt, and we'd have Wiener schnitzel and other German delicacies. It was the best! We hit many other cool places and hangs, and as Berlin is a very eclectic city with all nationalities living there, it was far from being short of restaurants. There was a plethora of food and cultures within the city to choose from. It was a treat to get to see it with Uwe, the "Prince of Berlin!"

After that amazing trip, I came home and started thinking that The Boys idea was not really for me just then. I was anxious to do a rock project. I started thinking about my visits with Uncle Max, and I revisited my initial thought to share his vision of the beauty of voodoo and to see if we could somehow make this all work as a rock band. That's when I started to form Voodoo X.

I immediately started writing songs on my own in New York. Here's how my thought process went: as soon as I'd come up with a concept, whatever it might be, even just a name, then all of a sudden, complete songs would start flying into my head. These songs included "I'm on Fire," and "Like a Knife," which I recorded and recruited Tommy Lafferty to play solos on. For "Voodoo Queen," our first single, I handled all the guitars, drums, bass and vocals, whilst Uwe handled keyboards.

Not long after that, I decided I'd go back over to Berlin with Tommy in tow to record yet another song, "The Awakening." Once that song was together, Uwe and I went to meet Michael Stark, Uwe's manager. We played him the songs, and he was blown away! Michael was a well-known longtime manager in Germany and had good connections, especially with Columbia Records, which just so happened to be my former solo label for the US. Michael arranged for us to meet with the president of Columbia in Germany. A deal was offered on the spot.

When Columbia Records offered this deal, it was time for me to bring my manager, Gary, into the fold. I got in touch with him and said, "Guess what, Gary. Remember I was recently just let go by Columbia Records US, right? Well, I've found a situation in Europe for my new project, with the same label." He was dumbfounded and anxious to hear more. I continued, "I found a situation for Europe where you don't have to recoup the cost of recording."

He said, "Now, Jean, there is no way. Nothing is for free. I don't buy it."

I said, "Gary, I'm telling you, this is the deal. You know that I know my business, so trust me."

I set up a call between him and Michael Stark. They had a long discussion, and Gary found out that, indeed, my information was correct: whether the recording portion of making the album was $200,000 or $1 million, it would not get paid back to the record company. Only the advance to the artist, video cost (usually at fifty-fifty), tour support, or other borrowed funds outside the recording budget were recoupable.

Once we were all in agreement with the basis, it was time for Gary and Michael to get rockin'. As Gary was the king of the big deals, it turned out to be a multimillion-dollar deal for two albums. Two countries had to join forces to consummate the deal.

This was a very interesting piece of business for me. I was involved in the negotiations throughout. I found it satisfying to make deals of this sort, keeping territories separate and other maneuvers that put you in a better position with record companies. In this particular case, as I had been let go by Columbia Records not that long ago, this new Columbia signing was big, but very unorthodox.

As the project was developing, I was really excited about it. Uwe's enthusiasm made it exhilarating to discuss. Being from the Plasmatics, I had a similar feeling of being a part of something more so like a character in a film, rather than just being myself. Maybe it was the ability to hide behind something that allowed me to feel less inhibited.

Let's say you, the reader, were asked to act out a role that was completely exaggerated and against your character. If they told you that you could wear a mask and no one would know it's you, you'd probably go crazy with that role. Then, if you were asked to take that mask off and be exposed, you'd be a lot more contained, self-conscious, and have all those other feelings you get when all the attention is on you. It was very much that same feeling being a part of the Plasmatics. And now I felt like that again in Voodoo X.

We decided that in Voodoo X, there would be five different images portrayed. Each member would be represented by a certain symbol. I would be the mask, Tommy was the snake that wrapped around the dagger, which was Uwe. Ivan Wrong, the bass player, would be the rose, and Ernie Lake, the drummer, would be the star in the center of the cross. Together, it was all intertwined forming the symbol and logo for Voodoo X.

I just loved fashion, but I loved things that were different. I was never a big fan of labels like, "Oh I have to wear Versace." I wanted my own clothes that looked cool. I loved to design things that sometimes cost less than you'd imagine but looked like nothing else, so when people would see it, it would be perceived as some amazingly expensive piece. In fact, it was its uniqueness that would make it valuable. It's like the guy who put the $12 champagne in a bottle of Cristal, and nobody knew the difference.

In any case, I loved putting outfits together down to the very detail. I could spend days looking for specific rhinestones to fit on a belt. I'd scour the garment district for materials, sequins, leather, snake and animal prints, metallic, whatever worked. I'd put studs or hearts down a leather pant leg. I found a clothing designer named Katharina in Sweden and worked with her for some things. Gittan Gooding was another talented designer.

At one point, I had my loft on Thirtieth Street across from another loft where girls would be trying on clothes all day. As you could imagine, my friends always wanted to hang out at my place. The girls, of course, knew that we were looking, and we just couldn't help it. I had floor-to-ceiling windows, and so did they. They were constantly showing off by getting naked, putting on clothes, and taking them off all day. It was very hard to ignore.

One day I'm in a nightclub, and a girl walks over to me and says, "Do you recognize me?"

I said, "No."

"Probably because I have my clothes on! I am one of the girls that you spend your days looking at across the street on Thirtieth." It was funny as hell, and we laughed our asses off! We became absolute best friends, and the naked shows did not stop until I finally moved out. When I did, that was definitely one of the regrets. Strangely enough, my friends visited much less!

So, being so into clothes, I'd hire these different people, as everything had to be custom made even if I found all the materials and dressings. Uwe and I definitely had this in common. He had his go-to places to get what he liked and what he needed, but he, on the other hand, loved to spend a lot of money on clothing! The other members weren't quite as fashion motivated as we were. I'd have to help them along a bit, but we got there and created some distinctive and fabulous outfits for everyone.

While we were focused on getting things together visually for the project, on the business side an executive at Columbia informed us that there had been a meeting in Miami. The label heads from Columbia around the world were presented with the upcoming year's artists. In these meetings, they were given the opportunity to showcase artists they were enthusiastic about. Everyone was excited to share, and the German and English record company heads supposedly got up and said, "Our important new signing is Jean Beauvoir for his project Voodoo X!"

It absolutely freaked out the American label rep. He got up and said, "Wait a minute. We just dropped him. How can you sign him, give him a bigger deal, excluding the US? This is crazy!" But the deal had already been inked. It was simply a good business move.

It wasn't all smooth sailing, though. My arrogance thinking I'd figured out a formula as to how things work in the music business would come back to bite me in the ass! Although Voodoo X had signed a deal for the UK, Germany, and the rest of the world, we weren't having any luck getting a US label to come on board. And we never would find one. The album was released solely as an import in the US, but later on for big bucks! I saw an original vinyl for sale on Ebay for $500.00!

As soon as the budget was in place for the recording of the Voodoo X album, it was now time to choose a producer. Once again, we had a generous budget, so I could pretty much hire anyone I wanted. The wheels were turning. I definitely wanted to coproduce as well.

I looked at various producers that I've admired over the years—Keith Olsen, Mutt Lange, and other greats who were well known, and not only in the rock world. Max Norman was mentioned by Seline Armbeck, who was one of my contacts at SBK, my then publishing company. I had also introduced her to my brother on one of his trips to L.A., and they were dating. Around this time, I met Jody Gerson and Dierdre O'Hara, who were also executives at SBK Publishing and Records and, at another point, EMI.

I listened to some different records I had received, and I was really taken by Max's drum sound on a record called *220 Volt*. It was just so slamming. I had already known of his work with Ozzy, which I was a huge fan of, so I reached out to him. We spoke, I shared my vision, and he shared his thoughts. He was very English and had a good sense of humor, so we hit it off right away. He really liked my work, which of course was very flattering. I decided to hire him. We started making plans for the recordings.

I had already recorded several demos in my apartment in New York as well as one or two songs in Berlin with Uwe and Tommy, so it was time to start bringing in the other guys to record. Very similar to my solo album approach, I wanted the recording experience to be fun, exciting, and adventurous!

I have fond memories staying at the Munich Park Hilton. I always enjoyed that hotel and the club P1, which wasn't that far away. I loved the vibe of that city and its people. I didn't want to record in New York or L.A., and I felt that it would be more inspirational to have the guys in a new environment to get their blood pumping.

Uwe knew a prominent German drummer, Curt Cress, who owned Pilot Studios in Munich. It had a unique drum room, one level below from the mixing board. You would be looking down at the drummer, positioned in this great sounding room. It seems he had built this studio for his personal drum recordings.

For the hotel, the woman who handled the bookings was a good acquaintance. I gave her a call myself to set things up. For some reason, it seemed I get better results that way. In this case, my long-time personal assistant, Robbie Coleman, had just left me for a girl he had fallen in love with in Sweden. Admittedly, she was better looking than I was, so I could hardly blame him. But, yes, my life was a bit in shambles for a while until I found a new assistant.

When I got her on the horn, she answered with a cheerful Munich hello before breaking the bad news that, unfortunately, the hotel was completely booked for weeks of fashion shows. All the rooms were being used as model and designer showrooms. There would be thousands of designers in the entire hotel, each having several models coming in and out to try on clothes. I could think of worse ways to spend our days! I thought to myself, *Yeah, baby, this is perfect, the guys are just going to love this!*

I started oohing and aahing and exercising my charm to the best of my ability, leaving her little choice but to offer up some kind of solution. We ended the conversation with her saying, "Let me see what I can do." That was a good sign, and before long, she reached back out and asked how many rooms I needed.

I replied, "Seven or eight."

She then said, "OK, I'm going to have to put you on the Laura Ashley floor," which was a floor designed completely with Laura Ashley bed covers and furnishings. They weren't exactly rock 'n' roll, but I loved those rooms. They were beautiful, so this worked out perfectly. I thanked her immensely.

Everyone was happy to hear the news that the hotel was all sorted. Uwe also had success locking in the studio, so we were ready to rock! We proceeded to book cars for everyone from my trusted car rental provider, which was Budget at the time, and we were given really beautiful vehicles—BMWs and Mercedes.

We all arrived in Munich, Germany, safe and sound. We checked into our hotel and then of course headed straight out to our favorite spot, P1. We just had to get our prerecording nightcap in! The next day, the recording would commence.

Max and I went in early to start preparing tracks. Later on, the band came in, and off we were.

We started off with drum tracks. Tommy, Ivan, and Ernie would play along as a guide, with Max at the helm and me listening. Uwe's keyboard work was quite intricate. He would layer multiple sounds to create those great effects heard on the record. He was working throughout, as this could be time consuming. I laid down some rhythm guitars, and we then moved on to the other guys' overdubs.

But then it came to the point where Max and I felt it just wasn't working or grooving. The feeling did not surpass the feel of the demos, yet we continued trying to make it work. It's a tough thing in recording and a problem many come across—though sonically you may be improving things tenfold, the end product just doesn't have the same effect. Colloquially, we call it "demoitis." Everyone in the band was a competent player, so that was not the problem.

I had already made demos in New York for nearly the whole album with me playing drums, bass, and guitar, including songs that Uwe and Tommy had played on. Some had been recorded in Berlin. Max came up to me one night and said, "Jean, it's time to fly in your tapes. It's just not gonna happen." So we did just that, and once we received the tapes, things started moving. Instruments were replaced where needed, Tommy added solos, and we did overdubs, including Uwe's keyboard parts.

We all had a blast while over there. We would order a whole fish for lunch from this little Italian place across the street. Those things were so tasty that I think we all ate it almost every day. At night we would hit P1, Nachtcafé, and some other hot spots, not to mention the hotel, which treated us to a daily fashion show.

During this time, I had a wonderful pet cat I brought to Munich with me named Mozart. This cat went everywhere with me, and I fell in love with the little thing. He was just so cute. He would sit in the closet or under the bed and wait for me to walk by just to jump on my leg, hold on for a while, and take off. He'd even take showers with me!

To be honest, he was more like a dog. I would take him in the Lotus and put him on the passenger side up on the dash. He would just lie there, and that became his favorite spot. I would bring him up to my manager's or accountant's offices on a leash. Now, just imagine a Black guy with a blond Mohawk, shoulder pads twice my size, and a little cat on a leash. That was me! That's where I felt comfortable. I'd also bring him to Central Park in the Lotus after a meeting, and I'd stop at the hot dog stand and get a couple of hot dogs—one for me and one for him. It must have been a crazy sight!

He flew with me from New York to Munich for the recording of the Voodoo X album and stayed with me at the hotel. Unfortunately, one day he decided to start ripping up the beautiful Laura Ashley chairs and sofas with his little nails. A million little strings and threads were hanging off the furniture. I was so embarrassed and didn't want the lady downstairs to think badly of me, so before checking out of the hotel, I bought one of those little fabric shavers, and I sat for hours and hours going over every inch of the couches and the furniture that he had done this to. He stayed with me all the way up until I moved to L.A., when I ended up giving him up to my girlfriend, Ann-Sofie, after we separated.

After recording was completed, it was time to get the visuals together. I knew a great photographer, Mark Weiss, who I had been shooting with since 1982. Mark shot every artist on the planet and was brilliant, so I asked him to shoot us.

We had our outfits together: Tommy was dressed in a snake outfit, Ivan had some exotic, velvet type of an outfit with feathers, and Ernie was wearing somewhat of a fringed, velvety leather outfit. Uwe was in his black-sequined regalia, completely rocked out, including his golden blond hair extensions, which he constantly pulled out by playing with them! He had to summon his hairstylist every couple of weeks to fly in from LA and fix his hair, wherever we were. I had a custom leather suit made that was decked out with sequins, rhinestones, and studs. I was into big shoulder pads in those days, somewhat reminiscent of a glamorous motocross outfit or road warrior jacket, with matching pants that had buckles down the side and a big red mask in sequins on the front of the leg. I still have that outfit.

Mark shot some great photos with über-creative sets, fully identifying the vibe I wanted to portray for the band. It was now time to shoot the video. I had grown up with Voodoo ceremonies at my uncle Max's Voodoo temple in Haiti, so I gave him a call and asked if something could be done for us. I wanted us to go down to Haiti to film.

He said, "OK, well, I'm doing a ceremony on this day, but as you know, Jean-Jean, nobody ever gets to film these ceremonies, but if you're there when it's happening, I will allow you to film it. I won't be able to do a ceremony expressly for you to film."

So it was decided that we would indeed be filming the video in Haiti. At this point, we were ready to audition girls for our lead part. Uwe would hold the auditions in Paris and London, and I went to Los Angeles and New York. We were looking for a special kind of girl to be the Voodoo Queen, and the girl we ultimately chose was from New York. She was a pretty biracial girl and a perfect subject for this minifilm.

The concept was that the girl would walk into a record store (filmed at Tower Records in downtown New York), see the Voodoo X album cover on the shelf, and be lured in by it. Our cover was beautiful, incorporating the Voodoo X symbol on the front in raised gold leaf. A Voodoo X tattoo came with the packaging as well. We would have never gotten away with this elaborate artwork in the US because of the expense for the label.

As our girl looks at the cover in the store, she feels strange and somewhat possessed. She runs out in discomfort but encounters a tall Black man dressed in a black tuxedo suit and top hat with his face painted white. This figure is a popular subject in Voodoo culture, Baron Samedi. She falls back from the shock and finds herself mysteriously amid a Voodoo ceremony in Haiti.

We first filmed some scenes in New York, where we built a soundstage, as you can see in the "Voodoo Queen" video. I hired my dear cousin, Estelle, Uncle Max's daughter, as a stylist, consultant, and choreographer for the scenes where the Voodoo Queen would be crowned. Estelle was also a well-known Voodoo priestess and, alongside Uncle Max, is referenced in *The Serpent and the Rainbow.*

We then prepared to head off to Haiti to film the remaining segments. Getting prepared for any trip is always an ordeal with me—the amount of luggage, preparation, making sure I have everything I need, the dozens of outfits, boots and shoes, makeup. I was worse than most of my girlfriends, and Uwe was not far behind!

I was in constant contact with my uncle and the Haitian government official who spearheaded our arrival, greetings, and arrangements. He was really excited about having us down there. I was already recognized from my solo success, and they were honored that I was coming back to film something of this magnitude.

You would think we were filming a huge-budget film with the amount of people, crew, and equipment that we brought down, so we were very well treated. Also, they understood that this was being done for Uncle Max, Voodoo, and for the country. I can't image that an artist had ever before invested this kind of money into filming something in Haiti in an effort to highlight the beauty of the Voodoo culture and of the Haitian people for global recognition. It would be seen by millions of people around the world.

The crew we had commissioned for this project were state-of-the-art, top-notch people from Germany and the US. Before hiring them, we conducted a worldwide search for a director willing to go to Haiti at that particular time—it was during an upheaval.

We had our eyes on several directors—Mary Lambert, Russell Mulcahy, and some other A-class candidates—but no one was prepared to make the trip during these turbulent times. Some suggested filming elsewhere, but that thought never entered my mind. Consequently, I was introduced to a director named George Seminara. He was hailed in the industry as a daredevil Emmy Award–winning producer who was rumored to be prepared to go anywhere for the challenge. He was a US journalist who had recently returned from a trip abroad, filming in the middle of gunfire during a revolution. He supposedly got great footage and was stoked about being in the middle of the turmoil. That sounded like our guy! I reached out to him, and he was totally into it. He later went on to become the Ramones' video director and has since also done some important films.

It was probably one of the largest crew and gear packages that had ever been brought to Haiti. There were three or four 35mm cameras, other cameras for different angled shots, a documentary photographer, videographer, assistants, hair and makeup and fashion stylists, and all the people we hired in Haiti.

I could see that my uncle was both impressed and proud. He always felt that I had a much stronger place in the religion than what I had opted for, and he hoped that I would someday be the one to move things forward in his place.

Our plan was that Uwe would be picked up first by the stretch limo in Berlin. He was thirty minutes late coming down to the car. When the car got to me, I was another thirty minutes late getting my luggage and hundreds of things together, which then had to be loaded into to the car. We headed to the airport knowing we were late but hoped for the best, as I'd been pretty lucky in the past. Through my solo career, planes had literally been brought back from the runway to pick me and my band up on numerous occasions when we were late.

When we arrived, we were told that we had missed the flight to Haiti. We sat in the airport complaining and crying to the gate attendant—we had to make this flight! It was costing us hundreds of thousands to go down and shoot! We could not miss that first day! Unfortunately, our charm held no water that day. They simply said, "I'm sorry, the plane's too far gone. It's about to take off and we just can't bring it back."

We had to resolve ourselves to the fact that the flight was a goner. The record company was freaking out. That lost day of filming would have resulted in throwing a small fortune into the trash. "OK, we have to figure out how we're going to get down there," I said. There were no other flights leaving at this point. It was getting late, and I was adamant about making it down there on time in any way possible. We started checking out the possibility of renting a plane.

Asking around, we were finally led to a Learjet operator, and we asked him if he'd be willing to fly us down to Haiti. He, too, was aware of the turmoil down there. He quoted us the price; I believe it was upwards of $30,000. When you have the controlling interest in a band, as I did in this project, you also pay that lion's share for any expenses that may come about. With this band, and with me prior to that, expenses came about quite often! So we agreed to the price, set a time, and headed out to his plane. As we're flying, we realized we were starving from this stressful day, so the pilot agreed to land in Florida. We sent our tour manager to go get Kentucky Fried Chicken for the plane. I was crazy about Kentucky Fried Chicken, and actually would fly KFC to Sweden sometimes by the buckets! We got our KFC and headed off to Haiti.

The government officials had been forewarned that we were arriving after the close of the airport, and they had agreed to reopen it for our landing. That was pretty considerate of them and definitely going way above the bar. We were thankful, and it was all very exciting, yet we were nervous. As we headed over Haiti, we could see the mountain tops with some scattered lights, but nowhere could you see the airport. It was a ghostly mysterious feeling, but really adventurous at the same time. As our pilot called down to air traffic control, they gave us the go-ahead to land as the lights appeared.

Upon arrival and landing, the runway had armed soldiers prepared to welcome us, including the government official who had been sent for the welcome. All had been arranged by Uncle Max. They went above and beyond by providing all these amazing services. I felt like the president coming into the country. Everything was smooth and seamless. The government official was cordial. Our film crew was still at the airport awaiting our arrival, so we could all head out to the hotel together.

We hopped into the cars and Jeeps that they had provided and headed to the hotel. We arrived at this old 1950s hotel and casino, and the only other guest was a Nazi. He had escaped from Germany to Argentina, as many had, and then after being kicked out of Argentina, ended up in Haiti. He was supposedly welcomed by the Haitian government and held up in refuge at this hotel.

The Germans in the crew were, of course, shocked. He was boisterous and not shy at all to talk about his times and contributions in the war. We all sat with some rum punches, listening to his stories that went on and on, and I could see the looks on both the American and German crew's faces, flabbergasted at what was actually happening out in the middle of the desolate woods of Haiti.

The ocean was across the street, crashing against the rocks and creating a spooky and very surreal soundtrack for this ominous setting. It was right out of a film.

The next morning, we arrived at my uncle's Voodoo temple, Le Peristyle de Mariani. It was early morning, and there was still dew on the ground. Waves crashed against a sea wall across the street where there were little broken-down signs of what once were fisheries. Restaurants and street merchants lined the streets as we pulled into the driveway.

The guardian opened the big red iron gate by hand and greeted us. We parked in the outer drive, and everyone started to get out to take a look around. Four dogs approached, barking aggressively. They were my uncle's protectors, but they stayed calm as long as he did. We entered and found ourselves surrounded by walls of beautiful Haitian paintings depicting spirits of the religion. The door shutters were painted as well, and there were many small rooms within the temple, each bearing its own significance, with some containing important artifacts from former times. Then imagine a half-circle miniature version of a Roman stadium, with seating reserved for special VIPs from around the world invited to witness certain ceremonies. There were *veves* (Voodoo drawings of various spirits) drawn in the sand around the *potomitan* (middle pole).

VIPs who had been invited here included Bill Clinton, other presidents, high-level political and military figures. At times, major press publications and TV journalists would come from around the world for a one-time glimpse on the Day of the Dead. The *New York Times*, the *Boston Globe*, the BBC, the *Guardian*, and many others all came to see the man who proved that zombies are real!

My uncle then appeared, statuesque as ever, and greeted us with his low, endearing voice. "Welcome!" he said, in a manner reminiscent of being greeted by Ricardo Montalbán on *Fantasy Island*. Our guests were intrigued, frightened, sensualized, and excited, all at the same time. This was all so new to them, something they would've only read in books or seen in a horror film. So odd to them, yet so normal to my eyes.

The Voodoo ceremony was about to begin, and all cameras and equipment were set up and ready to go. The entire experience was extremely thrilling. The ceremony began, and the Voodooists were summoning the spirits. Practitioners were also eating glass, walking on fire (where they felt no pain), drinking blood, and other acts common to this ceremony. As everything was going on, the crew were filming in awe, whispering, "I can't believe we're getting this material."

As planned, our Voodoo Queen landed in the middle of the ceremony, and the filming to this point was successful. She was getting pushed around from Voodooist to Voodooist, when all of a sudden, out of nowhere, Uwe's girlfriend, who had flown in from Los Angeles, came charging into the middle of the ceremony. She was possessed!

We thought she was fooling around at first, but she started flipping out! She was screaming with her hands up in the air. They were trying to hold her still, but when you're possessed, you're strong, sometimes stronger than humanly possible. So it was difficult for anyone to retain her, and she didn't recognize Uwe!

Finally, after a lot of pushing, fighting, and her speaking in tongues, she just passed out! Shortly after that, she woke up again with no idea what had happened to her.

My uncle, of course, as usual, was very calm about it and remarked, "It's no big deal. She was possessed. She's obviously highly spiritual and sensitive, so the spirits found their way to her."

As far as everybody else in the crew or band were concerned, this was one of the most shocking occurrences they had ever witnessed. Once she was removed from the scene, the filming continued for the rest of the day.

At its conclusion, Uncle Max was forever grateful for this effort and the money I spent to show people around the world what he'd been doing and for shining a spotlight on this beautiful Voodoo culture and Haiti.

As was custom, money was spread to the area, generous contributions were made, people were well paid, and everyone was taken care of as a show of my gratitude. Luckily, the captured footage will live on for eternity out in the world for people to see.

We spent about a week in Haiti, as it was a fairly complicated shoot. In addition to filming at my uncle's Voodoo temple home, we also filmed in a cemetery and in the woods. It took some time to get everything completed, but it all worked out in the end.

While in Haiti, we did have some interesting experiences along the way. We were pulled over by police while going to a restaurant one night. It was scary, and everybody was nervous, especially as we knew that people were being kidnapped, shakedowns were happening, and who knows what else. Luckily, as soon as the officer came over to me, he saw the Mohawk. We told him we were filming my next video for Voodoo X at my uncle's temple. Uncle Max had quite a bit of juice. They quickly turned around, wished us a good night, and left.

A more pleasurable experience was at the Belgian embassy. They got word that I was in town, so we received a special invite. They sent a car with an official to come pick us up and bring us to a lavish party they were hosting. Haiti may be perceived as an impoverished country, but it has different sides. You'll find some amazing restaurants and clubs in other regions such as Pétion-Ville, and they sure know how to throw a party! As did these folks at the Belgian embassy. We arrived, and there were European diplomats from around the world and lots of interesting people. It was a blast. I don't believe my band or crew were expecting to find a party like that in Haiti!

It was so different from that old hotel with the fugitive Nazi. We spent the evening drinking, having fun, speaking with all the various diplomats. And there were more than a few pretty girls milling about.

After we finished the video and the Voodoo X album was released, it came time for us to do a European promo tour in support. Uwe and I came up with the idea that we should do the tour on Harley Davidsons. How cool, right? He already had a Harley Sportster in Berlin and had a friend who had a 1200 Softail that I could rent for the trip.

I believe we started our trip around August or September. In Berlin the weather was still beautiful and sunny. We would cruise around the city with sleeveless shirts and leather jackets. It was fantastic! I stayed with Uwe for about a week prior to prep and get all our outfits together.

Since we both traveled with ridiculous amounts of luggage, it would have been impossible to carry everything on our bikes. We arranged for our luggage to be flown to each destination on the tour; it would then be delivered to our hotel ahead of our arrival. That said, we were still loaded down like pack rats, with backpacks, motorcycle bags, and items held on with bungee cords.

As we headed out on the road, the sun was shining, and it seemed like the start of a magnificent day! Uwe and I were giving each other the thumbs-up as we felt that nice breeze upon our faces. All of a sudden, the weather changed drastically. It started hailing, full blast. We didn't even see it coming. It went from warm with sunshine to hail, and it took us by complete surprise.

We immediately pulled into the next service station to reevaluate. Thank God they sold those ugly little orange plastic poncho suits! We bought a couple of those, and I said to Uwe, "OK, we have to head back on the road. We're wasting time."

So we hit it again, with our ponchos on. We were snuggled up and bundled up in every way you could think. We placed pieces of cardboard we found in the dumpsters out back on our chests to block the wind. We were still freezing our asses off! My roots are Caribbean, and cold is not my friend. If cold wind would so much as graze my neck, I'd get sick with a cold! I'd go skiing, but I'm the guy you'd find back at the log cabin drinking Swiss Miss instant cocoa, nestled up with a girl two feet from the fire, whilst my cohorts battle the snow-covered slippery slopes in the stinging, penetrating, cold atop a Scandinavian mountain!

After suffering for several hours on the road, we finally reached our next destination. At this point, it was time for Uwe and me to have a serious conversation. We looked at the weather forecast, which indicated it would be bad for the entire trip. This was definitely not something we had anticipated. However, we were adamant about completing our mission. We said to each other, "No, we must do this. We said we're going to do a motorcycle tour, so let's man up like true rockers and take it! Pain is not an option!"

We got back on the bikes and headed off. But we suffered so badly on that trip that we finally said, "Fuck it!" We made the decision that for the rest of the tour we would rent a truck, fly the luggage, transport the motorcycles to just outside of each town, and then hop on our bikes to drive to the hotel and make our grand entrance! We had interviews set up by the record company at every turn throughout Europe. All the popular rock magazines: *Metal Hammer*, *Kerrang!*, and dozens of others.

As the journey continued, our next destination was France, which was all good! But we were really looking forward to getting to England. I had our table waiting at Stringfellows and by now, we were ripe for fun. We left Calais driving impatiently towards London. Uwe for some reason or another was in front of me at times, and I'd observe as he'd fiddle with something on the engine contantly while driving 70 miles per hour! He was obviously distracted and had me perplexed! As we crossed from France to the UK, it was taking me a moment to adjust to driving on the left. Not paying proper attention, suddenly I saw a roundabout before me! At 70 miles an hour or more, I was bewildered and lost my bearings momentarily, unsure whether to go left or right. Either way, I knew I was fucked! I guess motor memory from my motocross days caused me to slam on the rear brakes, turning to the left and laying the bike down as it slid out from under me towards the center island! The bike headed straight for that island as I rolled further and further from the bike! I still saw it bounce around and slam into whatever was in that island. Pieces were flying off, scattering across the highway alongside my luggage.

As I lay on the road, I looked at myself thinking, *What did I do! What did I break! What about Stringfellows!* I stood up and saw nothing but a rip in my leather pants with a minor scrape. I was fine! But the bike was totaled. That was, for me, a very lucky day.

We called a tow truck to retrieve us, still hoping to make Stringfellows before it closed!

We did! The bike was taken to a local Harley repair shop, and Uwe and I were forced to stay in London for about a week while the bike was repaired. Oh well, we made the best of it!

I always liked to choose alternative ways to travel, as I was never big into touring in buses. I never felt I got enough sleep, and having to deal with the Mohawk, makeup, clothing, and everything else, buses were not the most convenient way to go from show to show. I much preferred staying in hotels.

When on tour doing smaller venues, the crew needs to get to the club the next day, early enough for load in, but the band doesn't need to be there until sound check time, which is usually several hours later. This means that if you travel by bus, the band and crew travel together. The band ends up either getting a day room at the hotel or hanging around the venue all day, which I really didn't like. It made me feel like I was back in junior high school rock band or my early band Topaz!

So when we looked at the budget for our upcoming tour with Saga, I came up with a totally different way of doing this. I found a great deal from a rental car company that would actually save me money, compared to traveling by bus. And it would be a lot more luxurious. I ended up renting three different brand-new cars from my dear rental car lady.

I had a Mercedes 560 SEC. There was also a top-of-the-line BMW and an Audi Quattro. That car was super fast. And in Germany, we could drive 160 miles per hour or more on the Autobahn, without any problem.

For this tour I invited a very special guest, a well-respected UK journalist named Dave Reynolds. He was also a friend, depending on what he wrote last, of course! He liked the band and my work a lot, and at the time he was working for *Kerrang!* magazine.

He wanted to come and take a little sneak peek at how the boys were doing out there. He was also very aware of my Beauvoir disco nights, and a lot of other fun that I'd muster up, so he was very excited to join the tour and spend some time with us.

On one particular venture, our German manager, Michael Stark, had come to watch the show. He also had a very nice car, a luxurious BMW.

After the show, we decided to set out on our next excursion, which of course was "Jean's famous disco night!"

I had arranged something fun in town, and we were anxious to get there quickly. We were all dressed to the nines and ready to rock. We jumped in our cars, revved up the engines, and started heading out of the venue parking lot. For whatever reason, Michael stopped his car suddenly, and would you believe, I hit Michael's car—hard!

These were very powerful cars, and everyone's adrenaline was going from the show and in anticipation of getting to the club. Well, one of the guys slammed into me, then the next car into him. All this happened in the parking lot, no less! The cars were all totaled.

We're all thinking, "Damn! Disco night ruined!"

What to do next? Luckily, I did have insurance on the cars, but I was still extremely nervous as to what the rental car company would say about this. I mean, it's one thing to call and say, "Oh, I had a little accident," and it's one car, but to say that you just totaled three rental cars, I was sure that I was not going to receive pleasant feedback.

Michael took care of his car, and meanwhile, I reluctantly called the rental car company. After I explained the whole ordeal to the woman working at the rental place, she said, "Oh, I'm so sorry to hear about this, Mr. Beauvoir. This is what I can do. I will have the cars picked up, so just leave them as they are. Take any transportation or hire a car to bring you to the next town, and I will have three of the same cars waiting for you."

I couldn't believe what I was hearing. This woman was amazing! I'm not sure if it was the rock 'n' roll, the Mohawk, or what, but she was so sweet and accommodating to me in every way. The next day, we arrived at the designated location, and the cars were waiting for us exactly as she had promised, and I believe she even upgraded one of the vehicles! Disco night was unfortunately missed, but we were successfully on the road the next day.

I was so thankful to her for that, and I ended up renting cars from her in the future. I kept the Mercedes 560 SEC as my European car for probably another year or so. I actually left that car in Paris with my sister, where she lived at the time, to drive for some months while I went back to the States. I loved those Mercedes 560 SEC cars. I ended up buying one when I moved to L.A.

By the end of the Saga tour, we were getting to the point where we were ready to tackle the second album. The time, of course, came to reach out to the record company and start getting the second advances and allocating funds toward video, recording, and the like.

It was then I was told that Columbia did not want to continue. They were terminating the deal! Mind you, Voodoo X had sold a good amount at this point relative to other artists—but not relative to the amount of money that had been spent on that first record.

In my mind, it was clear that we had a two-album firm agreement, and that the second record was always more lucrative than the first. I am always a stickler for defending my rights when it comes to contracts. There was no doubt in my mind that they were liable and could not just stop the deal at a whim. I immediately went to see Gary.

His response was "No big deal, Jean, they don't want to make another record. What can you do? Just accept it and forget about it. You've made millions." Little did he know, I'd been spending it like a fiend!

By now, our relationship had changed. He didn't really like the direction that I took with Voodoo X. He liked me as a solo artist, and he didn't understand why I would change like this when I had a successful solo career.

He was going along but not really feeling it. He may have even been happy that the deal went south, despite missing out on a nice big check coming. Money never seemed to be his motivation.

He didn't think as much about instant gratification as I did. He much preferred the long road, where you just stick to what you're doing, gather momentum, and eventually make your place in history. He actually wasn't wrong in the end.

I called my lawyer, who was also not very responsive. You see, no one liked going up against the big guns, the big labels, because many of them had other projects going with those labels that they didn't want to disrupt. For me, on the other hand, this was my life, and a lot of money. I had made commitments based on a commitment that they had made to me. I wouldn't let that go easily, but I was on my own.

Losing this deal was an attack on my very soul. With Uwe and I anticipating the income for the second album, I had foolishly incurred a few hundred thousand dollars of debt in preparation for that recording.

I came home to L.A. knowing that on top of all this, my girlfriend, who I had set up in L.A. and secured with CAA, one of the biggest agents in Hollywood (and who I had recently gifted a car), was staying with some other guy around the corner. I had found about it long before she told me, but at this point, it was still insulting and just added more fuel to the fire.

I knew I was facing a long battle if I tried to force a foreign country to honor an agreement. Things were looking hopeless. I was at the very edge.

Though I wasn't much of a drinker, I went to a liquor store on Sunset and bought a bottle of vodka, a big one! I drank almost the whole thing and found myself on my knees in front of my apartment building, looking up to the spirits in sheer disappointment of what they had allowed to happen.

No money, no girlfriend, no deal, and no support—even from my manager, whose reaction had so disappointed me. I really thought I was done, and it was over this time. I remember that Uwe, usually as dramatic as I was, somehow still kept a positive outlook.

I drove my car to the parking lot behind Petit Four, where there was a ledge and I could look down and see parts of the city below me. I was so out of it from drinking that vodka that I was nearly hallucinating. I said to myself, "All you have to do is push down the pedal to the ground. You'll go right over that ledge, and it'll all be over." I was so close to doing it. But then I found myself waking up behind the wheel in the wee hours of the morning with a massive headache and some of my sanity back.

After I spent some time hibernating and feeling sorry for myself, my brother came over to cheer me up. I just wasn't having it. He had grabbed the mail as we were entering my apartment, and he said to me, "Jean-Jean, did you see this envelope?"

I was uninterested and kind of said, "Yeah, yeah, what is it?"

He opened it and stared at me as if he couldn't believe his eyes.

"Jean-Jean, it's a big check!"

And that it was! A check from EMI publishing had come out of nowhere. I ran around the apartment like a child, so thankful. This check was enough of a sign for me to regain my strength and press forward with the battle.

I then decided, with full confidence and belief in myself, that I would find an attorney, on contingency no less, to support me in my fight against the wrongdoings of that company. I proceeded in finding the right attorney and explained the situation to him. He didn't see much of a problem, and he agreed with my point of view. I brought him in, and we went to battle.

We sent a letter to the label saying that I would be suing them for the entire value of the deal, plus any loss of work, time, or opportunities during the entire period where I should have actually been in the studio making another album for them. This is where the rubber meets the road in a situation like this. I was definitely in the right by law, so you would think it would be a slam dunk. But nothing is ever a slam dunk with the law, especially when you're dealing with Europe as an American.

The label has to think that if this goes all the way to court, and the judge just so happens to feel that they were indeed in an agreement, which they breached, and that everything I stated was possibly lost, they could have been be liable for millions and millions of dollars. Should they take that risk? That's my question to them. Most of the time, the answer is no, so the offers started coming in.

They were lowball to start, and then finally, they offered a respectable amount. It took almost two years to come to the settlement, but we did. I was paid a very handsome amount not to make an album. My attorneys told me that I was one of the only artists to ever accomplish this. It was a good deal for the label, as they did end up paying less than they would have making that next Voodoo X album.

This is something I truly wish to share with young artists or people coming into the business—or any business, for that matter: self-respect and self-belief. You never know how important you are and to whom, so stand tall. Fight for your rights, and don't let people walk over you, disregarding contracts and commitments. If everyone allows this, it will only encourage the industry to do more of it. Cases like mine set precedents and make the big boys think twice about this kind of injustice. There is always a way to fight back—ways that may elude you—but you have to use your most valuable God-given asset, your brain.

The interesting part about this whole thing was that in the end, the German president was very angry that he was forced to settle with me. It was fairly common for companies in Germany to take advantage of artists in deals regardless of contracts, or to make unethical agreements like publishing for life for using a studio, and other such nonsense, which would never fly anywhere else. The NSYNC situation was a good example, where evidently, their German deal was disgarded by a US court, which allowed them to make a massive US deal, leading to their US success. The German president probably never wanted to see me again (and thought he wouldn't have to), but it just so happened that not long after the settlement, I was on tour with Bruce Springsteen and the E-Street Band across Europe.

The Bruce tour was the quintessence of luxury. We had entire hotel floors to ourselves, police escorts, a beautiful plane, and they even found KFC to bring on the plane in Europe! They had everything else you could imagine on this tour.

One evening, a dinner had been set up for Bruce, the band, and his entourage. And would you believe it? The person who sat right across from me the entire night was the same label head I sued for breaching the agreement at Columbia! This must have been a troubling evening for him, having to treat me with full respect.

I looked at him across the table with full confidence and a smile, feeling satisfied that something had been made right, and I was wondering, *How is he feeling right now?* I feel bad if I have to take someone to the cleaners, but at the end of the day, he initiated it and got what he deserved. I told him, jokingly, that he got off easy! He could have had to pay the whole thing!

15

CROWN OF THORNS

SOME TIME HAD PASSED since the entire Voodoo X / Columbia debacle, and I was just starting to think about what my next move would be. I wasn't really actively looking, but I was about to begin. One day, I received a surprise phone call from Jimmy Iovine. We'd worked together and seen each other quite a bit while I was with Little Steven. Jimmy is a fantastic producer himself, having produced Bruce Springsteen, Fleetwood Mac, Patty Smith, Tom Petty and the Heartbreakers, U2, and many others.

I said "Hey, Jimmy, what's happening?"

"Well, I hear you're looking for a label and that you don't have a deal right now," he said.

I said, "No, I actually don't. I just went through this whole thing with Columbia, and I'm a free agent."

"Well, listen, I loved your solo album, so let's make a record," he said.

I was like, "OK, that sounds good!"

He said, "Yeah, let's get together and talk about it. I'm at Interscope now and have a good situation, money, good marketing, good people. Things are moving. This could be a good place for your next solo record."

I started making a couple of calls to my friends, since I was really excited about the whole thing. Although making my next solo album was the obvious next move, I was still in the mind-set of wanting to do another band project.

Through the years, I had kept in touch with Micki Free and Tony Thompson. Micki was a very good rock 'n' roll guitarist of Black and Indian heritage from the Midwest. He got his first big break playing with Shalamar. He's the guy who could be seen swinging from a rope, playing a guitar solo in the "Dancing in the Sheets" video. Both the song and Micki won a Grammy for its inclusion in the film *Beverly Hills Cop*. But though he was in this band, his roots were truly in rock 'n' roll.

Tony Thompson was most definitely one of the most successful Black drummers in the industry. He not only played with Nile Rodgers in the grooviest band of all time, Chic, but he also played on fantastic records like David Bowie's *Let's Dance* album and with Robert Palmer and some other A-list artists. Tony was anxiously awaiting the opportunity to play rock 'n' roll, and he was actually called to be John Bonham's replacement for some Led Zeppelin reunion shows at one point.

When I was traveling around touring and promoting my solo record, they were touring with all the bands or artists they were associated with. I'd run into them in clubs all over Europe. We'd always have brief talks about doing something together, something like, "Hey man, we should do that."

"Yeah, baby! Come on, bro, we gotta make this happen."

"Man, yo, we gotta do this. It's gonna be great!"

Then we wouldn't see each other for another year or more.

So I thought to myself that maybe this Interscope situation could be a good place for that project. I told Jimmy, "You know, I'm thinking rather than making a solo record, I want to do this band project. I feel that there just haven't been any killer Black rock bands out there, and I know a couple of guys who are the real deal. I'd like to put together something special."

He said, "Well, OK, I'm open to that, whatever you want to do."

I began making some phone calls and started with Micki and Tony. They were both ecstatic, of course, because this was me serving them my deal on a silver platter. Another call I made was to Paul Stanley. As soon as Paul found out, it appears he called Gene Simmons to let him know, although Micki had already called him because they were close friends. Gene had helped Micki in the past—he'd put him together with Diana

Ross—so he was a supporter of Micki's, trying to get him into something, and Paul was my friend.

Paul called me back and said, "Listen, Jean, I just spoke to Gene, and we'd like to somehow be involved in this. Let's have a meeting."

"Oh, OK," I answered, not entirely sure if I wanted to go in that direction, mainly because I had my eyes on Doc McGhee. I respected Paul and Gene, but I was concerned that with their own careers to focus on, they wouldn't have the time, which might put strain on our friendship. Plus I had always wanted Doc to manage me, as that's what he did, exclusively.

Micki and Tony were ranting and raving, "Oh, yeah, baby! Well, you know we can't say no to this. We have to do this. This is the right way. Come on, Voodoo!"

Tony would always say, "Yeah, brother, ain't nothin' but a meatball." Up to this day, I still don't know what that means!

I went with it. From there, they formed a company called Amazing Management, and we started having meetings about how to move forward with the Interscope deal. Gene and Paul felt it was best to turn the situation into a bidding war to try to get more money out of the deal. Again, this was a little awkward for me because I respected Jimmy very much. I'd known him for years, and to be honest, I didn't really like the idea of having a bidding war against Jimmy.

I found myself, once again, between a rock and a hard place. But I once again went with it. Micki and Tony were really good at talking you into things. They were preachin' hard! "C'mon, man, this is great. Oh man, man. Let's do it," they said. So, I went in that direction.

Based on Paul and Gene's suggestion to stir up a bidding war, we'd have to present something great to entice the labels. They suggested we record a few songs as demos, but in the highest quality. I started writing songs for the album. The eventual Crown of Thorns CD included a ballad I wrote alone called "Standing on the Corner for Ya." Micki would come over to write as well. Paul was also involved in some writing and producing.

I had an apartment on Burton Way in Beverly Hills, a cool pad with a good vibe for writing. I set up a studio in the spare bedroom. Because of where the apartment was situated, I could jam all night and make as much noise as I wanted to with no complaints! We recorded in various studios around L.A., and Paul and Gene suggested we hire Mick Guzowski to mix the demos. A great idea! They were, in reality, masters. He was, and still is, one of the best mixers in the world. He has mixed so many albums and hit singles it's mind blowing.

When mixing rock songs, he had a knack for taking out irritating frequencies, which made them much more palatable for radio, but he still kept that low-end punch and power. We had a method for the whole mixing process. Mick would come into the studio in the morning and get the song set up with a basic mix. I'd come in the afternoon and we'd start working together on all the tweaks, guitar and bass sounds, drums, vocal balances and so on. We'd have the mix done by the end of the day and take it home to listen. First thing in the morning, we'd communicate to see where we were at. If all was good, we'd print, otherwise we'd spend more time perfecting the mix until we were satisfied. We worked hand in glove, and it was a really enlightening experience working with, yet again, one of the greats!

When the six-song demo was ready, it sounded great! At this point, Paul and Gene started going to labels, and they introduced us to a very well-known entertainment attorney, Paul Schindler, who proceeded on the legal front.

It didn't take long before a bidding war was in motion. I don't know if Jimmy even paid this much mind. I think he had his mind set on making the deal with me, so he came in with the best offer. It was a seven-figure deal right from the start with options for eight albums, with various increases. With the min-max provisions in the agreement and with some level of success, the deal was astronomical. The royalty points given out were among the highest in the industry, on par with superstar deals only granted to a handful.

A sudden surprise came about while all this was going on. Prince reached out to me and wanted to meet. He asked that I bring Tony Thompson along as well. We set a spot to meet.

We said big hellos to each other, asked one another how we were all doing. Not long into our talk, he reiterated he had wanted to sign me in the past, and that he now heard about my new project, Crown of Thorns. He was a fan of Tony's drumming as well and was happy he was involved.

He asked why I was doing this rather than another solo record. I told him that, for some reason, I wanted to be in a band environment this go-around, that I'd had this idea for an undeniable all-Black rock band that I felt was missing in the world.

He then said that he was prepared to sign the new project and, furthermore, was prepared to substantially beat any offer that had been put on the table up till then. He had one stipulation. Micki Free, my guitarist, would need to be replaced.

He suggested getting a young, hot Black guitarist like someone he had seen. Of course, I asked him why, saying that Micki was a wonderful guitarist. We'd been working closely on this record with great results. He said that he thought Micki resembled him too much and felt different would be better.

Micki and I had been working very closely on this record, and I was already committed to Jimmy Iovine, Paul, and Gene, so this wasn't something I could really consider. I thanked Prince immensely for his offer and for pursuing me again but respectfully declined.

When Prince passed away, I was extremely affected by it. I was saddened as if I could've somehow done something to extend his life. I always respected him very much—all his talents and accomplishments. But of course, like most artists, I did see him as a competitor.

At times, when he would make me offers like this, I'd be quick to think that he was just trying to buy me out of the market. It felt as if, were he to sign me, he would somehow be able to control my level of success or even decide if my album would ultimately get released. As an artist you can become very paranoid and cautious about all situations because you never know what people's motives are.

It's almost as if a spirit came to me speaking nonchalantly and I began to see things clearly. From my time spent with Prince, it was evident to me that he really wanted to be known as a great rock guitarist. He would always compliment me on my guitar playing, as I would him for his. He'd also tell me that his guitarists were fans. He was a wonderful guitar player, and I believe that toward the end of his career, his desire became more evident as he traveled around Europe doing shows that were very guitar oriented. In reality, many people complained, as they just wanted to hear the hits!

He was so good at so many things, but it's really strange with artists—more times than not, they always want what they don't have. Musicians and actors are some of the most fickle people I've ever known, so Prince's case was not uncommon.

I've had many friends who were and are successful actors. I met them because I was the bass player in the Plasmatics, and what they really wanted to do was play bass. I wanted to talk about acting, and all they ever wanted to talk about was music and playing bass in a band and how maybe I could help them or urging me to jam! Famous singers that I've known want to be songwriters. Songwriters want to be singers. Drummers want to be up front. The guitar player who can kind of sing wants to be the lead singer, so he grits his teeth at the lead singer every night until they finally break up! It goes on and on. I guess this probably extends to many other professions as well.

So I started thinking, "What if Prince was interested in my Crown of Thorns project because . . . ?" He had heard something from someone we had in common, so he already knew it was a really good rock record. What if he wanted the guitarist gone so that in the interim he could have an opportunity to play guitar with a real rock outfit, even if it was only on the record here and there? This would've given him the opportunity to do something he really wanted to do without diluting his brand and what he was known for. Plus, he would have signed me, so that would've been out of the way.

This was only a theory of mine, but it came into my mind so powerfully that it made me start feeling regrets for rejecting his offers and efforts to reach out to me on those occasions. I was always very flattered, and it also made me feel pretty good that he would have that respect for me—he didn't seem to respect many.

In retrospect, maybe there was some real magic that could've come out of our collaboration. Unfortunately, I'll never know, and neither will the world, so it's something I'll always wonder about. I wish him peace and happiness wherever he is up there, and I hope he's jamming hard with the many other greats artists we've lost throughout the years.

Whenever you're engaged in expensive deals such as the ones I've been involved with, problems are unavoidable. Everyone wants their hands in the pie, and they come out of the woodwork! For example, when all this started at Interscope, there was a successful rock producer working at the company. He had some big hits under his belt and produced a couple of big rock bands in the '80s.

He wanted to be involved in producing this record, but it had already been decided that I was producing the album, and Jimmy was fine with that. He still tried to convince me to let him get involved. One day, he had the nerve to call me up and say, "Listen, if I don't get to produce on that album, I'll make sure that not even a snare drum gets approved!"

Now, that was an abuse of his position at Interscope, and I was furious! I called up Jimmy Iovine immediately, who was always there for me—as was Ted Field—to speak, to answer questions, and to meet whenever needed. Ted was an esteemed businessman and entrepreneur who came from the Marshall Field family and had gotten heavily into entertainment. He was financing and producing major blockbuster films, including *Revenge of the Nerds* and *Three Men and a Baby*. He had also financed Interscope, and he was working closely with Jimmy. I found it pretty amazing how much time they'd find for me with all they had going on.

Jimmy called me back a few days later and said, "The producer is gone. You don't have to worry about him anymore!"

Somehow, we ended up doing some work with him anyway, but there were problems that I can't remember specifically. I do remember Gene walking into the studio one day while he was working. He just said, "Abort, abort! Turn off all machines and stop all work!" to everyone in the room.

Gene liked taking on that role. I'd seen him do this kind of thing several times before. One time, after the name Crown of Thorns was final, we found out about another band with the same name.

Gene called up the band with a couple of us in the room and said, "Hi, this is Gene Simmons."

"Oh wow! Yeah, Gene!" They were all excited!

He then continued, "Do you have a band called Crown of Thorns?"

"Yes!"

Gene said calmly, "Not anymore!"

Just like that. He was pretty funny, but very serious when he did business. He said, "You must change the name immediately to avoid being sued, as you are infringing on the Crown of Thorns that I'm managing." Soon after the call, the band changed their name.

Ted and Jimmy were very involved in the day-to-day business, a lot more than you would think. They were always present at meetings and available to discuss any issues I might have. They really put their time into it, and I actually don't remember spending time with any other A&R at Interscope, except for the short-lived producer situation.

We'd also go out together. Ted enjoyed going to clubs, and it seemed he enjoyed hanging out with us. I had another very good friend, Scott Rabin, who was also a friend of Ted's. Scott is from a well-known family. Artie and Jason Rabin have a very successful apparel business, which houses many of the famous brands you see and wear every day. They've been partners with Jay Z, Beyoncé, and other celebrities. They also co-owned the New Jersey Nets, now the Brooklyn Nets, and were heavily involved in the Barclay Center and many other high-level ventures. Scott also had his own clothing business out in L.A. at the time, and he and Ted were good friends. We'd all meet up every so often.

Jimmy wasn't the going-out type. I'd see Ted out a lot, but not Jimmy. He would stay in the office and keep busy doing whatever he was doing, and he was rarely, if ever, clubbing around L.A. I'd see him perhaps at a nice restaurant like Koi, or we'd have dinner together, but that was about it.

Throughout all the Crown of Thorns recordings, Ted and Jimmy were usually together listening to the songs. They would take me out in Ted's Bentley, and I'd play them new material I'd just recorded, or something I had an idea about. They just loved the song "Standing on the Corner for Ya."

Jimmy actually said to me once, "Jean, that's the song, and as far as the rest of the album goes, it doesn't matter. That's the hit."

Ironically, that's the one song I wrote alone!

We were also working toward perfecting our look. I got into the absolute best shape of my life. I was doing martial arts daily. Micki and I both really enjoyed cool clothing, which we already had a fair amount of, but we had some great new pieces made for the band. We shot with some great photographers, Randee St. Nicholas and Neil Zlozower, who did a wonderful job getting the images across.

The ongoing recordings were a lot of work, but we did have fun. When we were cutting demos and working at A&M Studios, we all had, somehow, gathered some of the same things. For example, I had a decked-out Bronco, Gene a Range Rover, Paul a Pathfinder, and Micki an Isuzu Trooper. They were all blacked out with custom wheels and grills, four trucks that looked similarly awesome. It looked pretty neat when we'd pull into a recording studio!

Now riding in those big trucks, we all had little dogs. I had a little Yorkie named Noel. Micki and Gene both had Pomeranians. And Paul also had a small dog, though I don't remember what breed it was. When we'd bring the dogs to the studio, they'd sure enough see us coming! The four of us were quite the team. We'd put wee-wee pads in the studio, and a couple of the dogs were trained to go on them. It was hysterical!

I got to meet a lot of really interesting people during my time in L.A. The nightclubs were filled with people, many doing drugs. There was quite an array of places to choose from, dance, private, rock, and, of course, the famous Sunset Strip, with favorites like the Rainbow and the Whisky a Go Go. We were accustomed to high-end clubs, as we had all spent so many years sampling the best around the world.

We liked those high-class places that playmates, models, and actresses would frequent. Places where men always needed something they didn't have to get in. If we wanted to go see a band, we'd hit the Strip or one of the other popular rock clubs. The China Club was still rockin' as well. One of the nights, Elton John was there. He came up to me and gave me a surprising and mindblowing compliment! I don't remember the exact words, but it was something like, "You've got more talent than everyone or anyone in this room" and nothing more.

I just looked at him, deeply flattered that he'd say something like that to me. It was very special, as I so admired his and Bernie Taupin's work—absolute genius. It amazed me how they could keep such a good working partnership and friendship for so many years. That's an accomplishment that people should really look up to in the music business.

Bruce Springsteen also made a comment to a well-known artist that was recording with me once: "You're working with Jean Beauvoir? You should be honored." That was just as thrilling to hear. Another was Stevie Nicks, who approached me and told me that she had just returned from Australia, where "Feel the Heat" was a big hit, and told me that she and her girlfriend were dancing the night away to my song and how much she loved it! It happened a lot, and it's really inspiring for an artist to hear these comments from such legends. Especially when you didn't know some of them had any idea who you were! It helps you to stay the course.

You'd also hear from record company presidents, "Don't you ever worry about anything or money. You'll have so much that you won't know what to do with it." You'd hear other similar praise on a daily basis for years. It's enough to make any artist start to drink the Kool-Aid and let it go to their head. You can start to believe that you're invincible, which we definitely are not!

Thinking back, a "funny" thing happened around 1989 when I moved back to L.A., after losing the Voodoo X deal. One night, I headed out to the Rainbow, and at the door was somebody I hadn't seen before.

"Uh-oh," I thought. I had known the owner, Mario Maglieri, for years, as he owned all three spots—the Rainbow, the Roxy, and the Whisky a Go Go. But he wasn't around that night, and the doorman actually enforced their "no Mohawk" policy and sent me on my way. At the time, I was already depressed about being in a lawsuit with Columbia and breaking up with my girlfriend. The last thing I needed was this to mess with my self-confidence and mojo.

The worst of it was that my picture was hanging in the center of the back wall of the place! It was a big photo of me, shot by Mark Weiss, holding a sparkle guitar to my face, hanging prominently in a restaurant that I couldn't get into! I scurried back to my apartment, which was right down the road across from the Sunset Marquis Hotel in West Hollywood.

That aside, I think the times I spent in L.A. were some of the best times of my life. A lot of the metal bands—Guns N' Roses, Mötley Crüe, Poison—were all there hanging out. Not everyone knows this, but when the Plasmatics played in L.A. and the surrounding areas, it set certain precedents in motion at the clubs. These paradigms are what allowed the L.A. hair metal scene to blossom and flourish.

I'd run into friends at parties all the time. I had actor friends including Steven Bauer, Esai Morales, Laurence Fishburne, Scott Baio and Pamela Anderson (who were an item at the time), and Leif Garrett. Musician friends like Herbie Hancock, Ray Parker Jr., Richie Sambora, Rick James, and many others. It was a wonderful artistic community.

Wayne Gretzky was also a friend, as his wife was a great friend of my girlfriend, Playboy centerfold Cynthia Brimhall, so we'd all hang. I had tons of both celebrity and "normal" friends from so many different walks of life. It was a nice balance. It was very vibrant, and things were really happening in L.A.

All in all, I guess I'm happy to say that I was there.

My houses in L.A. were always a gathering place for fun. I was known for throwing some of the most entertaining parties at certain times of the year, like New Year's Eve. My friends from Europe would come to visit on a regular basis, and my dear friend Camilla Olsen, whom I'd known from Sweden, was quite the socialite. She knew many high-profile celebrities from around the world. Frequent guests were Mario Cugnata, who ran Elite Models in Milan, and his wife Rebecca, as well as my friend Sabino—a big-built tough guy, yet lovable like a big bear. Sabino would pass on years later, hospitalized after a fight and given too much pain medication. I really loved that guy—still miss him and the times we shared.

But back then in L.A., everything was good, and the revolving door of incredible guests turned onward. The famed Italian photographer Fabio Nosotti and the actor Billy Zane would stop over, as well as Grace Jones, who popped by to visit one day and cooked us a fantastic chicken dish! She was a trip and may have had a thing for one of my best friends, Marcus Schenkenberg, who'd stay with me from time to time, sometimes for weeks. He rented my New York apartment at the beginning of his very successful career, before he went on to become the most successful male model in the world.

I was married to the supermodel Tove Johansen at the time, and we had a place on Fifth Avenue. Marcus's girlfriend and my wife were best friends, so we spent a lot of fun and wild times together! Those women were out of control, a whole different level of crazy and drama, but they had us hooked for a while there! My wife, Tove, I had actually met several years before we married, and with no real interest in anything other than friendship on my end in the beginning. It's funny how your perception of someone can change so with time. I was eventually enticed as she was stimulating, intelligent, and worldly. She had powerful friends like Donald Trump and Fidel Castro. When she and I would go to restaurants in NY's Little Italy, we'd have two armed and suited bodyguards accompanying us, as we drew a lot of attention, good and bad! It was a passionate relationship that perhaps had just too much fire to stand the test of time. Marcus had met Maureen through Tove, also a Black African Supermodel. Marcus and Tove were both Swedish, so they already knew each other. I had met Donald Trump on a couple of occasions at parties in NY. The scene was actually pretty small in NY and the same people would frequent those VIP parties. During my divorce with Tove, I ran into them at a club one night. He was cordial and he asked me something like why was I leaving her or said that I shouldn't. I guess she may have shared with him something poignant that she had told me once. "You are my husband forever and you can never leave me." It made me stop and think that perhaps I was a victim of my former teenage issues and fears, since as far as I knew, she had always been loyal to me while we were together. I can't remember all the details, but besides good times, I do remember her once throwing a French gold record of mine out the window onto Fifth Avenue! I guess I may have upset her that day.

I encountered Trump again some years later. Some changes were happening in the Trump Building, where I was residing, and there was a discrepancy that I felt was unjust. Being someone who speaks his mind, I asked that my concerns be communicated to him. I got a call from his office with an apology and was offered a surprisingly good incentive, including an upgrade to the largest apartment in the building.

After Marcus and I parted from our significant others, I guess we got each other in the divorce and have stayed best friends ever since.

People have written that Marcus and I were romantic partners, but that was never true, just Hollywood gossip. When I'm with my very few, very close guy friends, the way we act at times might make people think that. We've always been touchy, hugging, joking around, and genuinely enjoying each other's company. Most of my guy friends have a bit of a feminine side.

We're also very jaded when it comes to women. We've seen a lot and been pretty fortunate in that department, so more often than not, a pretty girl, or a group of them, standing around us at a table barely makes us flinch. Sometimes that makes others think we're gay.

At this stage of the game, it came time for another one of those famous car rides to discuss Crown of Thorns. I was picked up by Ted and Jimmy. They started out by saying, "Jean, we have a problem. We're signing bands for $50,000 who are playing out of tune and having hit records, so we believe that the time of extravagant videos and all this big money being spent for arena video shoots and the rest is on its way out."

They were referring to the type of videos where new bands were playing to eighteen thousand people with girls crying and fans going wild. I wasn't blind. I saw time passing, and I watched what was appearing on MTV. I knew the day was coming fast, but not this fast!

They didn't think that the record would have the success that they originally envisioned, thanks to the changing climate of the industry. Things were moving toward grunge. Not only that, Jimmy told me, "Jean, this is really your fault. I came to you, and I offered you a solo deal, very simple. We could have gone into it, and it would have been flexible. We would have been able to move forward and be in business for a long time. But you chose to turn it into Crown of Thorns, form a band, and do this and that. It overcomplicated everything and made things take this long."

That was most definitely an eye-opener for me, and I wasn't sure how to feel. "Could've, would've, should've," but it was too late at this point. I could clearly see this high-speed train about to derail. It was evident from that backseat that this dream was about to be shattered, and I'd be left without the good fortune of this incredible deal. I lost the most because, at the beginning, I was the only one who had it to lose. For everyone else, it was gravy. Their lives would just go on.

It was a sad day, indeed. I had felt strongly about this record and concept, and we had put together a great album. It was sincerely unfortunate that it would never see the light of day. No doubt, I was bitter.

Everyone was advised of the situation, and I was just really angry and fuming. Two years of hard work had been put into this record, and the fact that it was all going to waste drove me mad. I think that prompted me to start going out more, getting into more trouble, and being destructive. I had lost upward of $30 million, or much more if you factor in all that we would've taken in making records with Interscope, which I believe would have happened if it was released. Now, what to do?

So I headed to Italy for a while to go hang out with some of my friends. They always made me feel a lot better. I had a wonderful Italian girlfriend who really helped me out during this time. She was an incredible girl, one of the most famous Italian models and known around the world. I know, here we go!! Her name was Greta Cavazzoni. She had come to stay with me in L.A., and we moved from Malibu to the Hollywood Hills together.

Greta and I had a great relationship. She was down to earth, smart, very resourceful, funny and beautiful! She was asked to move to Paris since her career was really taking off. She had graced many great covers of top fashion magazines and a lot of things were happening, and she wanted me to go with.

I just wasn't prepared to do that, as I was still not over losing the Crown of Thorns deal. I really didn't feel moving to Paris was the best move for me at the time. I was also worried about what trouble in paradise might lie ahead with her being a model, being in Paris, and all the bullshit that can go with that. Those teenage demons once again! I remember our conversation vividly. I explained my reasons to her and asked her candidly, stuttering and at a loss for words, "So what are your thoughts baby?"

She replied calmly in her endearing thick Italian accent, "You wanna know my thoughts? *Fuck you!* Those are my thoughts."

It was truly a sad day, and in retrospect, I should have had more faith in her. She never went down the wrong road. She had a very successful career as a supermodel and then started her own business, got married, and has been raising two beautiful children. Pretty much on the straight and narrow for the years to come. That's what happens when you think you know what the future holds.

When I lived in Malibu. I had a very cool one-story sprawling ranch-style home, with floor-to-ceiling glass windows throughout the house. My studio was in the guest house. I loved it! It was charming and quiet out there. There was action if you wanted it. Otherwise, you felt comfortably removed. But it was a bit of a drag driving into Hollywood to go out and the return home was real long some nights.

On one trek home from a club, I was driving my Lotus down the winding Sunset Boulevard at high speed. Why else have a sports car, right? One turn was just too sudden, and I found myself in a spiral ending by crashing into a curb at a Beverly Hills street corner! Thankfully, there was very little damage to my coveted Lotus! I'm sure I had slightly more alcohol in my system than would be acceptable. As I was recuperating from the shock and thanking my spirits for being alive, I saw flashing lights in the distance! "Uh-oh," I said to myself! My ass is cooked! The car approached and it turned out to be a Beverly Hills security car. He got out, checked to see that I was OK and was friendly as could be. He called a tow truck for me and waited until I was on my way back to Malibu. That's what I call good fortune! I couldn't thank him enough!

Remember my childhood fear of birds? On a daily basis, I would sit in my dining room in that house, which had nothing but glass windows, and birds would be flying toward me at insane speeds! They would crash into the windows and die. I mean, dozens of birds, of all types, as if they were trying to get into the house! To me! I was woken up several times with huge black birds pecking at my bedroom window. It felt deeply unnerving.

Birds have always followed me around pretty much wherever I lived, but in this particular instance I was feeling there might be some sort of spiritual significance. I rang up Uncle Max to get his thoughts. He laughed in that loud, jolly voice of his and very matter-of-factly said, "Birds are your protectors, Jean-Jean. They are watching over you as spirits. I know you don't like them or you're afraid of them, but don't fear them. They feel the need to be close to you, and you will always experience this wherever you go."

I felt really sorry for the birds that hit the windows, and I'd have to go pick them up outside of the house every day. The house was adjacent to a national reserve, so I frequently saw foxes, mountain lions, and even a family of the cutest little raccoons who loved to stop by and say hi.

There were four of them and they'd first walk up and start scratching on the windows at the back of the house to alert me of their presence. Then they'd cordially pitter-patter to the front door. One or two of them would stand up on their hind legs at the door, urging me to open.

I pretty much gave them anything I had lying around. They were so well mannered that I couldn't help but give in to their asks. One day, some cooked chicken, another time fruit, banana, bread, but believe it or not, their favorite delicacy was ice cream. I took pictures of one holding the spoon with his paw and with little assistance from me, eating the ice cream from it. They'd each get their turn and would then just hang around for a bit. It's as if one would finally say to the others, "OK, time to rock!" And they'd turn around and head back into the woods. That was a highlight living out there, surrounded by nature, animals, the woods, and most of all, the ocean. My time there was very pleasant.

My next move would be to a home in the Hollywood Hills, Caverna Drive, with a beautiful view overlooking Universal and all the city lights below. It was a four-story home; you entered on the top floor, and the home would go down three more stories, hugging the cliff. As soon as you'd walk in, you'd see a beautiful white grand piano, where I wrote a lot of my songs. It was a present from my ex-wife Tove.

My studio was on the bottom floor, and you could access that through a sliding glass door in the backyard. As a matter of fact, someone was constantly trying to access that backdoor to rob me. I got tired of seeing that the lock had been tampered with and knew it wouldn't be long till this guy got in.

Though I did have an alarm system, I decided to leave the would-be burglar a note. It simply read, "If you come here to try and rob me again, I'll be waiting, and I'll shoot you." That lock was never tampered with again.

There were birds visiting me at that home too. I remember once lying in bed and my brother called me. He was living in L.A. at the time and had married my publisher, Seline Armbeck. They had two beautiful daughters, Briana and Danielle. As I picked up the phone, a huge bird swooped right past my window, so close it was as if I could even feel the air from its wings. I just made a loud sound out of nowhere and my brother immediately said, "What was it? An eagle?"

Now, mind you, I made a sound, but had not mentioned anything about a bird, yet he was spot on. The eagle landed on a tree twenty or thirty feet away. I was shocked that he would say that out of nowhere. I replied, "Yes, it is!" That eagle lived there for months to come, and every time I'd get into my car to head down the hills, I'd see him every couple of miles along the way until I'd reach town, as if he was following me. I just accepted it.

I had a lot of fun in that house. The parties I'd have there would boast everyone from my Italian friends who'd fly in to band mates to new friends in L.A. The Milli Vanilli guys would also visit at times, as well as a girl named Lisa Fiorucci and her friend Sylvia, who were very close to them. I remember one night when Rob, one of the members, got a little bit too out of control. I guess he was sitting on the countertop in one of my bathrooms, and all of a sudden, I heard a loud noise, a big clunk. The whole sink and countertop had fallen down. I went running in there and said, "What did you do?" He was too out of it to even realize what had happened.

As much as I liked that house, I had one very bad experience there: the big Northridge earthquake of 1994! I remember it as if it were yesterday. I had some friends over, I believe Camilla was there and another girlfriend of mine from Germany, Loren Woka, a stunning Danish-German model I had desperately pursued at one time. But for some reason, I did not feel the same after we started dating. She had been coming to the US to get me to see things differently. My passions never did rekindle, and I don't know why! She was perfect in every way and was just so loyal! Her feelings for me remained for so many years, regardless of my situation, something that always really impressed me. I never really understood my reserve. I remember my friend asking me how things were going with her. I'd tell him that I didn't think it was going to work out. He'd say, "No, you can't break that off! No matter what! She's just too fine!" He was funny! Well one night, we were down in my studio listening to some of my recordings and for some reason I felt a deep bass, which I was particularly sensitive to. I was thinking "Hmm, a lot of bottom on that song. I think I'll have to roll off some 60K and below." Before my thought was completed, the whole house started shaking and the lights flickering. I immediately ushered everybody up the stairs, walking behind them as we were all getting shoved from one side of the staircase to the other. The girls were screaming and crying, and I was just trying to find light in the dark. You would not believe how dark it actually gets when all the lights go off.

I scurried about the kitchen, feeling my way around in search of a flashlight, a lighter, candles, anything. I found the light and the first main quake had subsided. It's as if you hear a hiss, accompanied by people screaming from other homes and the street, and a wide array of car alarms sounding simultaneously. A couple of people ran over to the house, confused and scared, so I let them in. They didn't know what to do. They just happened to be taking a walk.

Then we were hit with an aftershock. That's what they call them, when in reality it's just another earthquake! And you have no idea how many of these aftershock earthquakes you will have! Anything can happen. There couldn't be an uneasier feeling than that of knowing that the ground you're standing on has absolutely no certainty. It could split right beneath you, and you could fall straight down into the earth. Now, that's freaky!

Everyone started to calm down, but fear still surrounded the room. I stayed positive for everyone else's sake and to make them all feel safe. But to be honest, I was scared shitless! Everyone stayed over at my house that night, and the next day they all went about their business. Now, my business just became getting the fuck out of L.A., fast! I was freaked out for weeks to come. I would take showers with flashlights next to the shower door. Everywhere I walked in that house I felt anticipation of that horrid sensation.

I had witnessed a couple of earthquakes in L.A. before. You could just be sitting around, and suddenly your whole house shakes, and everyone's like, "Yeah, it's an earthquake." But this one was major! In all seriousness, I wanted out of that city. This earthquake business was just too random for my taste—no warning, nothing, you could be buried! And you know that can happen anytime, and it probably will happen someday.

With rock 'n' roll business still to be handled above ground and my US situation in the fray, I had yet to proceed despite this "force majeure." I started to get a bite here and there. It seemed that labels in Europe—Atlantic, Warner Bros., and the like—who would have received the record once it was released, had already heard advanced copies and were anxiously awaiting the go-ahead for them to release. They started contacting me and asking, "Hey, what are you doing with this record?"

Independent labels started reaching out as well. One was Mark Ashton's Now and Then Records. He was just so passionate about the band and the project. Even though he wasn't a major label, he was one of these guys I could tell had a lot of enthusiasm and could make things pop.

He was really gung-ho about the band, and he came up with an interesting offer. I signed with his label, as well as with Avex in Japan and Point Music in Germany, run by a man named Harry Enzian. He remains a dear friend to this today.

Before you knew it, I had country-by-country deals around the world, and I started working off that. It showed me a little bit of light at the end of the tunnel, but definitely not what it would have been under Jimmy Iovine and Interscope.

One of the first things we were offered in the UK was a show at the Marquee, the monumental club in London where everyone has played, from the Rolling Stones, the Who, and Led Zeppelin to the Sex Pistols, the Police, and Queen. We agreed and started putting everything together. Unfortunately, Tony Thompson couldn't join in because he had a commitment with Power Station, so we brought in the drummer from Mother's Finest, Dion Derek Murdock. The lineup was great, powerful, and the show sold out quickly.

That Marquee show went over fantastically! I can remember one Swedish article specifically that literally brought tears to my eyes. I don't remember what magazine it was or who wrote it, but it said, "Anybody in the world who wasn't there missed the show of a lifetime," or something like that but more heartfelt. For some reason, I started cryin' like a baby (and I rarely cry)! It must have been a buildup of all the pain from losing the deal and everything I had gone through. It had been a turbulent couple of years, and it felt amazing to see appreciation again after nothing but negativity for so long.

Micki was hyped as well, and it reignited us to start moving forward by doing things together and kind of double-teaming—using both what I was good at and what he was good at. We had a good thing going.

16

WOMEN

Going back to my younger years, I was an extremely jealous and insecure teenage boy, and girls could be at times really cruel. I had several occasions that marked me for a long time. I had a girlfriend, my first real girlfriend who I was crazy about. My dad was against me dating anyone. She won him over by bringing him brownies and other pastries she made specifically for him, so he finally gave in.

I went on tour for the first time and was longing to come home and see her. The whole thing was difficult for me because she was a few years older and about to go to college. I thought to surprise her by going to her house as soon as I got back to town. I was so excited that I could actually feel as if my heart was burning.

I headed over and walked into her backyard having the bright idea to tap on her bedroom window. As I approached, I heard familiar sounds that made my heart beat out of my chest! As I peered through the window, I saw the love of my life in bed with another boy—a Black boy, no less. Now, I don't know why this was, but it was one thing if your girlfriend would cheat with another guy, but to see her in bed with another Black guy was even more of a shock, one I was not prepared for. I remember running back into the woods where I came from to get to her house, sobbing, as I never had before. The pain was such that I couldn't bring myself to ever see or speak to her again. It took me the longest time to get that horrid vision out of my head.

Another time, I had just bought a street-legal motorcycle and this girl I was seeing proposed we go out to New Jersey where her friends were having a party. When we got there, I was totally uncomfortable.

We all started playing cards around the table, and I could see her looking at a guy sitting across the table. I was livid and could barely speak. I went to the bathroom, and when I came back, she and the guy were not there. I reluctantly started to look for her and approached a bedroom door, which was locked.

I could hear the moans from inside the room, and I can't explain the feeling that came over me. It was pouring rain, yet I ran out of the apartment and jumped on my motorcycle pissed off but in tears. I drove that bike at top speed down the expressway wanting to die. I never spoke to her again and I felt my heart was ripped out of my body!

I had another crush on a girl that I was starting to go steady with, as we'd say in those days. I had to go to Vegas to perform with the Flamingos, and we spoke of all the wonderful things we were going to do upon my return. When I came back home, I was yearning to see her again. She walked into my place only to tell me that she was pregnant by another boy! A teenage girl! I just couldn't believe it! I can't even explain the pain I felt, that would just not go away no matter what I did. These experiences hurt me so deeply that they changed my way of behaving with women probably for the rest of my life! These are just a few horrid experiences I had in my teens.

So when I wrote earlier on that I wanted to be on MTV and show the girls who had hurt me, these are precisely the reasons why.

It would take virtually nothing for me to end a relationship, and I could never fully commit. I would find any little thing, any sign or indication. If I even saw a girl I was with glance at someone else, I would disappear without notice, ending that relationship without any further thought.

I can still remember as I got older getting into relationships with girls who would say to me, "How can you let me go so easily?" Or, "Why are you so cold all of a sudden?" Even when I moved to L.A. later on in my life, where in the circles I traveled many of the women would go from guy to guy, looking for that golden egg. In L.A., you never know who that actually is! A Lamborgini could actually be a Volkswagen, fake Rolexes, film production companies that are actually someone's $20 answering machine and so forth.

I always joked that if a girl dates a guy because he drives a Lamborghini or Ferrari, which is actually a Volkswagen, that's what she deserves to be in. I had a girl living with me for a while and we went up to club one night. I would literally say that I'm going to the bathroom, go to the other side of the club and just watch her in anticipation of her doing something to hurt me.

One time while out, I watched a girl who was staying at my house give her number to another celebrity while I had walked away. I immediately left the club, leaving her there, and had my assistant take all her things out of my house and put them on the street out front. Safely, of course, I was still a gentleman despite. She called and left me a message saying that she looked for me around the club and couldn't find me: "Where did you go?" I never responded, and she would never see or hear from me again. I had women contact me many years later who were victims of my behavior, still asking why I left them. I couldn't trust any girl for the longest time, and my jealousy was just unbearable. If a girl I was out with so much as looked in the direction of another guy, I was a ghost, gone, faster than a speeding bullet.

My sister joked with me for the longest time and would say to people "My brother? He can be jealous of a poster!" This changed as I gained confidence in my later years, but not totally. I had to so believe and trust that a girl truly loved me for her to get past that wall I kept up for so very long. Women much later in my life would still awaken that emotion in me without knowing it. And when they did, no matter how much they said they loved me, or what they did, we were doomed. The more I felt myself falling for her, the sooner I would leave. No matter what I felt or how much I loved her, I could just stop myself from feeling anything in a heartbeat and just take that pain. I preferred to end it rather than living in anticipation of the pain I convinced myself would come.

Now, I know that many are curious about the women I've since had in my life. I've decided that rather than speak about everyone I dated over the years, I want to basically say that I'm very grateful to whoever it is up there that gave me something later on that women found attractive. This is following my teen years, which were as I've revealed, very difficult.

I've dated everyone from *Playboy* playmates, centerfolds, *Penthouse* pets, Bond girls, Hawaiian Tropic girls, pop superstars, dancers, supermodels from various countries and different ethnicities, Miss Europe, Miss Universe contestants, TV hosts, flight attendants, even high-level escorts who'd quit their job! It was always in an endless search for true love and a soul mate.

The women I dated were for the most part intelligent, clever, witty, and fun most of the time, and definitely some of the most desirable women on the planet.

I've also dated girls who were not famous or top models but were equally as beautiful and wonderful, such as my wife, Susanne. She was not an actress, singer, or a top model, but was indeed as beautiful as anyone I had ever met. She has been my wife to this day and has blessed me with two beautiful children, Darius Beauvoir and Izabel Sophie Beauvoir.

The biggest mistake men make when they're younger is basing everything on physical appearance. I could see a girl who I thought was beautiful from across the room and fall in love without knowing anything about her!

But there's a lot more to it than just beauty. What you have in common, likes and dislikes, point of view on different aspects of life, and many other factors make a relationship work or not. Beauty is also in the eye of the beholder. A woman you may have thought was stunning may end up looking very different to you should she do certain things you don't like or because of her personality, which may not jive with yours. Now, what do I mean when I say "beautiful"? You can be skinny with no butt, or a big girl with a big ole butt! You got freckles? You're dark, light, blonde or a crazy redhead? Whatever you are, you are beautiful!

I would come across jealous men oftentimes who didn't understand why I'd been so fortunate. Men who had a certain level of success, yet were still not given the opportunities that I have had. The world can be really shallow at times. Guys could think, "Well, my album/film/TV show, whatever, is number one this week." Or they feel they're more successful or richer than you are, so they're wondering, "What's he doing with that girl? Why does she like him? That's not supposed to happen."

As it's always been very easy for me to have friends who are women, I feel I can understand that most women are looking for a deeper connection, too. These women friends included ex-girlfriends, who could be married with kids, or women I may have pursued but then changed my mind and we remained friends. There were some I never made a move on, but we somehow met and just hit it off for some reason. A friend of mine, Rachel Hunter, was a good example of that. We had gone out to dinner platonically. I wasn't interested in her romantically, even though undoubtedly she was pretty. We went to Roxbury, where I introduced her to Rod Stewart, which is actually a long story—they were married shortly afterwards! But I've done this kind of thing several times. Even women who hated me for leaving them would usually become friends at some point.

We usually spent hours speaking about life, their husbands or boyfriends, family, or the guys they like or are pursuing. They ask for my advice. Some of my friends are young, some older, but I always give them a fair and honest perspective, which they seem to appreciate. It's almost as if they're speaking to a girlfriend with the benefit of getting a man's point of view.

One thing, though, that has always miffed me is that so many female friends of mine would tell me about guys they've met or were with, but rarely mentioned that they loved them. It often seemed to be, "Oh, he's got a nice job, money, nice car, solid, or he'd probably make a good dad," as if they literally made a shopping list that, once satisfied, would be good enough for them. I've always advised against that thinking, as I believe in the end, the heart always wins. So many people get in those kinds of relationships and find themselves unhappy. Even though they obtained the material things, they still don't have what they want or the love they long for.

I've cherished women friends my whole life. These friendships have given me a great insight into women, educating me on their psyche, thoughts, point of view on life, and their views on men. It can be really interesting, and they've sometimes set my ass straight!

I always had a bit of a feminine side, as many of my male friends have, though we're undoubtedly men. I imagine it's made women feel more comfortable around me. They didn't always feel like I was trying to get in their pants.

When I was living in L.A., for example, I'd have *Playboy* playmate friends call me asking to come by and do laundry at my house or something of the sort. They'd be walking around the house half-naked with their girlfriends asking me for soap, and it just wouldn't phase me. There'd be boobs and booty hanging out everywhere, and I'd be like, "Baby, you want corn with that barbecue chicken?" I love to cook! Actually, come to think of it, I've turned down booty for some KFC many a time! My friends tease me about that all the time—and it's even funnier that I actually played for the Colonel as a kid in Kentucky!

17

KEY WEST & THE GERMAN YEARS

I NEVER REALLY FOUND what I was looking for in a partner in L.A. Many girls would just jump from musician to musician or actor to actor. They were celebrity hounds, and you didn't want to be next in line. I just wasn't into it.

I didn't like being judged solely on the celebrity aspect rather than who I actually am. I mean, let's face it, if you're playing in front of thousands and thousands of people on stage, there's a hit record and all the fruits that come with that, it's pretty damn attractive. I do understand that people are looking for security, and, of course, when it's happening, rock 'n' roll provides security, fun, danger, decadence, excitement, traveling, cool hotels, and all the other trappings of worldly success.

It's a happening life, when it's happening. But if the success diminishes and things start to go in a different direction, which it almost inevitably does at some point for everyone, then sometimes the girls aren't quite as flexible as you'd like them to be. Next thing you know, they're off to the next guy who happens to still have that stuff going on. They leave with your house and half the things that you had, so it's not the best situation in my eyes to get into a relationship like that, a relationship built on false and superficial things rather than somebody who falls in love with you because of who you actually are.

My ideal way to meet someone would be if they didn't know anything about you at first, and when they later found out, or saw you on stage, it would just be a pleasant surprise, icing on the cake.

So alongside my deep-seated desire to leave this morbid life of decadence in Hollywood behind me, and on account of the recent misfortunes and feeling down, I found myself being self-destructive. I started doing blow, which at first gave me loads of energy. I worked out every day, and at first it felt really good. But it wasn't too long before I started feeling unhinged as I ventured down this road. After a while, I decided it was enough.

I also felt it best to relook at my choice of women. I thought that I'd like to find a girl who was not at all involved in the industry, which was extremely difficult for me to find in Los Angeles.

Before our London Marquee show, I got in touch with my dear friend Peter Stringfellow, the owner of the real go-to hotspot in London at the time, Stringfellows. Every time I'd come to town, he'd always take care of me, roll out the red carpet and the whole shebang. I had a friend named Ciro as well, owner of a place called Ciro's Pizza Pomodoro, and he would also be one of my first stops every time I'd get to London.

In any case, I gave Peter a call, and as usual, he was extremely accommodating and set things up for me to have a great table the night before the Marquee show. Micki and I arrived at the club, everything was all set up in the center of the room, and the place was packed and hopping. It's a great feeling to walk into a place and the whole center of that place is just sitting there empty, waiting for you to arrive. I'm like, "Yeah, baby."

So we're strutting in and there were two girls standing at our table.

With a little attitude (as I would have at times), but in a good mood, cheery, bopping up and down, feeling powerful, I said to the girl with a grin, "You know, didn't the waiter ask you to leave?"

She looked at me and said in a British accent, "Well, I like it here."

Even though she had a British accent, she was Swedish.

I said, "You like it here?" and I just started to laugh. This girl's got some spunk. I'm diggin' her! Meanwhile, she had a girlfriend with her, who was also cute, but not exactly my type. Micki liked her friend, so we said, "Well, maybe we'll let them stick around for a bit." This is why we have wingmen!

The one I was diggin', Susanne, was very spunky, and she had answers for everything. She just kept going, going, and going. At the same time, she was cute as hell—gorgeous actually—but she didn't yet know, 100%, how to show it.

I knew baby was a sleeper—a little this, and that, and voilà! She'd look better than the models, but without the model stress, so I thought! The more "Swenglish" she spewed, the hotter she got! She had this little striped top that only went down right below her breasts and had this tight little stomach, a six pack, blonde, blue eyes, a smile, that accent, and an attitude.

So we stuck around and hung out all evening. In fact, I called my sister from the club and told her, "I met this girl tonight, and I'm gonna marry her."

My sister was like, "What? You just met her."

I said, "I'm telling you. I don't know what it is, but I just know it. I'm gonna marry her."

The funny thing was that this phone call happened after she had insulted me for an hour or so. But the more she insulted me, the more I liked it. I invited her to the Marquee show, and that's actually when she said, "I hate rock and roll!" My words were, "Mrs. Beauvoir!" This is why she's the one. She was so opposite of everything that I was trying to get away from.

Trying to talk her into coming to the show anyway, I said, "Well, you know, it's not just rock 'n' roll. You'd be coming to see me, and blah, blah, blah." I must have been convincing, because as they say, the rest is history.

Susanne and I started spending a lot of time together in London. I extended my trip, and we were getting to know each other better. But the attitude didn't change much, and eventually it was becoming too much for me to bear. Micki was coming to meet us once, and she and I had yet another tiff. I said to Micki, "That's it, let's go. We're flying out of here today!" I told her goodbye for good, and that was actually my plan.

We jumped on a flight to Stockholm, my favorite place to go when I was heartbroken! I checked into a hotel under an alias. I think it might've been Damien Thorn from the film *The Omen*. I'd use that every so often.

I was staying at a nice hotel right in the center of town on top of one of the hot nightclubs, called Alexandra's. I called up my friends to make plans. Then my hotel phone rings, I pick up, and much to my surprise, it was Susanne.

I asked her how she found me, not knowing my alias, which I had never told her. She told me she called around to all the hotels in Stockholm until she found me. She wanted to apologize for her behavior and asked if I would please come back to see her. Now, that was pretty damn romantic. It definitely made my heart sing!

"Hey Micki! Let's go back to London tonight!" I said.

He replies, "Oh no, Voodoo! What you up to now, nigga! Oh OK, well, ya' know I'm kinda diggin' on that little friend of hers!"

I couldn't stop laughing as I called to have our flights rebooked!

I got back to London, booked the hotel, and immediately saw her again. We went to Ciro's restaurant, our spot. Micki had known Ciro for years and always said he was a really cool guy. Ciro always wore a customized motorcycle jacket, lots of chains and bracelets, and looked like a celebrity. And Lord, he had the greatest pizza! The place was a really cool hang, and afterward we'd always head out to some private London nightclub for some more fun.

I had a great time with her despite the lingering attitude, and I was head over heels. I actually did like that she had no interest in celebrities and fame. In what I do, you have to be careful about that kind of thing. You have to be really sure that your girl loves you, regardless of who is or could be in the room.

I talked about people settling before. Well, I don't want to be settled for. The girls who met me or dated me would probably meet every man they could've dreamed of at one point or another. Marcus Schenkenberg, the famous model, would come and stay for a month or more at my house, and you know girls love him!

Not long after I met Susanne, she found herself on the stadium tour all around Europe with Bon Jovi, Van Halen, and me performing. That was a great tour, and she got to see things first-class. Although nothing really impressed her, I believe she enjoyed it. At one point, she'd met many of the celebrities most women would be attracted to or idolize. Either she never flinched, or she was a great actress.

I was still living in L.A. when we first met, and she came to visit me there. It was all new to her. She met my dad and some of my friends. It remained a long-distance relationship for a while, and then that became difficult for us. Around this time, I was planning on moving to Key West. So I called her and said, "Hey, would you like to move to Key West?"

She was full of questions, of course. "What am I gonna do there? But . . . but . . . but . . ." But she ultimately said yes.

I had always loved the Florida Keys. I booked a flight and went down there to look and found a house right on the water. It was pretty cool. It had a lagoon going into the house, with parrotfish, barracudas, and lobsters under the house, tons of those little Nemo fish. I loved those little things! The house also had a boat ramp and lots of docking space, but you couldn't have too big of a boat, as the water was very shallow to get out to the ocean. It was completely different from how I lived in L.A. I packed up everything, got a moving company, and headed down to Florida. My dad came with me.

The house was on Sugarloaf Key, which is about fifteen miles north of Key West. It was a very cool neighborhood, reminiscent of the Caribbean. I just loved Key West! It had this old feeling with hippies and pirates running around, and everyone seemed so free and happy. It was an appealing place to me, and just what I needed. I was happy I made that move.

Susanne came after a few months, and we started to get everything together. The island was exotic, romantic, and something very different for both of us that we could enjoy together. I made a lot of friends down there, and I was treated well by guys like Terry Schmida from the *Key West Citizen* and Bill Hoebee, who was, and still is, the top radio DJ down there. They soon enough asked me to do some interviews for their radio show and newspaper.

I somehow felt it was a place you could just let loose and escape. I think a lot of people felt the same way, but the place had a decadent side. Some people were letting loose more than others. What happens in Key West most definitely stays in Key West!

People down there drank like fish, and they partied hard! Thinking I left drugs when I left L.A. was definitely an oversight. I later found out that planes had come and dropped kilos of cocaine close to my house.

There were also a lot of interesting characters who had really eclectic backgrounds and history. Upon my arrival to the neighborhood, my neighbors across the street, Nick and Bonnie Manetti, visited me. They immediately came over to welcome us to the neighborhood and made us feel right at home.

Nick and Bonnie turned out to be fantastic friends. He was one of the best-known fishing guides in the area, but he also had a really long history. He was a commercial pilot, as well as a private pilot working in South America and doing a lot of crazy things in his younger days—great stories. His daughter lived in Denmark, so he spoke a little Danish, which was also surprising.

Bonnie was a sweet woman with a funny personality. Well, they both had that. She worked at a place called Sloppy Joe's in Key West, and she'd been there for years, so they were both staples in town.

There were many people who seemed to have left behind completely different—often extremely successful—lives that they just got tired of one day. So they headed to an island and left it all behind. As a matter of fact, some years later Susanne had a friend who went down to Key West on vacation with her family, and she texted us a photo of a book cover. It was a book that was left in the hotel where she was staying: *Quit Your Job and Move to Key West.* It listed the most famous celebrities who had moved and lived there. I was honored to see that I was on that short list, alongside people like Ernest Hemingway, Harry Truman, Kelly McGillis, Calvin Klein, Truman Capote, Thomas Edison, Hulk Hogan, Roy Scheider, Tennessee Williams, and Hunter S. Thompson.

They made me a part of Key West royalty and history. I definitely fit right in, but I was grateful. I'll always feel like I'm a part of Key West, no matter where I am or where I go. That book is still widely sold.

In any case, we adapted nicely down there. We were friends with the locals, and I'd walk down Duval Street with a full Mohawk, a Voodoo cane, and a rottweiler at my side, but I kind of looked normal. When we first moved there, it was much different than it is today.

As small as the place was, I much later became friends with a fantastic songwriter and author named Andreas Carlsson. He wrote many big hits from Backstreet Boys to NSYNC to Britney Spears and dozens of others. He was partners with his fellow Swede the iconic Max Martin. I found out from Andreas that they had a house in Key West where they were recording most of their hits, the whole time I was down there! For some reason, we never crossed each other's paths.

When moving to Key West, I also shipped my twenty-four-track machine and a big mixing board that I had at the time. Mind you, there was not one technician in Key West who knew anything about this type of equipment, so anytime it needed repairs, which it often did, I'd have to fly somebody in from Miami. The machine did not like the weather down there whatsoever! Regardless of ample air conditioning and other precautions, being only about twenty feet from the water was causing serious problems, to the point where it became dangerous to even use the equipment, as it could ruin my existing twenty-four-track masters.

So, I decided to look into digital recording, and I started with a program called Cubase. I had pretty much the first version ever released. It left much to be desired. At the time, I was using a PC, and with that system, I was lucky to get twenty-four tracks to play without difficulty and hassles. Today my digital recording system can easily handle over a hundred tracks with multiple effects and instruments on all tracks. With my old system, I had to bounce tracks to record new ones, and I had to incorporate lots of workarounds to get anything out of it.

It turns out that I wasn't the only one willing to pull hair out to enter the digital recording world. Max Norman, the famed Ozzy Osbourne and Megadeth producer who worked on the Voodoo X album, was also interested in digital recording. I hired him to work on the new Crown of Thorns album, *Lost Cathedral*, which we would record in my house.

Steven Van Zandt and I had written a couple of songs together for the album in New York, "Motorcycle Loretta" and "Cold Blooded Bitch." I recorded these songs, playing all the instruments myself. (I played most of the instruments on this one and on following Crown of Thorns albums but did use my band at times as well.) I brought the band down to Key West and started adding parts to some of the other songs. Tommy Lafferty played some rhythm parts and some guitar solos, Michael Paige contributed some bass parts, and Hawk Lopez played some drums.

Hawk Lopez is a great drummer who had been suggested to me by my friend, Randy Castillo (a fantastic drummer who before his passing played with Ozzy Osbourne and Mötley Crüe). It was a good suggestion. Hawk is a very disciplined drummer, fantastic with a click, creative, showy, respectful, and funny! We had a lot of fun together both recording and on the road.

The digital systems at the time were just not powerful enough, which forced us to spend an enormous amount of time adjusting to the limitations. Despite all the headaches trying to get things on tape, we had a blast down in Key West. They all loved it! The town was just full of action and very artist friendly.

There were several strip clubs that we liked to frequent. We knew the girls, and they were all cool. I later wrote the song *American Trash* for an album Micki Free and I recorded with the same name. It depicts a fictitious strip club and pays homage to the ladies who work there to put themselves through college, support their families or boyfriends. These clubs have traditionally been watering holes for many musicians, and those ladies have supported many a rock star that we know today! God bless 'em! My friend Bill Hoebee and some other guys would be deejaying at times, so I could bring in mixes and try them out.

The place was full of music venues all in close proximity to each other. There would be a grunge club on top of the strip club in front of the reggae club. Then, a couple of doors down, there were rock clubs like Dirty Harry's or Sloppy Joe's, which mostly had cover bands, but very good ones. I'd get up there and jam sometimes or sing a few songs.

Cruise ships arrived all the time, so it was very transient, and a lot of people visited from all over the place. When people came to Key West, they all went nuts drinking those crazy frozen cocktails from establishments like Fat Tuesday's or the like, containing multiple strong liquors and bearing names I'd prefer not divulge! Many unique to Key West! After two of those, you'd be out for the count!

I also am a fan of boats and had a couple during my time down there. The first one was a twenty-foot runabout, which we would take out to the reefs or to go fishing. I then bought a Sea Ray thirty-foot cruiser, which had a cabin, kitchen, dinette area, two little state rooms, and a spacious deck. We went to some beautiful places in the Keys with that one, and of course, you had to be careful not to run aground, almost inevitable if you didn't pay close attention. The waters could go from fourteen feet to two feet in a matter of seconds!

It wasn't always perfect in paradise, though. While Max was staying in one of our guest rooms, we warned him to please keep his door and suitcase closed. Our rottweiler, Sasha (who was still a puppy at the time), was a thief and loved to venture into guests' luggage and steal things. One day she went into his room and took his hat—his cherished hat, mind you, that had been given to him by his wife.

Well, she ate it beyond recognition! He was so upset and deeply saddened when that happened, and so were we. Max is a great guy, so he didn't kill us, but I couldn't have blamed him if he did! I could feel his pain run through me as if I was the victim and for a very long time.

Max once gave me one of the kindest and most endearing compliments I had ever received. He said, "Jean, if you would really put 100 percent into this, you could make a seriously untouchable album. You're probably using about 10 percent of your talent now. The problem is that your 10 percent is more than most artists' 100 percent."

He was criticizing me, but at the same time he was making a poignant statement I took as a compliment. I took it to heart, as this was coming from somebody I really respected and felt had immense talent himself. He is truly one of the best producers of our time.

I really enjoyed working with Max and having the band down. I enjoyed all the people who visited us in Key West. One fun thing I enjoyed and was always inviting visitors to do with me was snorkeling. The water is absolutely to die for when you get away from the island a bit. It's totally clear, and you can see down to the bottom, even if it's thirty, forty, or fifty feet deep.

I remember going fishing with my buddy and neighbor Nick Manetti. We would just drop lines into the water some miles out from shore, and you could literally pick the fish you wanted, including schools of dolphin (mahi mahi, not Flipper!). We'd bring our catch home and feast. Granted, Nick was an amazing fishing guide, so he knew all the spots and where to catch the most fish. My friends loved it when I moved around, as it provided new places for them to discover.

The Sea Ray boat we had was too big to dock at our yard, as the water was just too shallow most of the time to get it out to the ocean. I kept it at a marina in Key West where we would live most of the weekends. We would stay up at the house during the week and work, whether it was me recording, administrative business, making new deals, or doing artwork. Susanne became very proficient in artwork and layouts. She was also a fantastic photographer and ended up shooting many of my magazine covers, press photos, and album covers including those for Crown of Thorns.

She became my real partner in crime for all these things. She was a quick learner, extremely efficient, and fast! It got to a point where she learned how to use Cubase, the recording software I used. There were situations where I'd be in Europe working, and she was able to go in and do a different mix of a song or make necessary changes I might need and to send over to me, should the record company need more vocal in a mix or whatever it might be.

When I had first invited her to come join me in Key West, she was very concerned about what she would do there for work besides being with me. I didn't want her working or going to a regular job, selfishly so that we could hang! Therefore, I tried to tap into anything I felt she showed a talent or knack for. There was quite a bit, so that was not a problem. She would also travel on tour with me at times.

Swedes are well-rounded people and know a lot in general. It makes them a little overconfident at times. They may feel they know more than you about certain things! She already spoke four languages: Swedish, English, French, and Spanish.

As I mentioned, we would spend the weekdays doing business. Every Friday afternoon we'd head down to the boat for the weekend, and it was party time! We'd make food on the boat and stay on it, and on Saturday and Sunday during the days we'd go out to various amazing spots around the Keys. At night, we sampled the variety of restaurants in Key West, and we'd head out to the bars to meet friends and go have fun. It was truly a beautiful place, and at times I regret leaving. It's funny how you can get jaded or take places for granted when you're there. After you leave, you then get more perspective and realize what you actually had.

One day, a friend from the neighborhood came over and shared with us that our lagoon was a lobster paradise. It had rock walls, and the lobsters would hide in crevices just below the waterline. He proposed, "Go out and run your errands or whatever else you need to do today, and when you come back, I'll leave some lobsters in your lanai."

We said, "Yeah, sure! Do your thing!"

We got back to the house, and sure enough, a few lobsters were walking around the lanai. I called the guy and said, "Hey! Thanks for that! What do I do now?"

He said, "Either cut off the head, or just stick them in a big pot of boiling water."

We didn't like either of those options, but figured, "When in Rome, do as the Romans do."

We put one in a pot and heard this high-pitched screaming sound! We were freaking out! We couldn't bring ourselves to eat lobster for months!

I never did that again. I'm very sensitive that way. I love eating fish, but I hate seeing the hook in the mouth, taking it out, and watching them die. I've always had problems with any type of cruelty to animals, whether it be chickens in Haiti during Voodoo ceremonies, fishing, or hunting. The same goes for crabs—but that said, all the little kids hanging around my waterfront property in Haiti would spend their days chasing crabs around, catching them by hand, and eating them on the spot! That's the Haitian way, which I most definitely should have been accustomed to by then.

I particularly loved flying in and out of Key West. Being remote as it was, you had to get to Miami or Fort Lauderdale for any international or national flight. I'd take a little puddle jumper plane that only held a few people to travel between Key West and Miami. When arriving in Key West, you'd see this thatched roof, very Caribbean-looking little airport in the horizon as you were approaching. It felt really cool and obscure landing at this tiny airport to get back home.

After our hit show at London's Marquee club, I had started to get more requests for the band to play in England. I met a tour manager and booking agent named Adam Parsons. He was well known in the UK and in Europe for booking these kinds of tours, so we went ahead to set up our next UK run.

We toured by bus, and Susanne came with us for some of the shows. She and I would take the back lounge for travel and stay in hotels at night. The band's popularity rose as we were doing a lot of press, and Mark Ashton, who ran Now and Then Records, had signed me for Europe. He was doing a great job of getting us greater exposure. When the Crown of Thorns debut album came out, it actually stayed on the UK rock charts for a staggering six months. Then a new opportunity came my way.

Micki and I were not seeing eye to eye on things, and I decided it was time to let him go. An opportunity revealed itself initiated by my friend Scott Greenstein, a top executive at Sirius XM. He was a fan of Crown of Thorns, and in one of our meetings he mentioned that it would be so great to see me on tour with Bon Jovi. They were about to embark on a massive stadium tour across Europe, with Van Halen also on the bill. Sounded great to me! Scott and I, and at times Steve Blatter, the general manager, would meet often for business as we controlled two twenty-four-seven channels on Sirius XM, or I'd drop by to shoot the shit with Scott, as we had a common love for Sweden and rock 'n' roll! He had offered me my own rock show on Sirius XM at one point, but that was deemed inappropriate with my current position at Renegade and therefore unfortunately squashed.

I said, "yeah, that would be cool, but I'm not gonna bring it up!" It's always been uncomfortable for me, though I have many artist friends, to discuss such business. So he offered to speak to Jon about it and come back to me.

I knew Jon was a fan of my solo record *Drums Along the Mohawk*, as he had once shared, so my appearing solo would have been more comfortable for him, but I was hellbent on promoting Crown of Thorns at the time, so I often turned down offers to tour solo. I had several back-and-forth talks and meetings with Scott in his office where he'd update me that things were looking good! He then called me to say that Jon and management were in! But he was wondering if we could get Steven on board to join for a few songs. He had not been out solo in a while, and as I was previously part of the Disciples of Soul, it would all make sense. We approached Steven on that, he agreed, and it all moved forward.

I'd known Jon Bon Jovi for a long time, since the early '80s, and this wasn't the first time he had invited me up on stage. I remember going to one show as a guest, it may have been in New Jersey. When I sat with him and the band, he told me that he loved my album *Drums Along the Mohawk* and that it was a favorite on their tour bus.

Def Leppard had also shared the same when I met up with them somewhere out on the road. It was flattering to hear from both of these iconic bands. Compliments were always welcome! What better place for bands to listen to new music than on those long bus rides!

In 1989, while I was deep into my previous project Voodoo X, Uwe, Tommy and me were all in Germany working on our album and coincidentally, Bon Jovi was playing the next night. I reached out to Jon to let him know I was in town. We were actually staying at the same hotel. As I'd usually do, I went backstage pre-show to say hello and wish them the best, then he asked me to join them on stage and also invited Uwe and Tommy.

Rudolph Schenker was also in town that night and joined. I vividly remember Rudolph in his thick German accent shouting, "Where's the sound!" referring to his monitor mix where he wanted to hear louder guitars! It was a great jam, but I don't remember what song we played!

For the Bon Jovi tour, all came together nicely, and Jon made me a great offer to do the tour, including generous fees, and everything first class.

As Micki was now out of the equation, I summoned my buddy Tommy Lafferty, once again, to join my camp. He was ecstatic to be called in, especially since his first gigs would be a tour of this magnitude. I always enjoyed pleasantly surprising him. In preparation for rehearsals, Tony Thompson had some other obligations and wasn't available, so Hawk Lopez took his place on the road.

I hired Adam Parsons as a tour manager, and Jamie Owens, another gent I met working in the UK, came with to handle finances and other duties. Everyone was stoked and ready to rock. Sammy Hagar was singing with Van Halen at this time, and they sounded fantastic every night, as did Bon Jovi.

We played nothing but stadiums of eighty to a hundred thousand people every night including two nights at Wembley Stadium. The audience just went nuts, and the whole stadium had their hands up as we performed. What a high that was!

I love big audiences, and playing to that many people is like playing in my living room for me. I feel at one with the crowd, especially when they're as responsive as they were at Wembley and throughout the tour.

The Van Halen guys were a blast to travel with, and we hung out every night and partied. They'd be hanging in our dressing room, and vice versa. Jon, Richie, and the band were also my good friends, so the tour was a breeze—never any trouble.

Well, except for one night at Wembley. I was wearing sort of a black pleatherish catsuit with high-heeled white sneakers. I went down to the floor doing one of my moves and suddenly felt air between my legs. *Oooh, nice breeze,* I thought. Some fans were pointing at me, and I thought they were just saying, "Right on!" In fact, they were trying to let me know something was hanging, literally! Then I noticed my pants had split completely from my dick all the way back to half my ass! The fans in the front rows had a clear view of my sausage and meatballs!

There was a girl on stage who somehow found some safety pins and urged me to the side of the stage, having Tommy play an extra-long solo while she secured the pants as best as she could until the show was over. That was definitely talked about for a while!

We separated from Bon Jovi for a couple of the gigs and did Rock Am Ring in Germany on our own to a super enthusiastic crowd. We were on fire! The band sounded great, and my voice was in tip-top shape. Hawk was kicking ass, and so were Michael Paige and Tommy. We played Spain, Portugal, Sweden, and so on, hitting it hard every night.

There were many journalists who were very supportive, such as Dave Reynolds, Dave Ling, and the Bailey Brothers, and they'd come to the shows. Mind you, we were a true rock 'n' roll band with the boys giving their all. Girls were flooding the dressing and VIP rooms, drinks and shots were flyin', and it was utter madness! Of course, let's not forget my famous disco nights!

Susanne joined me for most of the tour, and that was definitely a great experience for her! This was rock 'n' roll at its best!

I had kept in contact with Uwe from Voodoo X. We were speaking all the time, always trying to figure out some way to work together again. He told me that BMG was doing some fantastic work, and he thought it might be something for me to look into. I did just that, and I spoke to a gentleman named Hartwig Masuch. He was the big dog over there in Germany, heading up BMG Publishing.

I wanted to get out of my EMI publishing deal because I just didn't feel they were putting in the necessary effort in terms of getting covers and placing songs in TV and film. They were receiving a fair percentage of my income from collecting all around the world on all the songs that I had released over the years, which was a large catalog containing hundreds of songs.

Hartwig liked my catalog, and me, so he made me an enticing offer, which would include me having to spend a certain amount of time in Berlin to work with other producers and artists. There was an interesting movement going on at the time with bands such as NSYNC, Backstreet Boys, and Britney Spears handled by the infamous Lou Perlman. He was ultimately sent to jail for some serious wrongdoings over the years, but at that time he handled all these groups and would send them over to Germany and Sweden to be produced, have chart success, and then he would release them in the US.

After signing with Hartwig, one of the first songs I cowrote was for NSYNC (with Uwe Fahrenkrog-Petersen) and called "Forever Young." I was also very involved in some of the arrangements, mainly vocals, and this song helped them get their start out of Germany and Europe. They became massive, going on to achieve a diamond album in the US, one of the very few at that time and up until today. Their debut album went on to sell over fifteen million units worldwide, and they became a worldwide phenomenon ultimately selling in excess seventy million albums!

This was a good way to start my relationship with BMG. I had already signed agreements with several publishers consecutively, which included CBS songs, SBK, EMI, Polygram, and now BMG, and had managed to retain all my publishing rights throughout all the deals. I worked on several other albums while over there and also recorded a few more Crown of Thorns albums. Some I recorded in my studio, which I had built in this cool penthouse apartment that we found right in the center of Berlin.

The area was called Schöneberg, and it was around the corner from the famous Kurfürstendamm.

Hartwig also introduced me to one of his most successful writers, who had just had a huge success with a song called "Scatman." This song had broken records all around the world, especially in Japan where it outsold everyone, including Michael Jackson. His name was Tony Catania, a very talented producer and songwriter who had had also worked with Frank Farian when he first started.

He was the main producer who did the music and productions for the massive Milli Vanilli album, *All or Nothing*, which was later released in the US as *Girl You Know It's True*. A very well-produced album with lots of hits. It had also sold millions of albums, despite them being shamed and losing the Grammy they were awarded.

Hartwig set up a meeting between Tony and me in New York. We really hit it off and ended up doing a lot of work together. We spawned a couple of other hits with the Dutch hip-hop duo R'n'G, and also worked on some of my songs, one of them called "Monday." This song was released and, by surprise, went to number one on the main radio charts.

I also met Tony's girlfriend, Ilona, a sweet, warm but firm German woman who handled all of Tony's business. She also made fantastic chili dogs at 3:30 AM when Tony and I were working night after night in the studio.

I made several record deals while in Germany and worked with some good companies. Harry Enzian from Point Music and I made several albums together for Crown of Thorns as well as some of my solo works, which included my acoustic album *Bare to the Bones*. He ultimately retired and moved to Brazil. I released records with Andy Schilling, who ran another German label, Milestone Music, and SPV released some of my Crown of Thorns records. I also released a further solo album, *Chameleon*, through label UlfTone Music, owned by a friend of mine named Ulf Zick, who also went on to run Gibson Guitars in Germany. We released a single called "I Wanna Know" that was cowritten by Lionel Richie.

I met Lionel for the first time in Sweden, at one of his concerts I was attending. He found out I was in the audience and had me pulled from the crowd after the show. His show was amazing, boasting hit after hit and an abundance of great songs, from his solo material to the Commodores.

I loved both, so it was an honor. He asked me to take some photos with him and his significant other, who was equally sweet to me. He congratulated me on my work and also thanked me for carrying the rock 'n' roll flag for Blacks. He also said that Michael Jackson sent the same praise. They were quite close.

After spending a great time together, he gave me his number and said, "Anytime you want to work together, no matter what time, day or night, call me and I'll be there." One night, probably around midnight, I was working in my studio, and I had an idea. I thought about what he had said and gave him a ring. He came over as he had assured me, and we wrote "I Wanna Know." It was blast working with him, it was effortless, and we hit off well. It was interesting how he had a different take on the timing of certain melodies, that's one thing that really stood out to me and where we complemented each other. I learn something from everyone. His phrasing was so unique along with his mezmerizing, velvet voice. That's why he's one of the greatest artists and storytellers of our time.

For me, Germany was an educational time as well. Coming from Key West, where I had started messing around with digital recording, it was time for me to go back to school. All the producers over there were using Logic recording software, now owned by Apple, which was not the easiest to master. It was developed in Germany, and the instructions were not evident, but I needed this knowledge to stay current. Though I was already a successful producer, I wanted the ability to produce final works myself.

We had come to a point in the music industry where sending rough demos to record companies no longer worked. Back in the day, if you were an artist looking for a deal, you could record something on an acoustic guitar, go sing it to an A&R guy, or use other methods of showing your talent. Now, they wanted to hear the finished product. The songs and demos that you recorded had to be up to par, good enough for release. We'd use great demo singers, oftentimes better than the actual artist! We'd record flawless tracks and share the material between various German producer friends of mine that I worked with.

I perfected Logic and reinvented myself to not only be able to sing and play all the instruments on a song but also be able to produce it and engineer all my work using digital software, where previously I'd had to rely on highly skilled engineers. This added new tools to my toolbox, and I could now send songs to prospective artists, record and perform songs for films and TV on my own, and more. It was a welcome freedom.

I was always interested in film, as I had acted before. Berlin hosted the much-acclaimed international film festival Berlinale. I met some really cool and interesting people there every year, and one person, in particular, who was heavily involved in the Berlin film world, was Melanie Möglich. She was fun and a very cool girl who taught me a good bit about the famous Berlin film scene, and also introduced me to some folks for film music projects.

I did songs for three films while in Berlin. One was *The Guilty*, starring Bill Pullman. The director asked me to write the main song. Anthony Waller, the film's director, sent me some footage to give me a sense and a feeling of what he was trying to get across. I then wrote a song called "Here She Comes." It was also included on my acoustic album *Bare to the Bones.*

The other two films were *Berlin Nights*, directed by Gabriela Tscherniak, and *Flawless*, starring Robert De Niro. For the latter, Tony Catania and I produced and wrote the song "La Chica Marita" for my longtime friend Marcus Schenkenberg.

My newfound knowledge also allowed me to record more solo works and Crown of Thorns albums to completion in my own studio. This education has served me well up till now.

Susanne was helping me, developing her own successful Internet business, and learned German fluently within a couple of months. This was very helpful as Berliners, especially at the start, were not very open. I can remember when we first started spending time there, I felt people were really cold in comparison to Americans, and especially folks from Key West.

I would walk my rottweiler, Sasha, down the street, and I'd say to someone, "Hey, what's happening?" or "How are you doing?" I would get responses like, "Do you really care?" "Do I know you?" or other rude phrases that made you feel like an ass.

There was some truth to what they said, because in reality, there isn't a lot of thought put into those questions that we Americans throw out.

It was just a knee-jerk American habit to say something, even if it has no meaning or sincerity.

I did, later on, come to meet some wonderful people over there, and it was just a matter of better understanding the culture. Still, Berlin was indeed the town with the most happening. The Wall had come down, and there were cranes all over the city from all the construction taking place. It was amazing what was happening over there. But it was still not anywhere as friendly as Munich or the Cologne area, where people were a lot warmer.

Berlin was heavily bombed during the war, so it lacked some of the beautiful architecture that remained in many other cities. Instead, you had a lot of 1960s square block buildings with no personality. The architecture that did remain was incredible though—massive, beautiful buildings that made you look back and say, "Wow, they really had it together."

I had already spent a lot of time in Germany dating back to the Plasmatics, the Little Steven solo days, and Voodoo X, so I was familiar with the country. But it's different when you're partially living there. I still kept the place in Key West, and we'd go back and forth.

As I said, I did make made a lot of wonderful friends while there, who remained so for many years and, some to this day. Some of my friends, like Berlin promoter Nader Korayeim, ran the hot nightclubs in town, so going out was always taken care of. I also had the opportunity to visit East Berlin, which was really cool to see and to get insight on how people really felt about the wall coming down.

It's funny that some were not as enthusiastic as everyone made them out to be. It was a different world for many Germans who were accustomed to having everything handled and were not good at struggling in the "real world" and making their own way. As the saying goes, "It's a dog-eat-dog world out there, and not everybody's cut out to be a dog!" Fighting, competing, sometimes lying, and cheating, as so many have done to get ahead or simply survive.

Germany still had many regulations that, at least, prevented people from taking things too far, which some most definitely do in the US, with little regulation. For example, insurance companies canceling policies before fires or hurricanes with no consequences, or doctors charging whatever they want, and so on. That's what makes the US attractive to so many, and the truth is, it's basically because they can come here and get away with all the things they could never get away with in their own country.

Of course, all of what I'm saying has its positives and negatives. Those regulations that they have in Germany and in many other countries can also be problematic. The Germans did not miss a thing when it came to numbers, taxes, and other implemented rules that had to be followed, or there were serious consequences. They were meticulous and extremely efficient.

As an example, there was a specific date when currency was set to switch from Deutsche Marks to euros. When that date came, many other countries, especially the Latin countries like Italy, France, Spain, and others, experienced total chaos. Nothing was working—ATM machines, taxis, the banks were just a mess!

However, in Germany that shit was tight, and I mean tight! By midnight when that date came along, the entire country changed to euros on a dime, within a second's notice, as if the Deutsche Mark never existed! It was incredible to watch. Meanwhile, I had friends calling from other countries that were completely falling apart!

I went to France several years later and they were still using the French franc, even though it had not existed for years. I always found this to be pretty comical. We were actually looking for a house there, to rent or possibly buy. Looking at different properties, all the prices were in francs. I asked the broker, "Can you please give me this price in euros and how exactly are you calculating this?"

She barely had an answer and had to check to see what the price actually was. I was shocked and looked at her saying, "You know the French franc hasn't existed in years, right?"

"Oui, Monsieur Beauvoir, I guess not, but we still like our little francs here!"

Of course, I still loved the country very much. I had family living there, and the French had been so good and welcoming to me. Not to mention the massive success I had there (which they still looked at as if it happened yesterday). So there was no love lost, but I did think this was just crazy (but funny, no less)! It makes me think of Haiti. When there, it always intrigues me how most calculations and prices, in restaurants for example, are made in the Haitian dollar, which actually does not exist in a physical form, either!

I found that Germany was very open sexually. You'd see all kinds of nudity and sex-themed ads on TV. Kids, of course, saw it too, so they were pretty blasé by the time they grew up! There were also quite a few beaches you could go to where people would be topless or nude at times. It was no surprise to have an old naked fellow walk over to you when you were taking a walk in a park, dick swingin', to tell you he liked your dog! They also had some very specialized clubs, and one, called the Kit-KatClub, was really close to where I lived.

This club was for swingers. Literally, when you walked in, the guy who greeted you was actually masturbating while you walked through the door—for real—and he was not the only one! The concept of the club was that you'd just walk in, meet a person then and there, and just start fucking—right there in the club, at will and anywhere you wanted. So, this club was jam-packed with everybody fornicating, masturbating, or just standing around like they were at a normal bar, watching and not participating while all that was going on. It was reminiscent of old Roman orgies you'd see in films—really wild for a club right in the middle of the city!

Another thing that Germany is well known for, besides delicious Wiener schnitzel and bratwurst, are brothels. They can be found all over the country, and Berlin, most definitely, has its fair share. It appears the concept behind this is that after work (or at any time for that matter), men stop by their favorite bordello and get themselves some sex, or whatever they want, for about 50 to 150 euros. Some men make this a part of their weekly routine. I don't really know if it's actually accepted by the women, but the women sure are aware, as hundreds of these "paradises," as my good friend Tony would say, are everywhere! It's quite similar to the famous Red Light district in Amsterdam.

Something you just don't see here in the US, or in many other countries.

Not from personal experience, but I've heard that many of the women in these places are beautiful, and they're just ordinary girls trying to support their families, or themselves. Some guys I've spoken with argue that rather than taking a girl out, spending hundreds of euros wining and dining her, to the tune of hundreds or thousands of euros, in the effort to entice a girl to no avail, they prefer this convenient option. Mind you, I'm not one of those guys!

While Tony Catania and I were working together in Berlin, at times, it was really hard to convince labels to sign certain singers and artists because they were looking for artists that already had that extra pizzazz or star quality of some kind, to minimize the workload on their end. It came to my mind to reach out to my good buddy Marcus Schenkenberg. He had never made a record before, but I knew him very well and thought that his personality of always being up to a challenge and wanting to try new things could possibly work here.

I gave Marcus a call and said, "Hey Marcus, what's up? You wanna make a record?"

He was nervous at first and said, "Jean, I don't know. I never sang or performed a song before."

I told him, "Don't worry about it. There's a first time for everything, and we'll just work and make it happen! Just like you learned Italian fluently in three months or so to host the TV show you did. I'm not worried about you getting this together."

We immediately pitched a couple of labels and received offers right away. Amazing response! I had reached out to my ex-Virgin president for Germany, Udo Lange. He had worked on my solo record *Drums Along the Mohawk* and the hit single "Feel the Heat."

He was happy to hear from me, since it had been a while, and jumped on it. He wanted to beat everyone else to the punch. I called Marcus and informed him, and he couldn't believe how quickly this went and that he was about to make a record! We made a deal and prepared for him to come over to record a song that Tony and I had written, "La Chica Marita."

They agreed to a very big deal that included first-class travel and hotels for all of us and all the bells and whistles you could ask for in a recording agreement. I was actually surprised, as was Tony, at what was proposed. The only stipulation was that I would make myself available, whenever needed, to coach and support him. That wasn't a problem for me, as we were best friends.

Marcus was, at that time, spending a lot of time in Los Angeles since he was dating Pamela Anderson. Of course, the label was excited about this as well. It was built-in press for promoting the record, and Germany just loved American gossip. Marcus and Pamela were huge celebrities in Germany already.

We flew him to Germany and started to record. He did surprisingly well for someone who had never been in a studio before. I loved the whole thing because it was, yet again, an opportunity for me to bring something new to someone's life and where he was also handsomely paid.

The song was released, and he had the opportunity to perform on Germany's most popular TV show, Thomas Gottschalk's *Wetten, dass . . ?* They actually canceled another major artist scheduled to appear and put Marcus in the slot. It was his first time performing a song on TV with the entire country watching, and he rose to the occasion!

Of course, you had your naysayers as always, but he definitely had his fans who really loved his new venture. Marcus had previously appeared on some other big TV shows as a guest and was frequently in the press. The song entered the charts, and shortly thereafter, I received a phone call from Jellybean Benitez, the famous DJ and record producer. He wanted the song for the soundtrack of the film *Flawless*, starring Robert De Niro. That was another coup for the "Virgin" artist. Marcus enjoyed seeing these opportunities come our way.

When it came time to shoot the video, it was ultimately decided that it would be filmed in Los Angeles. Pamela drove up in her Viper to watch and also to help me get some Jägermeister into him so he could relax and feel comfortable. This was a completely new situation for him, and I think he came through with flying colors. The video turned out to be very cool.

His relationship with Pamela was pretty hot and heavy at that stage, and we were offering him TV shows all over Europe to start. He didn't feel comfortable knowing he'd have to be away for so long, and these requests would keep coming from around the world. He finally opted for Pamela and L.A. as his priority, so his music career never really moved much further. In the end, we never made a full album, but it was a great experience for Marcus and another accomplishment for him to add to his legacy.

In Germany I did a fair amount of performing with Crown of Thorns as well as solo, and I was doing interviews on a regular basis. One of the record companies assigned me a tour manager who made sure everything went smoothly, Dirk Lehburger. He was a good guy, and we worked very well together. After some time, he was asked to manage the "Metal Queen," Doro Pesch, and he thought it would be a good idea to introduce us. She was a really a cool girl I had known of since her band Warlock, plus we had friends in common like Lemmy from Motorhead, Gene Simmons, and others artists we had both worked with.

She asked me to cowrite for her album, and I wrote two songs with her. We first wrote "Salvaje" with just the two of us, and then she told me her band members wanted to be included in some of the writing. I suggested we do a session with all of us together. Johnny Dee, the drummer; Nick Douglas, the bass player; and Joe Taylor, the guitarist, showed up for it, and we wrote "Sister Darkness." It all went like clockwork, and both songs were recorded and included on her album *Fight*. Everyone was happy, and I believe it was the first time her band members were involved in songwriting for one of her albums.

I was also featured on the Doro DVD *20 Years—A Warrior Soul*, the movie and the concert, and I performed "White Wedding" live with Doro and "All We Are" with Doro, Lemmy Kilmister, and Mikkey Dee. I had been contacted by Dirk, my former tour manager and then Doro's manager, to come over as a guest for her twentieth-anniversary arena concert, which was being filmed. She staged fabulous concerts, adding cheerleading squads at times and pyrotechnics. It was always a blast to be invited to join as her guest.

Doro was also good friends with another friend of mine, Ute Linhart, who worked in the industry. I had met her at one of the big rock festivals, and Ute, on Doro's behalf, invited me to take part and perform at Doro's thirtieth-anniversary concert at New York City's Gramercy Theatre, which was filmed for her live DVD called *Strong and Proud*. She later went on to handle some of Doro's management business, I think primarily in the US, while she was working for the well-known merchandising company Bravado. Later, Bravado was absorbed, and she went on to join Live Nation.

Doro and I kept in touch over the years. While we were both in New York, we took the opportunity to cowrite another song, "Rescue

Me." Doro also contributed her vocals and cowrote the song "Shed No Tears," which I asked her to perform with me as a duet for my Crown of Thorns album *Karma*. I remember playing her the mix at a studio called the Bunker. It brought tears to her eyes to hear it.

While living in Berlin, there was also one occurrence that really marked me. We had brought our trusted dog, Sasha, with us from the US. Days before leaving for Berlin, she had started to limp. She was still just a puppy—I think six to seven months old—and the vet told us that she had hip dysplasia. He tried to point out his findings on X-rays, but no matter how hard I looked, I couldn't see anything! Yet the vet was convinced that if we didn't do the surgery immediately before departing for Berlin, we would have a lot of trouble with her.

To be honest, I can be pretty skeptical, and I didn't buy it. I'm not a big fan of surgeries, and I have to really be convinced before I take that route. Well, good thing, because as soon as we arrived in Germany, the limping stopped, and she never had any problem with that leg ever again for the thirteen years she was alive! She enjoyed her time in Berlin, and she loved the parks, lakes, cold weather, and the snow.

One day, we saw on the news that there were problems with aggressive dogs biting people, so the authorities made a list of dogs that were considered *Kampfhunde* (attack dogs). The list included pit bulls, of course, Staffordshire bull terriers, and some others. Strangely, rottweilers were not on the list. It troubled me to see this list being seriously implemented—all the listed breeds would have to wear muzzles at all times. We know that in the US, many, if not most, would ignore this rule, but not in Germany. It appeared that everyone, from one day to the next, muzzled their dogs. On top of that, it also showed on TV that should a police officer corner any of these types of dogs randomly and the dog showed any aggression, they could immediately take the dog and kill it. That freaked me out!

There's just something about people invading my personal space I just don't feel is acceptable. There was something about the idea of a policeman walking over to me as I'm peacefully walking my dog, and all of a sudden starts to menace or taunt her into a corner, a hallway, on the street, or otherwise. And should the dog react, as many dogs would, they could take her right there and kill her! That just did not sit right with me. It was insane, actually, but it appeared the people agreed, and as a matter of fact supported it.

I found myself walking one day into a video shop where two or three people started harassing me, following me around the store, basically saying, "Muzzle, muzzle! Kampfhund! Where's your muzzle?" As an American, I sort of looked at them like, "Do I know you? What business is this of yours?" and I felt really offended. The worst of it was that they were wrong! My dog was not on the list and did not have to wear a muzzle, so they were invading my space with no valid reason.

Even going back to when I made my first solo record, I wrote a song called, "This Is Our House," and the song depicted a little boy, actually in Germany, whose home was being invaded by the Nazis, and him crying out for them to leave his mother alone—this was their house that their father had built for them, and that they had no right to take it away. My lyrics, at times, can be vague enough so that they can be interpreted differently by the listener, to suit a situation that they are perhaps going through. I don't know if many people ever really knew that this was the story I had in mind when writing the song.

Though not the situation I wrote about those years ago, I did have a bit of the same feeling I had then come over me when I saw this going on—a lack of freedom, and a feeling that you were controlled. That somebody could take something so precious from you, just because they decided to, overnight.

It's a funny thing that there are positives and negatives to all different kinds of regimes. As I've mentioned, to a certain extent I love the fact that there are regulations and rules to protect the people in countries like Germany or Sweden, and I feel that this should be implemented much more than it is here in the US. However, having that type of regulation also comes with having a certain amount of control over the people, where once something is said, everybody immediately does it, as if it's ordained. That is something that is not American.

In the US I don't see myself parking in a spot where I shouldn't park and having three or four people run over to me yelling, "You can't park there, you can't park there!" In many countries, this is very common. To be honest, this was one of the reasons I decided to head back home to the US.

18

RENEGADE

Shortly after my return to Los Angeles, I received some bad news. My dear friend and former drummer, Tony Thompson, was in the hospital. He'd always had something bothering him around the stomach area but was told it was nothing, probably from working out too much at the gym. It was never taken seriously. One day he insisted on taking a closer look to see what was up, and it turned out he had kidney cancer.

Everyone who had worked with him was saddened by this and offered to help. Like many musicians, he didn't have medical insurance. Fundraising efforts were put in place, special events to try to save his life. Artists such as Madonna, Nile Rodgers, and many others, including myself, made efforts and contributions to help. Unfortunately, the cancer had been found too late to do anything about it. He passed on November 12, 2003, two months after the death of his Power Station bandmate Robert Palmer from a heart attack.

That was a very sad day for many, and the loss of an iconic figure who had helped redefine disco. He was one of the very few drummers to become legendary, even in the rock world. He played on countless hits and was even asked to perform with Led Zeppelin for their reunion.

I had kept in touch with Steven Van Zandt on a regular basis. We'd always discuss business over the phone, or I'd tell him of new deals I was making. He'd tell me what he was up to, and we'd just chat or complain about the industry's downfall, pitfalls, and solutions, what we could do to help. We had some very intelligent conversations that lasted sometimes hours on end, and we'd see each other every so often as well. One day, he came out to L.A. from New York, where I was living at the time.

We went to dinner, and he asked me, "Are you tired of making records yet?"

At that point, I had made lots of records—either as producer, writer, solo artist, or band member.

I said, "Actually, yes." I'd had so many releases at that point that I truly felt I needed a break.

He said, "Well, why don't you come run my company?"

I said, "Oh, tell me about this."

"You already know my company, Renegade Nation, as we've talked about it extensively. It has all the departments that I mentioned, including my syndicated radio show, which goes out to over two hundred affiliates across the States and around the world. There's also an agency, and I'd like to try to get bands out on the road. It needs to be based on sponsorship dollars. I'm also working on a lot of other things, including TV and film."

At the time, I had gone back to L.A. to pursue acting more seriously. I had previously been offered several roles, including one Jimi Hendrix role and a significant role in *The Mask* starring Jim Carrey in his first film, and Cameron Diaz, whom the director Chuck Russell had just discovered.

Chuck really shared a lot with me, and he was looking forward to having me involved. He had been sending me drafts of the film for a couple of years, and they were really good. Finally, he sold the concept and called me.

He came to my home in Malibu, and he was writing my parts in my office with me! I was in the middle of all the Interscope, KISS, and divorce drama, so I wasn't as focused as I should have been. I had to leave for Berlin exactly when he wanted to move forward with some filming. I couldn't get back in time to fit his schedule, and I wasn't in the best state of mind, nor seeing things clearly.

He moved forward without me, but he was very disappointed. When I got back, it was of course too late, and he was not happy when we spoke.

I called him again after the movie became that year's smash to see what he'd be doing next. I was in a much better state.

He invited me to a party at his house, but he wasn't open to offering me another role. I understood, and we just amicably enjoyed the party. This was one of the biggest career mistakes I've made.

I did some cameo parts for films such as the Vin Diesel film *A Man Apart*, which was directed by John Herzfeld; *Cellular*, a Kim Bassinger film; and a couple of other TV shows basically to get back into SAG (the Screen Actors Guild) and to really start going for it. Once I was in, I was about to start looking into some serious roles when Steven Van Zandt's offer came.

He said, "Ah, don't bother with that. We'll make our own films, we'll do our own TV shows. Rather than spending your time doing this, we'll star in them." So, to be honest, this sounded like a good opportunity.

Steven was always the kind of guy that wanted things to start promptly. So I asked him, "Well, when would you want me to start?"

He said, "How about Monday?" I said, "OK, what do we do?"

He said, "You'll need to move into an apartment in New York, but you can start by flying from Los Angeles to New York to work during the week and stay in a hotel or short-term apartment in the meantime."

So, I did just that on a weekly basis. I'd leave Los Angeles on a red-eye Sunday night to be in New York Monday morning. I'd stay in New York for the week, and then I'd fly home Friday to be with my family. My son, Darius, had recently been born in October, so it was really hard to leave him every week for so long.

As the CEO of this company, everything was first class, which was great. The offices were on Thirty-Fourth Street, and it was a great loft space. It was a light, airy, and vibrant office with the desks spread around the room. There were Underground Garage and Renegade posters hung around the place, which I hadn't ever seen, even though we spoke all the time. I never knew what the insides of his operations were like or all the details of what he'd been doing for all these years.

I was introduced to all the employees in the office as the new boss, or, technically, the underboss as he was the owner and chairman.

The first day was spent getting situated, and I was given a nice corner office. A couple of the girls helped me pick out the furniture, set it up, got my music system together, and helped me with anything else I needed. This was the first time I had worked at a company as the CEO and managing director, besides my own companies. It felt good, and it was a welcome change from what I had been doing before, which seemed to be getting harder and harder.

I was also pretty good at reading bullshit, probably from the many years of watching it get shoveled in my face! Initially, Steven literally asked me to get on calls that were happening with brands and the like and let him know, without being involved, what it was all about—whether it was a good or bad deal, what the guy was thinking, what I thought their motives or agendas were, and what I felt would or could happen in the future. He always looked at me as the "consigliere."

I rather enjoyed my role. It was exciting, and it was a good way for me to hear firsthand what was happening with certain deals and see what I could bring to the table. After our business calls, I'd report to him, and it was usually valid and useful information. We continued doing that for a while, and then I slowly started to take over negotiations, contracts, and writing the agreements, at times, for the different ventures of the company. It was also my job to try and save the company money, so I made a lot of cuts and reductions, which brought about big savings for Renegade.

I started getting into making certain deals, including sponsorship deals with companies like FYE, Best Buy, and Olympus—some unprecedented deals, to be honest. I also handled renewing and restructuring deals with Pepsi and the Hard Rock Cafe while creating new initiatives every year and getting them to renew. There were many, many clients that we had approached on a sponsorship basis, and many that we brought on board. The core of the company was Little Steven's Underground Garage radio show and the two twenty-four-seven channels we had on Sirius XM, two of the very first.

I had already received a rundown of what the company was doing from Steven while still in L.A., but here I got a chance to really dig in and get inside of all the activities. Steven knew that I was proficient with contracts and legal issues. He would always be intrigued at the way I would structure deals or how I would insert certain protections. He just liked the way my mind worked in that aspect, so that was going to be a major part of my role in the company.

I was also to take a look at the financial and structural aspects of the company, including the divisions, the corporations, and all other facets. I started bringing in people who I knew could help, including Jerry Eisner, a very good accountant. Steven had been working with big accounting firms that charged monthly and pretty much only did his taxes without providing any other real benefits.

I just felt that this was not the right way to go. As I always loved the contrast, I thought it would be beneficial to bring in a real street accountant for our business. I met Jerry through a woman named Carol Green who was involved with Richard Manitoba's bar. Jerry was a guy from Long Island, and his accounting chops were on the money. I let the other accounting firms go, and he became our new guy.

The next thing I looked at was our legal structure, and he had a similar situation there. I felt that the legal costs were far too high, so I implemented new practices in that department. I took over a good part of the legal myself, as well as hiring a house attorney for other things that needed to be done. I did, however, keep the big law firms involved for certain contracts or advice we'd need, but their involvement was minimized.

The attorney that I brought in was a young Haitian girl, Natalie Jean-Baptiste. She had just gotten her license and passed the bar with honors, so I felt it was a good thing to give someone like her this opportunity. Steven concurred. She was smart and talented, so she learned quickly and was able to fulfill our obligations, quite easily, most of the time.

The good thing was that she was young and not yet set in her ways, so she was still open to any and all unorthodox agreements I might have thrown at her, of which there were many! For as long as I can remember, I've had an affinity for fixing, addressing, and teaching a lesson to people who took advantage of others for whatever reason, or because they thought they had the power to do so. As I was fortunate enough to get my schooling in this aspect very young, I've always felt it my duty to protect the less knowledgeable, to share wisdom and experience with people who needed it. Friends and acquaintances knew they could call me if they found themselves in an awkward legal situation, if they were confused or unsure if they should take that deal, buy that story, accept those terms, and so on. I've always given my advice and help gratis if it would help someone circumvent a dangerous situation.

At this stage, traveling from L.A. to New York weekly was becoming pretty stressful. In addition, my mom had fallen ill and was living in Hollywood, Florida, so I found myself flying from New York to Florida and then back to New York, skipping L.A. some weeks altogether.

I came to the realization that it was time to move, and that living in Florida would be a lot easier on everyone. It was much closer to New York (a two-and-a-half-hour flight), easier to go to Europe as I often did, and Haiti was also only a couple of hours away. In fact, it was a pretty central location for me. Key West at this point felt a bit too isolated, and I really didn't like the East Coast of Florida—meaning Miami, Fort Lauderdale, or really any of it. Palm Beach, the island, was one of the few places I really liked over there.

I just opened a map on my computer one day and looked around Florida. Naples showed up, so I clicked on it. It was a beautiful, quaint place, with everything pristine, everything I liked. I immediately found a broker, picked some homes to go check out, and started my quest!

Arriving in Naples was enlightening. Everything was just so clean and neat, yet it had a lot of personality. On Fifth Avenue, for example, which is the main street in downtown Naples, there were a great selection of restaurants, little shops, and other attractions. There were some amazing houses in neighborhoods such as Port Royal, long sought after by celebrities and CEOs. I found out that over 50 percent of the world's richest CEOs have homes in Naples, and that Port Royal, in particular, is named the most exclusive and most expensive neighborhood in the United States by the *Robb Report*. Besides all the money there, which actually wasn't my motivation or that important to me, it's just a beautiful place. Schools are great, and it seems like you're removed from all the bad that exists elsewhere in the States.

So, I bought us a home, got out of L.A., and moved in to our new house in Florida. It was a beautiful house on a golf course and a great way to start with our new baby onboard.

The funny thing is that so few people knew about Naples, at least that's what I thought! When I started flying back and forth to New York, there were only a few seats in the first-class cabin, and I started meeting guys I worked with at Pepsi and major advertising agencies. They'd all be right there on that plane doing the same weekly commute that I was doing.

I always liked places that were as un–rock 'n' roll as possible. Conservative, quaint, beautiful—everything that you would think is the opposite of rock 'n' roll or punk. I believe it's the contrast that I dig. I don't know why, but some of my friends, such as Paul Stanley or other celebrity friends, also seem to feel the same way. All that said, I couldn't help but notice that there were very few Black people on the streets—like none—unless they worked in a kitchen or at Publix. Things haven't changed that much down here.

That disturbed me, and it was the first time I actually noticed it, but since I've always managed to make my way in so many of these situations before, I didn't pay it much mind. When I do think about it, however, there wasn't one Black family living in my neighborhood or anywhere in the vicinity, either. Sounds like my childhood, right?

When I bought my house, I had a broker find me a place that was not yet on the market in the neighborhood I wanted to be in. I remember seeing the daughter of the seller come out of the house one day, and I thought for the first time, "They're never going to sell me this house! Not a chance!" I kept that thought to myself.

Well, how wrong I was. Parents Tom and Barbara, daughter Kristin, and the rest of the family not only sold me the house but offered to help in every respect and turned out to be the most amazing people you would ever meet. They were originally from Wisconsin, and they've remained some of our best friends. It's never too late to learn valuable lessons. Do not prejudge people or assume. I remember a saying, when you assume, you make an "Ass of U and Me"!

I hadn't come across many problems being in an interracial relationship, nor had I been openly discriminated against for quite some time, but I did feel the most prejudice of anywhere I've lived down in Naples. Granted, I've really played down the celebrity aspect and pretty much disguised myself as a normal guy, whatever that is, and if that's possible! It gives me a certain freedom and the chance to see how I'd be treated if I weren't a higher-profile individual. Let me tell you, it's not good! But I can't say this comes as much of a surprise. It gives me deeper insight as to what many Black Americans have to endure on a daily basis.

Life is a potpourri, however, and it throws you for a loop every time. While this place was definitely mostly conservative Republican with some old South mixed in, wouldn't you know it, a journalist discovered that I had a house here and reached out to my office for an interview. A fun interview it was! I was placed on the front covers of both papers, the *Naples Daily News* and *News-Press*, the two biggest publications in Southwest Florida, plus a full-page cover in the entertainment section, Mohawk and all! Usually, there'd be a story about Obama in that spot, or Trump!

I have to say that I was shocked, but I have to give credit to Charles Runnells, the reporter who did the article, as well as the editor or whoever made that impressive decision. "Ahhh! Honey, honey! Look, look! A Black punk rooster icon moved here!" I'm sure it added some color to all the readers' lives that day.

The piece was to highlight a New Year's extravaganza that I was headlining in a newly opened Southwest Florida venue. Many attended that night, including our mayor, Peter Simmons. We became good friends after that.

For my kids, I wanted Darius to have the best upbringing and education he could possibly have, without any of the challenges I had to endure as a child. I also wanted a safe haven for my family. Two years later, my daughter, Izabel, was born, so this place became even more suitable for now raising two kids.

I also had a beautiful apartment in Trump Tower, New York. The family came up to visit from time to time, but the Naples move made things much easier for seeing my mom and helping her get treatment. She had hepatitis C, and her liver was scarred to next to nothing. She had gone through breast cancer before that, a stroke, and now this! It was terrible and truly disheartening watching her slowly decline. My mom and I were always very close, and even through the bad times when my dad refused to see me, she was always there as much as she could be under the circumstances.

When Darius was born, she was there, and it was a wonderful thing that she had the opportunity to spend some time with her grandson. Our amazing rottweiler, Sasha, was also with us at the time. She had lived in Key West, Berlin, L.A., and now Naples. She was so good and protective of that little toddler running about the floor, it was amazing to watch. My mom still lived in Hollywood, Florida, but she would come visit and spend weeks with us. It was only an hour and forty-five minutes away.

It came time where it was imperative for my mom to have a liver transplant. I remember her looking me in the eyes and just saying, "Darling, I don't want another liver, please save it for someone young who will need it. I've lived a full and beautiful life, had wonderful children, but I feel I've lived long enough, please let me go in peace." As hard as it was to swallow, that was her wish. I understood her and respected her decision.

In her time spent in Hollywood, she did have spare time and would sometimes get herself into trouble, like buying a $3,000 vacuum cleaner from some door-to-door salesman. I'd have to go and get her money back. She also succumbed to the Jehovah's Witnesses, and they had her pretty deeply involved. At first, I didn't think much of it and felt, *Great, it's something to occupy her mind when we're not together.* But it was truly disappointing when she arrived in hospice with her family around her, and, as distraught as we were, people from her Jehovah's Witnesses group would be at the hospital, sneaking around, trying to get her to sign anything and everything she had over to them—on her dying bed, while she could barely speak! I found that appalling.

My mother, Eddie Sylvain Beauvoir, left this world on April 3, 2006.

A funeral was held shortly thereafter, and as she wished, we took her ashes out on a beautiful boat near Marco Island, Florida, and spread them in the ocean. The ocean was something that my mom and I had very much in common.

As I continued my work at Renegade, I was proud of some of the deals I was able to make happen. One was a deal with Best Buy. Steven and I had been discussing having our own section in record stores for a while. I was trying to find the proper partner to make that happen. Best Buy, one of the biggest retailers in the US, housing a fairly large music section in almost every one of their thousand-plus stores, was one of the first targets.

I ended up connecting with Lon Lindeman, a top executive at Best Buy, who was known for being ahead of the curve when it came to marketing ideas for his brand. We went back and forth for a while based on my original proposal to him, but we finally came to an agreement. We forged ahead toward a different and unprecedented deal: Renegade would receive a hundred slots and the prominent endcap display in all Best Buy stores in the US. In return, they would buy product from us—no returns—plus buy time from us to have that section promoted on our *Little Steven's Underground Garage* radio show.

It was a very good deal that had never been achieved before—by anyone, anywhere. I was especially proud of that one. Steven was ecstatic, as that's exactly what he wanted, but with perks, including getting paid to have it!

These were the kind of deals I enjoyed making—deals nobody else thought of that went against all the people crying, "But you can't do this, you can't do that, blah, blah, blah. If you want to have record slots, Jean, you'll need to pay for them."

I'd be thinking, *Thanks for the newsflash and telling me what I already know. You go on doing that.*

After this, I had major and independent labels calling me constantly asking to get slots in our section, most of them completely miffed as to how the hell we got that section in the first place. I didn't believe in rules or things that couldn't be done. I'd start from scratch with every deal, and I would never follow in anyone else's footsteps or subject myself to any limitations that others have accepted.

Such limitations often came from attorneys. They became so accustomed to a deal structure that they'd use over and over again for artists, and it literally became a template. Then when I'd walk in, eliminating a third of the clauses and revising it completely, they sometimes looked at me like I was crazy.

"That's never gonna happen. They don't do that," they'd say.

Meanwhile, Steven would be nodding yes in the corner.

Some of my attorneys enjoyed it and were up for it, however. Now, mind you, this indicates absolutely no disrespect for my attorneys over the years. I've been fortunate enough to be represented by the best and most powerful entertainment law firms in the US and around the world, and they all, most certainly, know their stuff! Let's just say that often, they have a lot more cobwebs to get through than I do: who they're already in bed with, or the last similar deal they made with a particular company—where they might feel awkward presenting an entirely different contract to that company, a company that, in the past, said no to certain clauses, so they anticipate pushback, and they wouldn't want to try. So as an artist or businessman, you have to think of their position sometimes when negotiating an agreement on your behalf.

It's like a musician who's not formally trained. He's not stuck in those musical limitations. For example, the Beatles were never musically trained. They never learned to read music, and everything they knew they learned by ear. This is much more common and applies to more of the biggest artists in the world than you'd think.

The Beatles created chords, sounds, and note combinations that would, perhaps, be taboo to a classically trained musician. It allowed them to create unique pieces of music that will live on forever and to become the most successful group ever.

Someone created dissonant chords, minor and major chords, major fifths, augmented chords, and everything else. They didn't just fall out of the sky in a notebook for everyone to learn. That's what originality is—experimenting by doing things that have not been done before, just like Thomas Edison did when he invented the incandescent lightbulb. He didn't go to school to learn how to do it. He had to try, fail, and finally create and invent it—just like every other creator or inventor that has given us the wealth of everyday items and luxuries that we all have and oftentimes take for granted.

There's nothing wrong with people going to schools to learn what has already been invented and perfected, like a violinist going to Juilliard or Berkeley to learn what already exists and has been performed by thousands around the world. Perhaps he or she becomes the best at that reproduction, and that has its purpose in the world. Now, should that violinist be of an overly creative nature, he or she can go on to use what he or she has learned and further incorporate that genius to create and invent something new, utilizing that tutelage for a better good and breaking new ground. Not many, however, have that ability.

What the world always needs more of are those inventors and creators, or originality would simply cease. The best creators and inventors usually start with no limitations to work from or use only parts of something that already exists.

For some reason, after I left high school and my cover bands, where I always incorporated original songs, when a guitarist or other musician would be at a rehearsal with me and they'd start playing cover songs, I could feel my hairs stand up, and I'd get really annoyed and uncomfortable, like something out of my control. This also happened when singers would constantly sing cover songs around me. I'm not sure why my very being reacted in this way.

Although I've played covers before, and even recorded some, I noticed that whenever a guitarist, for example, starts playing in my presence, I'm immediately writing a song. I'm very sensitive to people's presences. When I'd walk into a rehearsal space, before the person I'm working with even plays a note, I'll hear and write three or four songs in my head. As soon as I see them or they're close to me, songs start coming to me that are specific to them.

This kind of thing happens often, and there have been very few artists I've written with where the results were not as positive—less than a handful. I guess that's pretty good odds.

A venue that personifies this striving for originality, CBGB, was facing a fight against a landlord who was raising the rent, forcing Hilly Kristal to give up the long-loved space. Being from the Plasmatics, producing the Ramones, working with Debbie Harry, and loving the New York punk scene, CBGB was an important part of my youth. I had been a regular there, and I knew Hilly pretty well.

It was a venue that was very dear to me. Steven was a fan of that era as well, so in commemoration of the club, we decided to put together a charity CD and bring in some of the world's greatest artists to contribute songs to the album. It would be the first product in our new Best Buy section!

The bands who graciously contributed songs to our cause included U2, Foo Fighters, Blondie, Green Day, Patti Smith, Good Charlotte, Talking Heads, Audioslave, Velvet Revolver, the Damned, and the Ramones. We included the controversial and award-winning Ramones track, "My Brain Is Hanging Upside Down," the song that I cowrote and produced. The CD was *CBGB Forever*, and it was personally endorsed by Hilly Kristal. The proceeds went toward the fight for CBGB, but despite all our efforts, this fight was ultimately lost. The truth is that I spent a lot of time personally trying to convince the gentleman who initially wanted to close down the club to not do so. He was a real estate developer and clothing mogul. I was ecstatic about the prospect of reversing the situation. We would speak on the phone night after night and meet to the point where I had convinced him to buy the club and keep it as it was. He came to understand the value and importance of CBGB after our talks, to the point where he made an offer, which was actually accepted. Doing his due diligence, he realized that documents and licenses were not in order in several countries, which he felt were important to protect and preserve the brand. So he called me one night to inform me he was backing out! That was very bad news, but convincing him otherwise was futile. I was disappointed to say the least. He later called me quite upset one night about the outcome and went from not knowing or understanding anything about the history and significance of the club to informing me that thanks to our talks, he went ahead and bought the brand Max's Kansas City.

We did many innovative and successful things with Renegade, including MTV Battle of the Bands and a Cheap Trick or Treat Halloween Ball, which was filmed at the Hard Rock's newly built venue in Hollywood, Florida. One of our biggest undertakings was an ABC/ESPN New Year's Eve television special that we produced in 2005. I was an integral part of making that a reality and worked very closely with David Saltz, ABC Television, ESPN, many lawyers for the bands, and various clearances that had to be obtained. We had to work with the city to get special permits to close off full blocks adjacent to the ball drop for our recording trucks, dressing rooms, and green rooms.

Hard Rock International was a partner, and the show was hosted by ESPN's Stuart Scott and Little Steven atop the NY Hard Rock's awning, which was directly across from the ball drop. We had our bands performing, including the New York Dolls and the Troggs (performed "Wild Thing" on the mayor's stage). We included our Garage Girls a Go-Go dancers, all performing in Times Square in cooperation with *Dick Clark's New Year's Rockin' Eve* to more than eight million viewers.

We also arranged for *The Sopranos* TV show closing party to be held at the location in Hollywood, Florida. Hard Rock Hollywood's team were wonderful longtime dedicated sponsors of the show, and I personally became quite close with the CEO of Seminole Gaming and Chairman of Hard Rock International, Jim Allen. He is a remarkable man who went from being a franchisee in Hollywood, Florida, with his Hard Rock Hotel and Casino, to ultimately purchasing the entire brand globally, including worldwide hotels, casinos, cafés, and all merchandising, on behalf of the Seminole Indians. It's been hugely successful, generating billions of dollars per year.

I also became very close with Dave Miller, who mainly ran the Tampa Hard Rock Hotel and Casino, which was also going through the roof solely from slot machines at the start, previous to their obtaining the exclusive license for gambling in Florida, as well as Henry Pisano, an entertaining guy who handled casino operations in the Hollywood location and worked closely with Jim Allen. Not to mention the other wonderful executives I worked with here and around the world.

I secured deals with them such as including CDs for sale in all the rooms and guitar-shaped jerky, produced by my brother's and my company that I placed in all the in-room minibars. We worked on a variety of initiatives together over the years. It was an exciting partnership, and Jim was always forthcoming, honest, and open to ideas or deals I'd present.

I made a similar deal with FYE as the one I made with Best Buy. I remember the woman that I worked with there, Jodie Evans, SVP of all Entertainment for Trans World Entertainment / FYE. She was tough but a real pleasure to do business with, a smart and effective executive and lady.

I also became close with the Pepsi team and remained so even after my departure from the company. Same with the NASCAR guys I met—Chris Stewart, Tom Knox, and Jason Garrow were really great to work with, and those relationships also survived my departure.

One memorable day, I went to a *Sopranos* shoot in Jersey. I was in a scene in the Bada Bing, but I never actually saw it. James Gandolfini found out I was from the Plasmatics. He was a fan, so he offered to take me out that night to hang out. We headed out and had a great time! A night of debauchery, I must add, which took us into the wee hours of the morning. I even remember us climbing through someone's window! We went all over, talked and talked till we could talk no more, at least I couldn't! I was definitely out of practice when it came to all-nighters with a full day of meetings booked for the next day. I told him I just had to go and bailed when the sun came up. I remembered that feeling all too well! We did have a blast—he was for sure a fun and entertaining guy! Everyone started calling me the next day asking where he was, where I left him, as he was supposed to be on set that morning! I actually didn't know! Turns out he showed up a day or two later.

An interesting trip I took during my tenure was to Beijing, China. Steven and I were invited to meet with parliament about the possibility of a partnership with Little Steven's radio show. It was a very long flight. Steven stayed about two days, and I stayed an extra few days for follow-up meetings.

The parliament meeting was a riot! They had several women who'd constantly serve us these alcoholic shots that were strong as hell! We kept asking serious questions, trying to get information and get into business, especially Steven asking specific questions about the parliament, which they never seemed to answer. It was quite amusing actually. We were getting drunker and drunker by the minute from these shots and their constant toasting where they would shout "Ganbei!" (cheers) at every turn.

We were then taken to dinner where they presented us with a veritable smorgasbord of Chinese specialties. It wasn't easy choosing what to eat, as the only thing we recognized was rice and roast duck! I may have seen some chicken feet in there somewhere! I had the opportunity do some sightseeing, going to the wall, markets, and even Inner Mongolia to watch some authentic Chinese performers. It was over the top and without a doubt a trip to remember. A strange thing I remember is that I didn't see one bird anywhere in sight during the entire journey into the mountains! Not one! I found that extremely odd and always wondered what that was about.

During my time with Renegade, I met some great people and some not-so-great people. Some tried backing out of deals at the last minute, and others made some unethical moves, but ultimately, I'd say we got the last word more often than not. Working in an office was an immediate change from being an artist where you run your company, make your own hours, and work at your own leisure, even though that can still be very intense and time consumming.

Sometimes as a self-employed person running your own company you don't know when to stop, and you just keep going and going around the clock. At least here, you kind of had a fixed time—though to be honest, I would spend most of my time in the office, and Steven would, too. When we'd go home from the office, we'd get back on the phone most nights and just catch up on the day, discuss new ideas, new plans, and things we wanted to do, so this was a real full-time job.

The radio show was based on selling a certain amount of time on Steven's show, which was a two-hour weekly program going out to about 230 different affiliates within the United States and more around the world. We also had two twenty-four-seven channels on Sirius Satellite Radio, which became Sirius XM. The main executives I dealt with were Scott Greenstein, who was an old friend, and Steve Blatter, with whom I had a very good working relationship. I handled all negotiations including our on-air talent, which included Joan Jett, Kim Fowley, and Kid Leo.

For example, working with NASCAR gave us the opportunity to go to North Carolina, meet Richard Childress and his race team, and get a bird's-eye view of everything that happened with NASCAR. As I remember, I was invited to South Carolina for some meetings in regard to a partnership, and believe it or not, Steven and some others in my office were very concerned about me going there.

Racial issues still resonated in everyone's mind, and we were wondering seriously if it would be safe for me. It turned out that it was, and as a matter of fact, it was one of my most surprisingly endearing experiences.

When I got on the NASCAR track, I was nervous looking at the hundred thousand people in the stands. I got some hearty cheers when I stepped out on that track, which was surprising to me. There were very, very few Blacks at a NASCAR race, as you can imagine, but it was great, and the people I worked with—Tom, Jason, and Chris, were very cool making sure that my team and I were totally taken care of.

It was actually even more ironic when one night while on that visit, I decided to head out to a bar. People were telling me, "Oh, don't do that. Don't do that, stay in!" The first place I walked into was kind of a pub. It looked really cool, kind of punky, and wouldn't you know it, I went to order a drink and directly behind the bartender was a huge Plasmatics poster with me on it!

I couldn't believe it! I thought, *Wow, times have changed!* As soon as folks in the place found out I was there, everyone started coming over to meet me and get autographs and photos. I left with a completely different perception than I came with, which will last me a lifetime.

Another highlight that ensued was while Steven and I were on a trip in Norway for some other business. Our attaché for Norway was Therese Asker (aka MissFixit), a vibrant, energetic young lady who, in all seriousness, would schedule her days off following a party if she knew she'd be drinking! Efficient as hell, though! She informed me of a couple who had an interesting TV script about a Mafioso placed into the witness protection program in Norway—specifically Lilyhammer, a quaint ski resort town.

I found the concept compelling and agreed to book the meeting for Steven and me with the writers, Anne Bjornstad and Elif Skodvin. At the time, we were on a trip shopping an international producer TV series that we had written and were to both star in. We had received a green light from two of the production companies we met with at the Grand Hotel in Oslo.

I did realize that *Lilyhammer* could be a conflict and would probably ruin my chances of being on-screen in a series but didn't really give that much thought.

We listened as they shared their idea, and it was a good one. After the meeting, Steven told me in his usual tone, "No way am I gonna do some TV show in the fuckin' cold in Norway!" I laughed, as usual. I personally liked the concept and thought it would be a great move for him and, what with him being my dear longtime friend, I wanted to see him score something soon. I saw a shot here for him to get what he'd been yearning for.

Steven was not an easy person to convince. I kept bringing it back up, but he was still dead against it. This was far from the first time I'd experienced his resistance towards proposals that were good for him. As CEO of the company, I had a lot on my plate, but this proposal stayed on my mind. After me pushing relentlessly, he agreed to at least await their offer. His expectations were low, though, and he was probably thinking the anticipated lowball offer would get me off his back!

A gentleman named Lasse Hallberg from the production company Rubicon was spearheading the project and serving as the executive producer. He reached out to me with a proposed fee which was, indeed, too low to consider and offered no further incentives.

Of course, Steven said, "You see, Jonny, fuggedaboutit, no way!"

I told him, "Ignore that figure, Steven, I'll pursue and see what I can do."

He reiterated, "What the fuck am I gonna do in the fuckin' snow in Norway, Jonny? Forget it and let's move on to other things on our plate."

He was only interested in scoring an American TV series, which did not seem to be in the cards at that time. I knew that *Lilyhammer* would be quite an undertaking, but we needed something to shuffle those cards a bit. Things just weren't clicking in the US like Steven wanted, even with CAA on board and the massive success of *The Sopranos* under his belt. It made no sense to me, but that's how life works sometimes. You never know what that eye in the sky has in mind, the bigger plan. I told him, "You never know how things happen, Steven, sometimes you have to go the long way around to get what you want here"—as had been proven many times before! But it fell upon deaf ears.

After some reflection, I was certain that there was no way they could do this show successfully without him or someone else from *The Sopranos* or a similar show. The actor would need the necessary knowledge and experience to bring to the table for the show to work, at least in my mind. So at this point, I was on a mission! But to be honest, while I was confident of my negotiation skills, I had never negotiated a TV series deal before, so I was a bit at a loss.

When I returned to NY, my first call was to our attorney. I wanted to pick his brain and get an idea of where to start. I asked him what he felt would be a win for Steven, in line with TV industry standards for a series such as this one. He told me that 5 percent would be extraordinary. Once I had that number, I knew I was on my own! I thought to myself, *Just do what you always do, Jean, it doesn't matter if it's TV. Fuck the rules and other actors' deals and go for what you feel in your gut is deserved.* Looking at all that was on the table. I felt strongly that Steven's participation was worth far more than that! I felt he should be an equal partner at 50 percent, and I had a strong pitch to support it.

I set a meeting with Lasse and the Rubicon team to discuss the matter further in Norway. I was met at a location in the center of Oslo, and they escorted me to their offices—"not too far away," they said! I remember the perilous journey for about half an hour through snow, ice, and treacherous stairs, all while sporting the high-heeled snakeskin boots I'd often wear, anticipating falling on my ass at any given point! Scandinavians love to walk, so they say, "Oh, the office is right around the corner," but it never is! They'll have you walking for miles rather than jumping in a taxi! After this trek, we finally arrived at the office of Jan Morten, their attorney. Perhaps their objective was to wear me out prior to the meeting to soften me up!

I entered the room and sat across from the Rubicon team, which included Lasse, who would be executive producer for the show, Jan Morten, and other executives from Rubicon. I was the sole representative from our side. Following cordial introductions, I proceeded to explain in detail that I felt Steven should receive 50 percent of all income and why!

At first, they looked at me as if I was severely delusional! An expression I'd grown accustomed to over the years. I explained that this was an opportunity that they'd never had before and how Steven, a recognized figure from an uber successful international TV series, would add significant value to their cast and would also potentially mark the first real

TV cooperation between the US and Norway of its kind! And in turn, this would heighten their visibility on the world stage and open doors significantly for future cooperation with the US.

Someone mentioned that there was another cast member from *The Sopranos* that they could potentially bring onboard for what was offered. I shot that down, but it sure didn't make the negotiations any easier! I continued by mentioning how the publicity would be massive and the long-term benefits derived from this collaboration for the company, network, and country would far outweigh my humble request.

At the time, Norway was having difficulty trying to gain credibility in the entertainment sphere, with their neighbor Sweden having so much success with music and for so long. At this time, A-ha had been Norway's last claim to fame. One of my goals was to help Norway achieve a competitive presence, like we had previously discussed with Trond Giske, the then–minister of culture, but had not yet achieved. In my mind, this was much bigger than just getting Steven an acting role.

I went on to say how this deal would be groundbreaking and would help to put them on the international map in the TV and entertainment world. I also proposed Steven's inclusion in the writing, based on his experience with *The Sopranos*, which had given him in-depth knowledge of the inner workings of the Jersey mob, and explained how this would be key to the success of the show. For good measure, I requested an executive producer credit for Steven, which I always insisted on anyway. I was unsure, truthfully, as to how they would reenact the story authentically without him or someone else who had similar experiences or abilities.

They listened openly as I spoke for a fair amount of time. I was convinced it was worth 50 percent, and I knew if I could pull this off, Steven would be ecstatic. It would give him another shot in the TV world, contrary to his belief.

We took a break and after some deliberation, they came back in and said, "OK, we discussed, understand your point of view, and agree." I held back my excitement and told them I'd come back to them.

I flew back to NY, went to the office, pulled Steven aside, and said, "Guess what I got you?

"Whaa?"

"Fifty percent of everything! Will you do the show now?"

He grinned at me in amazement. I could see in his face that he couldn't believe it. He said, "OK."

So now, we were prepared to move forward. I felt great, of course, as I really loved making deals like this, breaking down barriers and changing the game.

I still had some issues I wanted to resolve to finalize, as I knew there'd be a lot of downtime while writing and so forth before things could get rolling, so Lasse flew into NY for a two-hour meeting. He and I finalized and drafted the deal memo, which contained all agreed points for the cooperation. I had a very good feeling about this and truly believed it could be successful. Norway was already in place to air the show on the National TV channel, NRK, with a substantial budget for filming already allocated. In theory, the other territories would just be gravy, and Lasse and I were already discussing a plan for distribution in the open territories. I felt the whole concept was unique and exciting.

Not long after this negotiation, I parted ways with Steven and Renegade. But the terms I'd fought for were honored, the deal was consummated, and Steven went on to do the show in Norway.

Lilyhammer was revolutionary, in terms of both the unique deal I negotiated for Steven and the show becoming the first Netflix-original TV series. It boasted three successful seasons of eight episodes each and accumulated multiple awards around the world, including "Best TV Drama" and "Best Male Actor." The show was a smash, making them a shitload of money!

I watched its success, and I wasn't surprised to see that I wasn't credited or mentioned anywhere. But I must admit, it was disappointing and disheartening, as this was, without a doubt, one of my better negotiations. I never watched the show.

In retrospect—and thinking selfishly—if I hadn't forged forward and pushed as hard as I did for *Lilyhammer*, we might have consummated a deal for our producer show. But—perhaps stupidly—that wasn't my style. I felt *Lilyhammer* was simply the better idea.

As with most experiences in my life, my time with Renegade was educational and armed me with more knowledge and experience. My departure allowed me the freedom and time to pursue the life I had put on hold. I really wanted to pursue cementing my legacy and further promoting my work, my own brand and me. I went back to Florida to resume pursuing my own goals and aspirations—and I've been doing so ever since.

19

DAD'S INFLUENCE & OUR CONNECTION TO THE ARTS

THOUGH I MAY HAVE MADE MY FATHER out to be such a mean, bad daddy—which he could be—he was also the single biggest influence in my life, and we had a very strong connection with the arts that was unique to us. My father always knew that I had something special when it came to music. He badgered me as a child, but with a purpose—he wanted me to be the best I could be. He started "training" me early in his own way by playing me all these legendary records and, in retrospect, showing me that he was actually fifty years ahead of his time in understanding what would stand the test of time. He was never off the mark, from Janis Joplin to the Beatles' *Magical Mystery Tour* to ABBA, Led Zeppelin, the Supremes, James Brown, and others.

Every weekend he'd say, "Sit down, boy, vagabond. Listen to some good music and learn." He had a powerful Marantz stereo system with speakers in all four corners of the room (he was definitely an audiophile). It was, of course, vinyl back then, so you'd feel the room shake as the music played.

He would come to some shows when I was younger, and all he did was criticize and tell me how I was really nothing and had such a long way to go. One day, I played a concert at my school, and it was packed! My dad came to watch, and he saw all the kids running up afterward telling me how great it was. As we headed home, he said, "Don't think you're something because some kids applauded. That was nothing. You're a nothing."

I thought he was discouraging me from continuing in this field, which he probably was. But in reality, perhaps, he was preparing me for what was to come—little did he or I know.

I think, in the end, he may have wanted music for me. He saw it in me, and we had somewhat of an understanding. But in his logical thinking, he decided there was no chance I could succeed in that world under the circumstances. It was just too far-fetched to imagine, even for him, and he had quite an imagination.

Years later, when we reunited, only then was he able to be properly introduced to my music. He was thoroughly and sincerely impressed, as if it awakened some feelings in him. He understood details, ones that you wouldn't think would draw his attention.

Mind you, he had a wonderful baritone voice himself that we'd only hear in the kitchen occasionally when he was cooking. He was also a fantastic accordion player, which we'd hear at special times of the year. Not to mention a great harmonica player and an amazing painter. His oil paintings, in my opinion, were more beautiful than those of top painters from Haiti.

He had a musical yearning within him that seemed to come alive around me. I always respected everything he did, as he was good at lots of things, whether it be building a house, changing an engine in a car, going to get his pilot's license on a whim, being a top-notch engineer, a designer of the World Trade Center, or pretty much achieving anything he set his mind to do. In his head, there were no limitations, except for the ones that were placed on you unfairly by others. I guess me wanting to be a rock star fell into that category in his mind.

After reconnecting years later, he became very familiar with my songs and projects and was extremely supportive. At this point, he was always deeply impressed with anything that I played for him. In his mind, I was with the best of the best, at any level. He met the KISS guys and Nile Rodgers, and he'd go out to clubs with me in L.A. and meet lots of people and other celebrities. He felt a part of the scene and was living a life he would've never thought he'd have the opportunity to experience. He'd sit and speak to Tony Thompson about drums for an hour. As for my Mohawk, he paid it no mind, and he got a kick out of all the crazy clothes I had, though they couldn't be further from his reality!

One of the most poignant moments I remember was when we were in Key West together at my house. He asked me to play a song of mine, "I Keep Holding On." I put it on, and he was actually cleaning a pot or something in the kitchen. I looked at him, and his face was drowned in tears. He was crying as I've never seen him do in my entire life. I asked him, "What's wrong? What's going on?"

He said, "I can't believe something so beautiful can come out of something I created." Few things in my life have ever touched me as this did.

He loved that song, as well as another song called "Happy Birthday" from the Voodoo X album. He was also head over heels about the first Crown of Thorns album, as he was there at that time. Actually, the same thing he used to tell me when I was a child he said when he heard this record for the first time: "This is real music, these players are champion players." He was incredibly impressed and very proud.

He ran back to Haiti and shared this music with all the people around the land where he lived. It was extremely flattering, and of course gave me a lot of satisfaction that I finally had an undisputed seal of approval from my father.

On October 4, 2008, at eighty-one years old, my father left this earth. I had received news of him falling ill. It was a bit mysterious as no one could actually tell me what was wrong. We brought the children to visit when he had a short stay in a hospital in West Palm Beach. He was summoned by his partner and kids in Haiti to return back home, as they wanted him to die there. There was little I could do but go spend some time with him there during his last days, which my brother, sister, and I did. There was a beautiful ceremony on our gorgeous seventy-plus-acre beachfront property in Haiti, with many attendees, including family and townspeople, who he had been so helpful to when he was alive. In my father's case, I can feel his spirit often, as he rests in peace.

20

RECENT YEARS

When an unexpected earthquake devastated Haiti on January 12, 2010, I still had a lot of family living in Haiti.

My cousin Nathalie Brunet, a really together and intelligent woman, was one of my first calls to get info about the damage. She has studied in the States and recently went to Harvard to get her degree. She has two beautiful sons. Her parents, Yves and Nancy, and the whole family there are wonderful people. I'd see them often when I'd visit Haiti.

When my mom passed, she left me a medical clinic to oversee in Haiti. It was completely destroyed, flattened to the ground with no insurance. A silver lining, however, was that it afforded me the opportunity to disengage from the woman who had been managing the clinic. Before the earthquake she was becoming difficult and proving to be a problem. She was starting to feel that the clinic was hers.

We had a shed behind the main building where all our personal belongings had been stored for years—personal items brought from the States when my parents moved to Haiti. That space contained all our childhood photos and Super 8 films (thousands) my dad had taken of the entire family, plus other family heirlooms. One day, she just decided that she wanted that space to use for other purposes. She took it upon herself to burn and throw away all the contents from that room. All our precious memories were lost forever!

I was so angry and upset that I was now dead set on getting her out, but she was being difficult. When the earthquake happened and there was nothing left, she was left with no choice but to leave.

The earthquake came as an utter surprise, devastating a country that was in no way prepared for such a disaster. So many people died, so many were injured, families were torn apart. There was no electricity, no fresh water, nowhere for people to live. People were in dire need of help in so many ways. It was heartbreaking to hear about and to witness.

My relatives on our property in Léogâne, two sons fathered by my dad while he was still married to my mom, Serge and Daniel, and another son, Raoul Jr., born years later, and the mother of all three, Comena, who lived with him after my mom was forced to leave, also suffered from the devastation. The children, all good boys, and Comena, a strong and capable woman, had a lot to contend with. Our property incurred damage; the sea line changed and everything was in shambles. The entire town of Léogâne suffered greatly. My half-brother Daniel was responsible for multiple camps, working with various nonprofit agencies from France and other countries, including the Red Cross. My cousin Nathalie was also very involved in relief efforts working with USAID.

I decided at that point to start my foundation, the Beauvoir Haiti Foundation. I paired up with a wonderful organization out of Orlando, Florida, called Clean the World. They recycle hotel soap and hotel amenities to send to countries in need. The organization was headed up by a smart and creative gentleman, Shawn Seipler, who I had the opportunity to spend a fair amount of time with. I teamed up with Daniel to organize taking the recycled soap and other products and delivering them to camps throughout the region. We did what we could to lend a hand.

We had a plane full of clothing and supplies ready to be sent to Haiti, pledged by Donna Karan through my good friend Camilla Olsen, who has always been prepared to help. Unfortunately, planes were not being allowed to enter at that time, so I was unable to take advantage of this generous gift for the Haitian people. I remained extremely thankful to them for the efforts they made to support our needs and my foundation.

Once I flew down, it was disconcerting to see the devastation and the corruption surrounding this force majeure. I was alerted to the fact that many nonprofits were not willing to even give up full tents as housing and would only donate tent tops to save money.

All the ads in the US about food needed in Haiti, raising millions of dollars, were often misleading. Food was not even allowed into the country by the government and had not been for a long time. The Haitian government, in actuality, felt that food was not the issue and donated food would only hamper the ability for Haitian merchants to continue to earn a living and would compromise the economy. This did not apply to everyone, as there were indeed organizations that brought much-needed medical help, clothing, water, and many other necessities to the country. But others were just lining their pockets and deferring the raised funds to staffing their organizations in other countries or other uses that had nothing to do with the problem at hand.

It was disheartening and demoralizing to observe. I'd walk down the street and want to take a photo of someone living in a tent in one of the camps. That person would say in Creole, "Pa gen foto jiskaske ou peye m" ("No picture until you pay me"). They believed these photos were being taken to go solicit on TV in the US and get money that none of them would ever see. It was sad to hear them say this, but I understood their feelings all too well on this subject.

My dad truly loved my song "I Keep Holding On" and would play it to everyone he'd see or meet in Haiti. I changed some lyrics and made it specifically dedicated to the Haitian earthquake and the people who endured it. A video with photos was used to try to convey the situation and give people in Haiti hope, courage, and belief that they could overcome this tragedy.

The commissioner Samuel B. Ings of Orlando, Florida, who was heavily involved in supporting Haiti, declared an annual holiday to commemorate the losses and pain felt that tragic day, and he wanted me to share my song. He asked me to come perform at a special event in Orlando. I was asked later to perform the song in Seattle for a very concerned, passionate, and captive audience.

It was such a satisfying feeling when I sang that song and showed the video on big screens. I watched the entire hall stand up, giving me a standing ovation, with many in tears as they praised my performance of the song. It's an amazing, heartwarming feeling to cause people to feel something as strongly as they did. This is why I do what I do.

I had started to notice that, at times, having multiple projects on the go could confuse people. Fans who knew me from producing the Ramones didn't know I was the guy from Crown of Thorns, and some people didn't even put together that I was the guy who did "Feel the Heat" if they were a Voodoo X fan, and so on. So to try to clarify things, I decided to release two albums under the moniker Jean Beauvoir entitled *Rock Masterpieces, Vol. 1* and *Vol. 2.* They featured about thirty songs that I'd recorded either as a solo artist or with one of my projects, Crown of Thorns, where I had recorded numerous albums and Voodoo X. As I had written most of those songs and many times played all the instruments and produced, the albums included full credits and information so that folks could see clearly in one place what work I'd done up to that point, as an artist. The albums were thankfully received with rave reviews throughout the rock press.

I decided as well to tour solely as Jean Beauvoir, including songs from my entire catalog, projects, and even titles like "Shocker" that wasn't being performed by anyone, and hit singles that I wrote with KISS, the Ramones, among others.

I also wanted to further pursue television and film (acting and producing TV shows), touring, and writing this book, in addition to taking more time for myself and my family. So much time was lost while at Renegade that I pretty much missed seven years of my kids growing up. I wanted to be around for the next part of their lives.

I noticed that much of my previous work started to gain more attention. The Ramones won the Lifetime Achievement Grammy award, and our songs were getting placements in films and becoming more and more notable. In addition, singles I had written with KISS were really being highlighted, partially due to the ever-loyal KISS fans who rule the rock 'n' roll world.

I felt that it was important for me to inform young Blacks and other minorities of things I had accomplished with the purpose of paving an easier road for those yearning to get into the rock 'n' roll world (or any world, for that matter). I wanted them to know that anything is possible if you put your mind to it.

I started playing big festivals in Europe again, and I realized how much I missed performing and touring, something I regrettably took for granted in the past. Working at Renegade, I felt I had lost my identity. That role prevented me from pursuing interests that were important to me. I did get several offers to appear on TV shows while there, with and without Steven. For example, while I was pitching the Underground Garage TV show, our New York agent called me to say that A&E were not interested in that show, but they were interested in doing a show with me. They had recently done well with *Gene Simmons Family Jewels* and proposed a show idea highlighting the different facets of my life. Rock Star, CEO, and family man. It would have focused on exploring how I managed to balance these different roles on a day-to-day basis.

I knew it wouldn't be deemed appropriate in my current role and Susanne wasn't keen on a crew infiltrating our private life, so I had to let that go. But it was one more reminder of the limitations Renegade placed on me—limitations it was time to rid myself of. I wasn't getting any younger!

I wanted to start writing songs again. For that, I would go to Norway annually and work with a very talented group of producers and writers called Dsign, introduced to me by an old friend and admirer of my work from Sweden, Pelle Lidell, a widely respected and extremely successful CEO and European publishing and A&R executive. Pelle was responsible for over 140 million records sold and the commencement of Swedish songwriting and producer teams, who spawned iconic producers and writers including Denniz Pop, Max Martin, and Andreas Carlsson, who I also worked with. He invited me over to come work with some of his current writing teams, which included Erik Lidbom, Harry Sommerdahl, K-1, and other talented writers. From those collaborations, I achieved two number ones across Asia and on the US *Billboard* charts with the

K-pop group Shinee and the artist Jonghyun. His single was also *Billboard* magazine's most-watched K-pop video in the world. I also had music featured in the world's first hologram musical and soundtrack, *School Oz*.

I served as a judge for the Norwegian National Songwriting Contest alongside Pelle and Uwe Fahrenkrog-Petersen. This was part of what they called a songwriting camp that would span over one week. The winner was chosen by the judges and would receive a publishing agreement with Universal Music Publishing, which Pelle headed up. The following week, the international songwriting camp would begin, where I'd take part as a writer. This camp brought together over a hundred writers in twenty different studios, all working simultaneously. Label executives from Korea to Japan, the US to the UK, and the rest of the world would attend in search of hit songs for their artists. This was very motivating for the writers since songs could be pitched and placed right there.

As not only rock 'n' roll has its quirks, writing pop songs with crazy Scandinavians, Germans, and every other nationality is quite the experience! The camp was held in Trondheim, Norway, and the Norwegians had wine, beer, and alcohol ready to go at 9:00 AM. They'd be drinking all day as if it was Evian. Personally, I don't generally start any drinking until nighttime. God forbid I would start drinking red wine at 9:00 AM—I'd never be able to write shit, plus I'd be passed out by 1:00 PM!

The rooms were separated into teams of four, usually with a producer, a top-liner or two, and someone who could sing the demo (most writers over there are talented singers as well). I ended up in a room with a Norwegian girl, a top-liner guy, and a producer who previously had a huge European dance hit. He came with a big duffel bag, and as we were about to start the session, he pulls out a double-sized vodka bottle and started going at it.

Scandinavians are known for being heavy drinkers, and when I say these people can drink, I mean they can *really* drink. After the bottle was almost empty, he reached into his bag and pulled out a suit—a pink bunny suit with a white cotton tail. He slipped it over his clothes, and with his crazy Finnish-mixed-with-English accent, he started saying the most outlandish things about what he wants to do to the girl we were working with on our team.

He said how he was gonna do it, right then and there, while he was hopping around the room as we were trying to finish this song. These sessions had time limits, and you'd get two to four hours to finish a complete song—recorded and ready to go. Then the teams would switch.

Now, this pink rabbit guy had a personality such that all this wasn't really coming off as offensive, even to the girl! We were all just in tears laughing and trying to comprehend what the hell was going on. In between these outbursts, he'd run back and forth to his laptop, doing more work on the track—and believe it or not, it was good! Finally, as the session wound down, so did Pinky. Right after laying down the mix, he was out of it, and sprawled out on the couch. Thank God it was the last session of the day!

Free from my Renegade obligations, I was able to take the time to really get to know my kids and participate in things that they were doing. I had put my son, Darius, in tae kwon do once he could walk. He was a high-energy kid, and martial arts teach discipline, among other things. I also wanted him to learn, early on, how to protect himself. I can remember him tugging on my leg as we were walking in the dojo, and I believe he was four years old. He trained in tae kwon do for years and achieved his junior black belt, then continued, starting over on the adult level, to eventually receive his second-degree adult black belt at the age of ten years old.

I wanted to share an appreciation of martial arts with my son because during my teens, I boxed in New York, New Jersey, Floyd Patterson's gym, and anywhere else I could find. I later added karate to the mix around the Plasmatics time, and I have trained ever since, finally achieving my black belt.

I later moved on to Muay Thai and mixed martial arts. When working with Renegade, I would arrive in New York at 6:00 AM and go straight to an MMA gym and train before going into the office. When I left Renegade, I had the opportunity to spend more time training. I've always found martial arts to be amazing for the body and mind, and it's played an important part in my life.

I have two dear friends involved in martial arts, Palau Lopes, who has reached eleventh dan in karate. He lives in Gothenburg, Sweden, and we've trained together for years. When I spent time in Gothenburg, I would teach classes with him. My other dear Swedish friend, Pentti Von Fürstenrecht, also a high-ranking black belt, owned a school in a town called Borås in Sweden. He unfortunately was diagnosed with cancer, which stopped activities for him for quite a while. Being one of the first to receive a fairly new procedure at the time, he beat it, thank God.

In Berlin, Germany, I trained mostly in Kyokushin karate, which is full contact, and in New York, besides boxing and MMA, I trained privately with the internationally known Krav Maga grand master Rhon Mizrachi.

One day while training in Naples, Florida, I injured my knee badly, tearing my ACL. I had also further damaged my meniscus pretty severely. It had originally been damaged from wrestling in high school and then again from a car accident.

I had to have surgery and did so with acclaimed Naples sports surgeon Dr. James Guerra, who had been suggested to me by Crafton Wallace, a professional MMA fighter I also trained with for a while.

I had an ACL reconstruction where they used cadaver tissue to recreate the ACL and secured it with two screws. I felt a little like my childhood hero, Evel Knievel! It took me about a year to recover with medicine and rigid physical therapy, which I followed religiously. Thankfully, as the doc had assured me, everything healed, and I was back to normal.

For the record, the martial arts or boxing that I've done during my life has never been because I'm an aggressive person, like to fight, or agree with the violence that is constantly seen and promoted on TV. I am not a fan of this by any means. I've done it for sport, skills, body conditioning, and for my soul.

Now that things had changed, I could also pursue some of my hobbies and passions, like boating and yachting! I've always loved the water, the ocean, and marine life. My mom loved the sea as well, and I reckon I got it from her. Before my mom passed, she did have the chance to spend time with Darius, who was very young and still in a stroller. I would often take her to the beach, as she loved going there. I wish she would've lived longer to see him grow up into the tall, handsome, intelligent, and loving son that he's become.

I also wish she would've been there for our beautiful daughter Izabel's birth. She grew up to be an amazingly talented, beautiful, and very intelligent little girl. Much like Darius, we started her in dance at age four. She was really shy when she was young, and would hardly talk around other people, but meanwhile she was actually able to fully speak at around two years old.

At home around the family, she was far from shy. She would entertain us endlessly, dancing for hours on end and putting on little shows. She was also the most flexible member of the family; she could do full splits, back tucks, and flips at a really young age. She also took gymnastics classes, which she became great at. It got to the point where they wanted her to compete and travel, but it would have just been too much with school and the other activities she had going. Apparently, gymnastics ran in the family; Darius also has mad gymnastics skills.

The first few years of Izabel's life, I only saw her on weekends. When I came home on Fridays and went to get her from school, she barely knew who I was, as I spent such little time at home. Now, I was able to spend those priceless moments with both of our children, and that became the most important thing to me.

She has now grown up to be a beautiful young lady at fifteen years old. She has kept up with dance, and she started competing some years ago. She's also taking acting classes, continuing with gymnastics, and she's a straight A student. She's got a good little head for business, too. I'm extremely proud of her!

I also just wanted to enjoy life without feeling business pressures every damn day. I had to remind myself that this was the reason I decided on rock 'n' roll in the first place. But like most things, nothing is as it seems. I would always say, "We are in the music business, and without business, there is no music."

Since I was a kid, I've always been into motorcycles. I raced motocross when I was young and later got into street bikes, eventually Harleys. So when my son was growing up, I bought him a mini 125cc dirt bike.

We'd take our bikes out to some local tracks, and I'd teach him how to ride. We later got two bigger motocross bikes—for him, a full-size racing Suzuki RM 80 and for me, a Yamaha YZ125 motocross bike. Back to my childhood! They had recently built a professional motocross complex with five different tracks reasonably close to where we lived, so we'd go there to tear it up! We had those bikes for a few years, and that was a lot of fun—a great way for a dad and son to spend time together.

Besides martial arts, Darius had an affinity for basketball. I put him in leagues early on, and he progressed quickly. When he was a baby, his doctor told us that he would be great at all sports. Somehow he knew, and indeed, he is a natural. He played on a travel team (where I was shocked to see that many Black team members had Mohawks, even blond ones!). And the school team as well. When he reached eighth grade, he started playing varsity basketball.

He has since joined the varsity football team as a wide receiver and cornerback, which he loves. We were apprehensive at first about him playing football, even though I had played football in my teens. It's much different now with up to 400-pound sixteen-year-olds charging at you like a bull with one intention—to destroy you! No parent wants to see their kid, a little 150-pound boy, eye to eye with that guy! Yet when he was younger, I felt he needed to play that sport for other reasons. Later in life, you will get pushed around, roughed up, maybe punched, whatever the case may be, and you'll be ready. Playing football prepares you and gives you a chance to see what it feels like getting hit hard, pushed, or jumped on.

Well, one day, Darius was that young kid looking in the eyes of the bull. Bam! He went down! Not moving as the seconds passed, we started running toward him on the opposite side of the field. We saw him move a little bit, and by the time we got there, he was able to stand up! "See ya!" Mom said, "That's the end of that!"

After we had enrolled him in private school, he started working us to play football again. He wanted to contribute to building a strong team for the school. He hadn't played since he was about ten years old, but it was a small school, so they needed players since several seniors who were an integral part of the team had just graduated. A good friend of mine, a captain in the sheriff's office and bodyguard, Mark Baker, happened to be one of the football coaches. He approached us about Darius joining the team.

Besides that, he is my son, after all, so he could be pretty convincing when he had his mind set on something. I remember that my mom would put her fingers in her ears and say, "I don't want to hear it. No, no. I know you're going to talk me into something again!" Darius also has that talent. We caved, and he ended up joining the team. It's been great so far, and the team has done amazingly well. And believe it or not, it's time to look at colleges.

Darius has been a straight A student his entire life as well, as is his sister. We consider ourselves so fortunate to have such a well-rounded, tall (6′1″), handsome, and talented sixteen-year-old son. We couldn't have asked for more. They grow up so quickly! I can't believe that he is now driving, has his own car, and is so rapidly becoming a man.

For music, everyone asks me if I've involved him in that. I walked into his room a couple of weeks ago, and he had about six songs recorded. He did everything on the tracks: production, vocals, lyrics, and all the rest. I couldn't believe it! I had bought him Logic Pro music software, which I've used for years, a computer, pro speakers, a nice microphone for his birthday, and some equipment and tools to try to get him interested. I also had him sing background vocals on several recordings of mine. He has incredible pitch and learns parts on a dime, a talent he had at a very young. I have no idea how he got to this level of proficiency right under my nose and in such a short time, but he got there and improves every day.

My children have lived a blessed life and thankfully, they have not encountered racism. They've been totally accepted by all races and looked up to as leaders at times. I believe this is because of who they are—their talents, intelligence, humor, kindness, manners, and ability to make friends. I'm so proud of both of them, and I am so grateful to my spirits for being so generous as to have chosen us to be graced with these gems.

One day, I received a surprise phone call from Lasse Hallberg, one of the heads of Rubicon and the executive producer of *Lilyhammer*, whom I had negotiated with for Steven back in the Renegade days.

Lasse told me that *Lilyhammer* was coming to an end and that he was no longer with the company, but he remembered and admired my business sense in our negotiations. He informed me of another TV show he was producing called *Kanal Valen*. It starred a very talented Norwegian impersonator, Kristian Valen, who I had met before through another friend of mine, Carina Ryerson. He informed me that he wanted to add an American flavor to the show and shoot it in L.A. He had some ideas to cast Hollywood actors and internationally known musical artists. He offered me the chance to executive-produce the show. It was a big-budget series with a great team and crew, being aired by SBS Discovery. I told him I was in.

I had been very involved in producing several TV shows before this, including the ABC/ESPN New Year's Eve show I did at Renegade, which was really successful. But for that, I was barely credited, so this would actually be my first executive-producing role for a major TV show. It was exciting!

I hired some people, gathered the stars, and organized everything with Lasse in Norway to film in Los Angeles in Kristian Valen's house, a beautiful multimillion-dollar home way up in the Hollywood Hills. It overlooked the city with all-glass doors and windows as a backdrop and the city lights behind that. It was a perfect location.

The entire Norwegian film crew—including the stylist and the woman we had as our liaison in L.A.—were fantastic, efficient, and totally professional. Accomodating the various guests, making all the arrangements, hair, makeup, transport, call times, and all else involved, were all on point.

The guests that I brought in were Sharon Stone, William Shatner, Steven Bauer (*Scarface*), Esai Morales (*La Bamba*), and Lita Ford (the Runaways) to perform a duet with him where Kristian did an incredible impersonation of Ozzy Osbourne. I was also an interviewed guest and performed a duet with Kristian. So this was a triple role for me!

The reactions from some of the guests were particularly comical—especially Sharon Stone and William Shatner! They'd enter the mansion and be introduced to the entire crew, but I was saved for last. Our producer would then say, "Now we'd like you to meet our executive producer!" I'd come down the stairs rocked out with one of my Western hats, over-the-top shoes, and whatever garb I felt like sporting that day.

When Sharon first saw me, she looked as if she was in shock! She made some comment about my shoes or something to that effect and maintained her cool, but she was obviously surprised that I'd brought her in and would be the boss that day.

When William Shatner arrived, he sat down and waited as I approached, then uttered, "How the hell did you get this gig?" I grinned and said, "Nice to meet you too! Well, it's time to get to work," then got the crew in place to start. He turned out to be a nice guy. He heard me speaking French to someone and said, "You speak French?" I told him yes, and he proceeded to tell me in French that he was from Canada. He was also a rocker, which I didn't know. We spoke and laughed for a while, and that broke the ice. We made him comfortable, prepared him for the interview, and started to film.

It was obvious that they were both surprised to see a Black guy—a rock 'n' roller, no less—running this ship with a full Scandinavian crew! It was something I actually wouldn't have thought twice about, until they brought it to my attention. But once everything started going and ran like clockwork, they quickly changed their tune and were very cool. I admired them both! This plays well into my theory on the importance of "setting examples."

Even the live recording of the duets, which can be difficult, went smoothly. After the show aired, Lita's song "If I Close My Eyes" (the duet with Ozzy) jumped up to number five on the Norwegian charts, and the new version I produced has since reached a surprising seventeen million views on YouTube and is poised to surpass the original version she did with Ozzy, which, as I write, is at eighteen million. I also wrote with Lita. We had been seeing each other around for years and were suddenly running into each other more often, so we got together. We worked for a period of time in my studio in Florida. She flew in a couple of times and spent a few days, and I flew out once to the studio where she was working owned by her manager.

Norway was a country where I had not spent a lot of time. It's a gorgeous country with scenery to die for. The fjords are spectacular. Marcus and I shot a pilot for our television series there, where he and I would travel around the world as Supermodel and Rockstar who are best friends, exploring unique places and sharing adventures. An adventure it most definitely was! We drove a classic Mustang through the mountains all the way up to the glaciers. We met Norwegian celebrities like the world champion triathlon winner. We had some unique experiences, and it was breathtaking, to say the least.

While I was at Renegade, however, Steven and I did do some work with some international bands, including a female group, the Cocktail Slippers, who came from Norway. We went over there to produce an album for them and to try to get the Norwegian radio and TV to support their own act. It's a strange concept in Europe at times, that acts that succeed in other countries or in the US are rarely supported by their own country and sometimes actively shunned. When they get the success, then the country wants to reap the benefits.

We went as far as discussing this with the minister of culture, Trond Giske. We had met him long before this and had become friends, so when we realized that the band was getting no support from radio in Norway (or anywhere else in the country, for that matter), we decided to discuss it with Trond.

As I previously mentioned, my view remained the same. Since he was the minister of culture funding the radio stations and hiring the programmers, he should inform them that there was a well-known American entertainment company, with its own radio network, willing to support this Norwegian artist and invest a fair amount of money into marketing and promotion, including tour support. In addition, we felt that if they wanted success for their Norwegian artist, they should support the act and play the record on radio.

He replied that this was impossible. In Norway, you don't control people who were hired to do a particular job, even if you have the power and outrank them. They have to decide on their own if they like the song or not.

I replied, "But they don't have enough information to make an educated decision, as you're working toward a global goal to enable Norway to be known again as an international exporter of music, which last happened with A-ha in the '80s! Your neighbor, Sweden, has been achieving this for many years." I continued, "We don't play that in America. If someone owns a radio station or network, and that owner calls the station to get a record played, it usually gets done."

We told him, "If you don't give your girls a little support over here, there's not much we can do or are willing to do."

He stood fast and truly felt he couldn't do anything to persuade or even explain the big picture to the stations. I had a hard time understanding the concept that this was not even open to discussion, owing to that famous principle I mentioned before, *Janteloven*, (Law of Jante), which at its simplest describes the way that Norwegians (and in fact, other Scandinavians too) behave: putting society ahead of the individual and not boasting about individual accomplishments. Here are a few of the rules attached to this law:

"You are not to think you are anything special."

"You are not to think you are more important than anyone else."

"You are not to think you are good at anything."

"You are not to think anyone can teach you anything."

There are several other rules connected to *Janteloven*, and this has dictated behavior in Scandinavia for many, many years.

We of course continued working with the band and helped them to move forward as best we could. During my trips back and forth, I had met a guy named Borge Johansson, an ambitious fellow who had some ideas for business partnerships. He reached out one day and told me of a brand called City of Friends, an animated children's property that housed three seasons of a popular kids' TV show and about forty books they had released so far in addition to some live shows and other interesting activities they were doing.

He asked me if I want to meet with them to discuss possibly working together and me coming on board. I really wasn't that interested in getting into yet another corporate-type business situation, but in this case, it sounded interesting, and it was in entertainment. They sent me some episodes to screen, which looked really great and were being distributed in a lot of countries, but they wanted help to expand and possibly bring in some partners.

After seeing the material, I agreed to a meeting, which was then set up by the company. I flew over and upon my arrival went to the hotel and freshened up. I was to take the day to recuperate, and we would meet the next day. They had planned to take me to the owner's summerhouse somewhere on the outskirts of Norway next to the sea. The funny thing is that everyone in Norway has a summerhouse, it appears, no matter who they are or what they do for work—they all have a summerhouse!

I had been told upon my arrival that on the first day there was to be no talk about business and that this day was reserved for us to get better acquainted with each other, enjoy some nonbusiness time, and so on. It was only the next day we could commence talks about our possible business together.

Well, this was an amazing summerhouse! Lots of glass, big rocks right next to the sea, and they had arranged a feast for me! They pulled out all the stops. We walked into a beautiful glass room, where you felt you were outside on this gorgeous sunny day. There was a long table all dressed in white and neatly organized with fancy dinnerware and silverware.

When we stepped outside to the deck, a chef came over and introduced himself. He had been hired specially to cook for me. He had fish on the grill and in close proximity stood a gigantic boat filled with ice, like an old Viking ship about twenty-feet wide and probably six-feet deep. It was filled with premium seafood, all kinds of lobsters, crabs, and shrimps, different fish salads, and condiments. It was really incredible, and I was so grateful that they would think to take this much time and effort to welcome me to Norway.

After everyone had taken their food, we all sat down for a wonderful meal, and we did really get to know each other better. I ate so much that I believe I fell asleep in the car on the way back to the hotel!

The three principals in the company were real estate developers, restaurant owners, astute and recognized businessmen in the Norwegian community: Jan Olav Jørgensen, Bjørn Ostbø, and Harold Sletten. They had acquired this company from the creator and controlled it at this point.

The meeting was set for early morning the next day, and everyone arrived in a business head, much different than the day before. They had a very long table—very corporate—where all the principals sat, and several other employees joined all on one side while Borge and I were on the other side. It was time to make my pitch and clarify that after what I had seen, I could help them to move things along further. After hearing what I had to say, they took a moment, looked at me and said, "Welcome to the company."

I was then hired as the US CEO for the company. I worked with them for a year or so to help expand their business initiatives. A Netflix deal was struck, and at that point, I decided once again to go back to more creative work and my own initiatives.

I started getting invited to various KISS-themed events that would feature previous KISS collaborators and members, as there were not that many who were a part of KISSTORY. We'd be available for meet-and-greets, photos, autographs. We'd sell merchandise and would usually perform a few songs. As I was one of the very few cowriters and bass players who played on numerous KISS songs and albums, these invitations became more frequent—New York / New Jersey, Indianapolis, Finland, Florida, and Sweden.

Of course, you meet a lot of people at these events, and one of them was one of my favorite hosts and rock music critics, Eddie Trunk. I ran into him and Doug Pinnick, and Eddie told me he was a big fan of my first album, *Drums Along the Mohawk*. I was honored and also knew that he's one not to mince words when it comes to his opinions about bands or their music. For some reason, I ran into him very often after that, and we became friends. I had the opportunity to do some great interviews with him, and I remained very flattered and thankful that he's always had good things to say about me.

For one of my tours and by invitation from Jack Frost, a great guitarist I added to my band, we rehearsed at a School of Rock in New Jersey that Jack was managing at the time. I used their all-star band to open for me at a warm-up show of mine, and it seems the word got out to the CEO, Rob Price. He was happy that I chose to do this and with the press it garnered, so he came out to L.A., where I was headlining a show and inducting Max Norman, the famed producer of Ozzy Osbourne and Megadeth, into the Metal Hall of Fame. We took photos, met, and discussed the irony of the start of my career being in, and heading up, essentially a school of rock as a teenager.

The Hall of Fame also showed an informative film highlighting the importance of bands working with brands called Band Versus Brand, directed by metal afficianado Bob Nalbandian, where I was a featured interviewee. I was actually promised an induction into the Metal Hall Of Fame two years in a row, but both years, my induction was pulled a couple of months before the ceremony for some obscure reason.

Thankfully, the years and times that I spent doing the corporate business ventures were not a waste, and every experience for me was a learning experience that prepared me for things to come. I've always believed that there is something to be taken from every situation and everyone you meet, regardless of who they are or what they do. Be it a homeless person, a cab driver, someone's assistant, some guy who stops me walking my dog, or a CEO of one of the biggest corporations in the world.

In keeping with my resolution, no matter what happens in a deal, I usually make money from it, and sometimes much to the other person's surprise, as they never know what's coming and when. This I learned from many years of suffering. You develop a shell like a turtle, especially growing up as a New Yorker. New York is a special kind of place, a melting pot of immigrants going back generations, who came here and had to learn the streets and how to survive. They created the streets and the rules that go with them.

There are rules that you need to abide by—loyalty, honor, respect, and keeping your word. For those who come here thinking that just money and education prevails, they oftentimes end up back where they came from with their asses kicked and nothing left after going a few rounds in NYC.

I have learned from everyone. I learned important lessons from the Hells Angels, the Mafia, and other streetwise folk. I spent a fair amount of time on the streets when it all began, and my life has run the gamut. I've had absolutely nothing at times, fighting for lunch money as a child daily to sleeping in boxes with roaches and rats climbing over me at night, and I've slept in the seediest motels imaginable, scraping the floors for coins when the maids opened the doors to clean, just to buy one corn muffin a day for dinner—raging war with mice that were trying to get that corn muffin before I did!

I've been beat up by police with my face in the snow and officers piled up on me taking swings at me with nightsticks, much like the many instances of police brutality today. I've been jailed and other indignities I dare not mention.

At the same time, I've experienced and led the most luxurious of lives imaginable, sharing meals with royalty, private planes, the Concord, MGM Grand Air, airport greeters and many other first-class perks that even some billionaires have not experienced. I won't say I've seen and experienced it all, but I've definitely experienced my fair share.

One day when I was back in L.A. for some meetings, I had lunch with one of my good friends, Lonnie Burstein, a great guy I met while I was running Renegade. He was the head honcho over at the production company Debmar-Mercury. They produced some great TV shows, including *The Wendy Williams Show*, which just so happened to be one of the top-rated US shows at the time. The possibility of my appearing on that show came up in our conversation, and when I got back to Florida, I received a call from Siobhan Schanda, who was the head of talent. She had previously worked with Ellen DeGeneres and was brought in to secure more A-list talent for *The Wendy Williams Show*.

She introduced herself and went on to say that Lonnie mentioned I might be interested in appearing. She sounded excited and said, "We'd be honored to have you on as a guest. What days would work for you?"

I knew the show focused more on pop artists like Jennifer Lopez, P. Diddy, and other chart-toppers, and the closest guests invited that even resembled rock 'n' roll were Michael Bolton and Lenny Kravitz, both friends of mine. She just asked that I didn't choose a fast, loud punk or hard rock song, so as not to blow out the audience's eardrums!

Originally, I wanted to do a full band and had reached out to friends of mine, Frank Ferrer and Richard Fortus from Guns N' Roses. We had been speaking about playing together, jamming, or doing something for quite a while, and thought this might be a great opportunity to do that. Believe it or not, very few rock artists, no matter how big they are, ever get the opportunity to appear on major network TV shows.

They were happy I asked them and would have loved to do it, but unfortunately, there was a scheduling conflict. It was a shame because I wanted to put together a real killer band (and these guys are the shit) to kick some rock 'n' roll ass on mainstream television!

After speaking with Siobhan again, she suggested I do the show acoustically alone or singing live to a track. I decided rather than using something I already had, I would rerecord "Standing on the Corner for Ya," Jimmy Iovine's favorite song on my Crown of Thorns album. I decided to do a scaled-down version with piano, orchestration, and choir-style vocals. I recorded the song alone, played all the instruments, and sang all the parts. They loved it!

It was a really early call time. I believe I had to get up at 4:00 AM. I was looking forward to this show, as it was major exposure. I had found a clothing designer locally in Florida and came up with a great black leather-ish suit to wear for the performance. Come the day of the show, I decided to try the outfit on at about 4:30 AM, and I noticed some of the seams were starting to come apart! I couldn't believe it! When I stood up, more started falling apart to the point where I realized I could not wear that outfit. I was seriously bummed, but luckily, I always travel with suitcases worth of clothes and shoes just in case anything comes up.

The performance and interview went well, and it aired during Christmas break, which was optimum for viewership. Wendy pointed out that when Wendy O. Williams, the lead singer of the Plasmatics, had passed, her phone rang off the hook from people thinking that it was her. She also mentioned that she was one of "those girls"—meaning she was secretly into our band, punk, and rock but was almost embarrassed at the time, as so many other Black fans were, since this was not what she "should" have been listening to as a Black woman. We hit it off and got along great on screen and behind the scenes.

Around the same time, a good friend of mine, Darren Dewis, and his wonderful family (his brother Tod and their mom), who had been extremely supportive of my work for many, many years, had been trying to put me together with the guitar player from a Finnish band, Lordi. They were the winners of the Eurovision Song Contest and put Finland on the musical map. After four years of us communicating, I was invited to appear at the KISS event in Finland, so I took the opportunity to get in touch with Lordi's guitarist, Amen. We finally set up a writing session and went to work. I also wrote with and became close friends with a very talented Finnish rock artist, actress, and proficient martial artist, Jessica

Wolfe, on that trip, who was also a special guest of mine at Germany's Heat Festival, which I had recently headlined.

Lordi is an amazingly flamboyant band who dress up as monsters. They are never seen out of costume, and they have an incredible stage show. I was definitely curious about working with them. I walked into the room, met Amen, and we spent a little time getting to know each other. He then pulled out his guitar and started playing me some riffs. I immediately heard melodies, and we forged an instant connection. He said, "I've been trying to get a melody for this riff for years!"

We knocked it out. Then he played another great riff—and boom! Another one down. He had some great ideas, so it really flowed. We probably put down three songs in a half hour or so.

Then, Mr. Lordi, the lead singer and leader of the band, showed up. We said our hellos and quickly brought him up to speed. As we started playing ideas we had put down earlier, he was hearing parts and countermelodies, and before long we were at six or seven song ideas. It really felt natural. Although most of my writing sessions have for the most part gone quite well, there was some magic here; we just felt things similarly.

We came in the second day and worked on perfecting and adding parts to the initial ideas we had from the day before. At that point, Mr. Lordi mentioned a great plan they had for the next album. They wanted to record songs as if they would have been written and recorded in the past. They would record songs fitting for each fictitious period, using an appropriate engineer, microphones, instrumentation, and recording techniques to reproduce the sounds of that time.

So this would be assuming they'd had hits in years prior to their existence: 1983, 1986, and so on. They mentioned doing that for the year 1989, and my little noggin lit up!

"Hey guys, I got a song that Paul Stanley and I wrote in 1989 that I think would fit perfectly for your album," I said.

Now these guys are avid KISS fans, so the thought of having a song written by Paul Stanley and me on their album was exciting! I happened to have the song on my phone. Takeaway? Always be prepared!

I played them the song, and they loved it!

It turns out that it is one of the only songs cowritten by Paul Stanley that wasn't earmarked for one of his albums or for a KISS record. I rang up Paul and told him the good news: Lordi was planning on rerecording the song, and as it turns out, it would be the single!

That was definitely a pleasant surprise! They made a fantastic animated lyric video for the song. Shortly after its release, the album came out. It charted at number one in Finland and thirteen in Germany, the band's highest entry there. It also charted high in other countries, so we had a hit!

Pretty good fate for a song that had been lying in my drawer since 1989! Paul and I were both pleasantly surprised. Two songs, one I wrote with the band and the other with Paul Stanley, are included on their latest album. A historical release beating the world record for the most albums released—seven—simutaneaously by an artist or band. An incredible accomplishment for Lordi!

My day-to-day life has been quite different down here in Florida, as compared to life in N.Y. or L.A. I have a recording studio in my house, where I can record pretty much anything, besides big orchestras and live drums. I do lots of virtual work with my partners in Norway, Finland, Sweden, Germany, Korea, and so on. Artists and producer partners of mine always love coming down here to the Florida sun! I'm still boat crazy after all these years, and I've collected some beautiful yachts. I record on the water at times, because it's great inspiration to be writing out in the deep blue sea with Rocky, my Great Dane assisting! I plan to take kids out to teach them about modern digital recording, as so much can be accomplished these days simply with an iPhone. Marine living has afforded me friends from different walks of life. Geoff O'Donohue, a longtime marina owner and yacht expert who knows very little about my business, has become a dear friend. I've always found it interesting to be able to have conversations on subjects outside of the music biz, and he's got tons of stories. Billy Zaccaria is another bud who comes from where I grew up on Long Island. We are a unique breed! He's a fun bloke and a blast to hang out with. He actually makes me feel like I'm back on Long Island with my original posse! Even some of my old "connected" friends pop up here and there, retired of course. I serve on a city council committee called Outreach. We meet with the mayor and help address needs and concerns of the community. We donate toys, Thanksgiving dinners, and Christmas gifts to the less fortunate, stage events, and commemorate individuals who have gone the extra mile to improve the community. I've always enjoyed being a part of these types of initiatives and lend my time whenever possible.

On the music front, Tony Catania remains a dear friend. He came to visit me once years ago, fell in love with the place, and he and his lovely lady Ilona packed up and moved right down! We work together whenever we can. For the most part, I have to travel to L.A., N.Y., or Europe for touring and collaborations, but I thankfully still manage to knock out a hit from here every few years. And the music biz is not too far. Doc McGhee, who I've known for a long time, and Gaby Hoffmann, manager, songwriter, and dear friend from the band Accept, are both nearby. Tim Rossi, a great guitarist from Blackfoot, is a bud of mine and joins me on the road sometimes. Stet Howland from W.A.S.P., Patrick Johansson, who's worked with Yngwie Malmsteen, and some other top-notch players and industry luminaries also reside close by.

So, folks ask me, what's next? Writing this book gave me a bit of a break, and COVID stopped touring dead in its tracks, but I plan to do more of it all. I'm getting back in the studio as we speak, contributing vocals to a well-known German Punk Band, Lustfinger, and continuing a couple number-one K-pop hits I've had recently. I also had a nice hit in China with a song I cowrote with Harry Sommerdahl, "Fashion Show," which was recently used for a popular Chinese TV series. You can also hear my voice on TV quite a few times a day here in the US, in the UK, and I believe now in much of the world, singing "Born to Be Wild" for the popular Procter & Gamble Pampers TV commercial.

I'll be releasing new music and touring more starting spring of 2022. Sweden Rock is a major festival coming up this summer, and I'll be there. I'll always stay as busy as I can, so stay tuned, as this is what I was born to do!

21

FAMILY

MY WIFE, SUSANNE, whom I met in that famous nightclub Stringfellows in London, is a beautiful, very intelligent, practical, and resourceful woman. She has been a wonderful mom to our children, especially considering that she never intended to have children in the first place.

She's a talented photographer, web designer, web business CEO, videographer, digital artist, and more. She speaks five languages, one of which she learned to speak fluently in about two months (German), and has also been an integral part of my life in so many ways, including my business, Voodoo Island Entertainment Group. This woman can do pretty much anything well.

Having said that, this relationship, like most, has not always been a walk in the park! From the first day we met, we were at odds about certain things. You might remember her "I hate rock 'n' roll" interjection initially! There were other differences we shared at the start and over the years, but such is life. Relationships are never easy!

Undoubtedly, she has never been interested in other musicians or celebrities, which eliminated those possible issues so many other relationships in my business experience. All that said, "I hate rock 'n' roll" doesn't only apply to other bands; it also applies to *my* rock 'n' roll! It's not meant literally, as I'm sure she likes some songs here and there, but basically, it's not her cup of tea.

It's not easy to live with someone who has little interest in your music, who you are, or what you've accomplished. I guess it's not that different than family members or parents much of the time. Artists can be big babies and often need to be pampered, lifted up, made to feel important or special, among other things. That balances the many challenges you have to succumb to in this business to carry on, but that doesn't always sit well, nor is it obvious to all.

The Swedish philosophy on this is that everyone is the same, referencing once again the tradition of *Janteloven*! Yes, I agree that everyone is created equal, but they believe that whether you're a president, rock star, or world champion boxer, you don't deserve to be treated or respected any differently than the gardener or a thief boat mechanic. Now, I personally make every effort to treat everyone the same at the start, but like most of us, I do have a tendency to delineate without much thought the president, a boss, a famous inventor, or others who have reached a certain level of success or accomplishment.

That said, my having a number one record is about as exciting to Susanne as my dog taking a poop in the yard! Slightly exaggerated perhaps, but you get the idea! Now, that doesn't mean she hasn't done everything possible to help me with business, the kids, been loyal, or hasn't given me support. We've found ourselves at odds many a time, and she is Swedish! Remember, they did rid themselves of the minor issue of male dominance way back in the sixties. The women claimed the role, which was actually accepted culturally as far back as then, and all the respect went right along with it!

The men surrendered and opted for a country populated with millions of women who now run the show. At the same time, the women did forgo those luxuries and perks that women customarily enjoy in the rest of the world, including gentlemanly gestures like opening the door for them, paying for their dinner, going to work, and paying the household bills, buying them jewelry, cars, and other presents,

Now picture this, when a Swedish couple is out to dinner and the bill arrives, you may see the man leaned back in his chair with his arms crossed, lips puckered as if to say, "You better take out your wallet biatch, cause it's all you, baby! Oh, and open the door for me while you're at it," as they're leaving the establishment. Or when planning a family vacation, she has to hope she'll be invited, unless she's paying for herself! Now, this is a general observation and of course not everyone is the same, nor do they all have the same philosophy—but most do!

I remember being at a Swedish beach a few years ago, and I watched a pregnant woman getting out of her car, packing a baby stroller—so packed that you could barely roll it on flat ground—but in this case, it had to go over a big sand dune to make it to the beach, which was nearly a quarter of a mile away. Now, the husband was nearby, about ten feet away looking at his phone while she's preparing this overloaded stroller and beach basket with kid in hand to take the journey above the sand dune and to their final destination, the beach, which to me, looking at that load, was quite the trek.

Everyone with me didn't pay much attention, as they were used to this, but I stopped and started watching to see what was going to happen, thinking this guy is going to help her any minute now, but he didn't. She started pulling that wagon with all her might, moving a foot at a time, while the guy walked beside her still looking at his phone. When I realized that he had no intention of helping her, I had to run over and assist. People looked at me strangely, and the guy just moved farther away to look at his phone. So that's an indication of where things are at over there and the cultural differences between our societies.

Now, as Eddie Murphy so eloquently put it in his hit comedy show *Raw*, when he was discussing Oom Foo Foo—for those who haven't seen it, he was describing the woman that he would go find in Africa, butt naked on a zebra with no assets, money, or expectations. This is because he was tired of certain expectations from American women. But as he said, and this totally applies, do not bring your nice sweet bush bitch that you find in Africa to America, because the women here will throw a monkey wrench in your whole program!

So as a Swede, not only will she want to be the boss, a right that has already been claimed in her home country, she will also want all the perks that American women want! Therein lies the discrepancy. . . .

Now, I must admit that I have been a fan of Eddie Murphy's *Raw* film for years, and my friends and I have taken many a saying from that film and laughed our asses off many a night! He hit so many things on the nail. I can vividly remember when it came out, it caused quite the stir in the US. Girls were wondering if what he said was true or not, and guys were wondering if their wives were doing what he said! It was hilarious, but eye opening.

I am of Haitian descent; I am a bit macho and believe that women and men are not meant to be the same and that each have certain roles in society, roles that each may be better suited for. I feel that if those lines are blurred too much, social chaos can erupt. My thinking is much in line with that of Italians, French, Spanish, Japanese, and other cultures where men don't enjoy being bossed around or disrespected! This has been an ongoing problem with Swedish or, even speaking broadly, Scandinavian women and Latin men! Now, I'm not saying that every case is the same, as I do know one or two Swedish/Latin couples who have survived this predicament!

Despite these challenges, we've managed to weather through it, making this, by far, the longest marriage or relationship I've ever had! Having children plays a big part in this, as it's not just about me anymore. My hits, my desires, my tours—that all takes a backseat now, and it's about the children, what they need, and what's best for them. If you choose to be a parent, I believe you accept the fact that you're now destined to fulfill your true purpose in life. Which, going back to before all this "gravy" (as I call it) was brought into our lives, was the following: you were born, yes, all equally, as we all have the same basic purpose—to find a mate, procreate, and die. Everything else you do is extra, "gravy." Your children take over to fulfill the same task, and so on and so forth.

If our world did not progress in many ways for the next thousand years—meaning, no iPhone 14 and 15, taller buildings, more or new designer clothes, a better-looking Corvette, fancier and more expensive homes, apartments or a plethora of other man-created additions and developments, with many just rooted in self-indulgence, it would make absolutely no difference when it comes to our basic purpose, which is simply as I stated above. Now, I know that this can evolve into a much deeper conversation, so I won't carry on any further!

After losing our beloved rottweiler, Sasha, at thirteen years old after enduring two bouts of cancer and diabetes, we found our new puppy rottweiler. She was much different than Sasha, having a lot more energy as compared to Sasha as a pup, who always had a more laid-back attitude.

Kiki was a gorgeous female standing taller than most rottweilers and looking more like a male of the breed. She, like Sasha, came from excellent bloodlines and world champion fathers.

Kiki was very opinionated, and it took a while for her to understand who was the boss. Darius was a little older at this point, but Izabel was just a toddler. She was great with the kids and a great addition to the family. She was also a ferocious guard dog when she needed to be.

Now, at the same time, she was extremely loving and did the goofiest things. She had her own Instagram site with thousands of views, and she was featured on the front cover of the Southwest Florida newspaper *Florida Weekly*. Susanne had shot a really cool photograph of Kiki doing "peekaboo." She'd lie completely on her back putting her paws together and trying to hide her eyes, which was very unusual for a rottweiler. The magazine was having a competition and loved the photograph, so out of thousands and thousands of submissions, it won first place and the front cover.

Kiki unfortunately also battled cancer when she got older, and more than once. But this time, it was just not possible to save her. Our last days with her were horrible. She passed away on May 7, 2019, which was an incredibly sad day for all of us. The house felt like a morgue to me after her passing. Everyone was sad, and everywhere you looked, you were reminded of her. I'm sure many of you have dogs, and you know that feeling when you go to the fridge and your mind is so accustomed to her showing up that you start to imagine she's there, everywhere, but she's not. It was really affecting the family vibe, and the air in the house was a little too thick for my taste. Susanne, however, did not want another dog—at least not yet.

My objective in the beginning was to breed our rottweilers so that the kids could experience them having puppies and have the chance to hold them when they were first born, and then take care of those puppies and witness the beauty of procreation. But this would never come to pass.

I had already started secretly looking at other rottweilers by looking for a rescue. I had been to some shelters, and it was a really sad and demoralizing experience. Though I think it's amazing, the craze I've noticed here at home and around the world of people taking such a passionate interest in rescues. You wouldn't believe the amount of people I run into who tell me they've got four or five rescues at home! I've always wanted a Great Dane. They were seemingly impossible to find as a rescue or to even purchase; there appeared to be none available in Florida. At last, I found one place that housed rescued Great Danes for adoption on the East Coast of Florida.

I called, and the owner told me that since she had a fairly new establishment, even though she loved the photos I sent her of the house and yard and believed it would be a good home for the dog, she wasn't willing to send a dog across the state in case something went wrong. She did say, however, that she had a friend who was selling Great Danes from a recent litter—a private breeder. I immediately called her up and made arrangements to come by. When I arrived, I saw these cute black and white Great Dane puppies. There were actually three, but a buyer was taking one away. She had a male and female remaining. I (or we) had never had a male dog before, except for the brief time I had with a male Doberman in New York. So I just wasn't sure. I finally decided on the male, and as we were getting everything together, the woman said, "I only have one left, and I'll give you a better deal if you take both of them."

I knew this was a crazy thought. I was thinking that Susanne was going to lose her mind, but the kids would be super excited. I leaned toward the latter and took both!

I was visiting my cousin, Nathalie Brunet, at the time and I told her what I was doing. She thought I was definitely out of my mind and that, yes, the wife would kill me!

I headed home, called Darius and told him I'd pick him up from school with a surprise. When I got there, he saw the two dogs and couldn't believe it. He jumped in the car excited but a little apprehensive. Darius has always been a sensitive boy, and I felt that he was still thinking about Kiki.

I called the house and asked Izabel to meet me outside so we could all together surprise Susanne with the puppies. I came with these four-month-old Great Dane puppies running into the house full of energy! She was extremely pissed off, and we fought about it for days! I wasn't necessarily intending to keep both of the puppies, but I just didn't want to leave the other one there alone. I thought I'd figure it out and maybe find someone around us who might want her.

So at least the three of us enjoyed the pups for a day. We named them Rocky and Rosie. Then all of a sudden, they both started getting lethargic, just lying down with no puppy energy, and we, of course, wondered what was going on. They were throwing up pieces of metal, plastic, half a collar—you name it, it was coming out of them.

The vets were closed, and we figured we'd give it a day to see if they'd feel better after throwing up all that stuff. Two days later, before we could take them to the vet, Rosie died! It was devastating, even though we'd had her for such a short time. I ran with Rocky to the vet as soon as they opened. A surgery clinic did some tests and assessed that he had parvo. Rosie must have had the same but just further along. This disease is so lethal that it will kill a dog within days. They offered a treatment plan including a week in the hospital, and we were a bit unclear about what they'd really do as they didn't seem too confident. We were also apprehensive because he wouldn't be supervised at night. It didn't feel right, so we went to our usual vet instead.

They had been really great with Kiki, but they also could not supervise at night, so I decided to get all the medicine, prescription bags of fluid, baby food, and whatever else necessary to try and save his life myself. He lay on the couch incapacitated, just looking at me with those sad eyes. He would drink a bit of water, and I was trying to spoon-feed him, but he could barely move. He'd hold the water bowl with his chin as tight as his weak body would allow when he didn't want me to take the water away.

I gave him antibiotics and other medicines, as well as bags of fluid intravenously every three hours, day and night! It turns out the key was to keep him hydrated, no matter what. That would keep him alive while the disease ran its course and the medicine was doing its thing.

I slept on the couch with him for days. Susanne and the kids would come in and help sometimes as I was passing out on the couch from no sleep. Susanne was warming up to him by now. This went on for days with no sign of recovery.

I was determined not to let this dog die! Suddenly, about the fifth day, I woke up and saw him clamber off the couch himself and slowly go to his water bowl. I started jumping up and down like a kid at Christmas. His pulling through definitely earned him the name Rocky. He was a true fighter!

This was the start of his recovery, and in about a week, we started to see his real personality. Those TV shows like *Marmaduke* and *Scooby Doo*, which depict Great Danes, are very accurate. They are goofy comedians—loving, loyal, and smart, but can be spooked easily, at least at the beginning. This changes with time as they start to learn what everything is and feel more comfortable in their fast-growing bodies. I've never seen anything grow so fast, right before your eyes!

He became the focus of attention in our home and really helped the family by being the focus, which was a healthy distraction from grieving over Kiki. It was as if this dog was psychic, a spirit sent down—which he may well be, knowing my family! He learned the sea life early on as he spent much of his life on the boat, and he has such an amazing temperament. He gets along well with my daughter's guinea pig, Bella, and he's a registered service dog trained in case of an emergency. He's been a wonderful companion to me as he follows me around like a shadow and has also been great with the entire family.

My parents were surprised that the rambunctious one not only ended up with the many music accolades I managed to attain but became a corporate CEO, dealing with the world's most powerful corporations despite never going to college. But my dad felt that by throwing me out early on to make my own way, he was giving me the best education I could receive. I remember watching a TV show where a Harvard graduate and a Brooklyn high school dropout competed to complete a certain business project—the street-smart guy won hands down.

Now, I don't discourage education by any means and will continue to help my children receive the best education possible. As a matter of fact, my son Darius has invites to Harvard and some other top schools as I write this. But should one of his or my daughter's talents reveal itself and seem undeniable, I will support and encourage them to pursue that.

My point is that the world has changed significantly, and half of the richest people in the world never went to or finished college: Richard Branson, Mark Zuckerberg, Steve Jobs, Ralph Lauren, and Henry Ford, to name a few. Not to mention many legendary musicians, artists, actors, athletes, and inventors, who have created most of what we hold dear in life every day. Whether it's accompanied by lots of money or not, many have succeeded in leaving behind an everlasting legacy using their God-given gifts. There are many ways to make a mark on this world, and it's up to you to decide what's most important to you and how you want to be remembered.

All that said, it's funny how things seldom work out as you plan. There's a lot of luck connected to success. I've heard people say that they make their own luck, which is naive and, simply by definition, impossible. *Luck* means success or failure brought by chance and not as a result of one's actions or abilities. Someone winning the lottery, Stallone seeing my video at the perfect moment, an American music executive hearing a song by a European artist while on vacation and bringing it back to an American radio friend, leading to a major hit that changes that artist's life forever—that's all good luck. Getting ready to film a series you've been doing for years and dying in a car crash, as was the case for Paul Walker, or a sports celebrity who falls and is paralyzed for life—that's bad luck, which could never have been planned for.

Preparing yourself for opportunities, though, is another story. For that, I am a strong advocate. I don't believe you can control destiny, so I advise my children to always do their best, follow their instincts, be thankful for all good things that come their way, and stay humble! I am thankful every day for all I've been given and every day I live and breathe on this earth.

22

RACISM, ROLE MODELS, & SETTING EXAMPLES

To DEFEAT RACISM, there are many layers that need to be peeled—bit by bit and individual by individual. There's the history of each person—how they were educated and brought up. I believe upbringing plays a major role in whether a child grows up a racist. It's dependent on the environment and influences they are exposed to while growing up, be it at home, school, or otherwise. I disagree when some Black folks say that nothing has changed. Though some may perceive it that way, I just don't believe it's true. A Black president, rappers making millions of dollars chanting absolutely anything they please, our new vice president, Black athletes included in and dominating sports including tennis, golf, gymnastics, and many other fields—which, not long ago, would have never seemed attainable. Though I remain one of few Black rock artists, despite Jimi Hendrix's huge success.

I will say that I've never met nor did business with any other Black CEO, president, head of marketing, or other leader in all the companies I've encountered as an executive or as an artist. This could be partially due to my choosing to be fundamentally a rock artist, despite my mainstream pop hits. Nevertheless, I found this to be a bit disturbing, and I hope it will change.

Here's how the US works: after the Black Lives Matter protests of 2020, almost overnight, a large portion of the new commercials, TV series, and films began using interracial couples. I'm talking very conservative brands. I'm not fazed, as I've been in interracial relationships most of my life, long before this. But I can remember members of my family who would naively say, not that long ago, "Oh, you have no idea how your kids will suffer being mixed." I'd just look at them, knowing how wrong they were. My kids have not suffered at all, and they have been treated with full respect and have not encountered any racial issues, thankfully.

As more and more visual media depicts interracial couples as the example of a perfect family, I assure you that those types of relationships will now increase exponentially. I smirk when I imagine dinner conversations in a conservative White US household where interracial marriages are not yet commonplace or have been embraced. The blonde teenage daughter sits at the table and asks her dad, "Did you see that commercial, you know, where the interracial couple both had diarrhea? They took that product, and they're all relieved! Can I have a Black boyfriend, too, Daddy, please? Everyone's doing it! I wanna be as happy and relieved as they are!" Perhaps a silly joke, but not pointless. Mark my words, and let's see what the US will look like in ten years.

Now I'm not saying it's a bad thing. It's not much different than my appearing on those massive TV shows in the US with the Plasmatics—the only Black guy with a blond Mohawk. The next thing you know, it's gone from that to now, when a big part of the Black culture all proudly sport blond or different color Mohawks or express themselves in some other way with their hair as was never done in the past. I find that the US has always been very easily influenced by the TV, radio, media, press, and film, and of course, the Internet, and the same applies in other parts of the world.

My philosophy remains the same—Just Do You. If you fall in love with somebody White or Japanese or Indian or African, do it because it's what you want, not because a TV commercial tells you it's hip at the moment, like cigarettes were at one time.

Nevertheless, I am grateful to those companies for making an effort in perhaps a way that they feel is best to contribute, but I feel they miss the point. Not every Black or White person wants to be in an interracial relationship. I hope that companies will go further than that and perhaps put qualified minorities in the executive positions to make those decisions. Perhaps use a Black family for a Charmin commercial—after all, we do wipe our asses too! Black and other minority groups are screaming for equality, equal opportunities, the same pay for the same work, the same rights as anyone else, to be treated fairly in any situation—whether by police and judges or in the workplace, schools, and everyday life.

Those who achieve a certain level of success must realize how many eyes are really on them, and the significance of their actions and example. Everything right or wrong they do can influence millions. So they must respect their positions and always remember that they actually do carry part of the world on their shoulders. I always acknowledge and respect the importance of the role I've been granted, and always will.

Everyone, regardless of their own success, will be judged by the actions of another member of their race, creed, or any other affiliations. Role models are of vital importance to our society. Their actions, good or bad, resonate not only where they originate but throughout the entire world. The examples they set shall remain engrained in our youth for years to come.

Take Muhammad Ali, for example. Boy, did I love that man! With his wealth of confidence, intelligence, wit, and sheer talent, he was untouchable. But despite those qualities, I so feared his defeat, which we all knew was inevitable. I remember as a child being allowed to stay home from school the day he lost to Joe Frazier. I can also still remember the photographs from magazines that lined the shelves of Ali lying on the floor as it was yesterday.

The pain, sadness and anguish I felt about it is unexplainable. The Rumble in the Jungle, where he fought George Foreman in Kinshasa, Zaire, was surreal! The world believed he had no chance, but with absolutely no love lost, he was adored! Then he triumphed! One of the greatest moments in history, where the entire world, united, took to the streets screaming and yelling exuberantly! It was a sight to see.

Some days, when I've felt weak, indecisive, or a bit lost, I think back to the confidence and self-belief that this one human being could possess against all odds, and it makes anything I'm confronted with seem like a walk in the park. The roles Al Pacino portrayed in *The Godfather* and *Scarface* are also empowering—not because of the crimes, but because they were powerful men.

Simone Biles, beyond being the most decorated gymnast in the world, shined a light on mental health and the pressures associated with competing—all that is expected, being the celebrity that she has become. She highlighted that no matter how superhuman she or these athletes may appear, regardless of their astounding abilities and accomplishments, they are, in fact, humans who have their own issues to contend with. Her success will empower millions of young girls around the world, and her helpful words will influence and aid athletes for many years to come. She is truly a Black American hero.

I've always strived for and believed in integration's importance. I believe we must embrace other cultures and races, learn from one another, and use that acquired knowledge to move society forward, rather than languish in discord and dismay.

I spend a lot of time thinking about all the young African American, Spanish, Caribbean, or Japanese kids, and others, who have felt limited their entire lives because they thought they were not welcome trying or pursuing certain things in life that they at their core yearn or dream of achieving or becoming. Whether it be making music, becoming a record executive, promoter, race car driver, pro golfer, or corporate CEO. Whether it means doing what I did, running several simultaneous careers at the same time as a producer, songwriter, recording artist, music industry CEO, executive, or otherwise. Or, as someone recently brought to my attention, being the only Haitian or Black artist—possibly artist of any color—to ever achieve gold and/or platinum status across five different genres of music: pop, rock, R&B, punk, and most recently, K-pop. I hope those that come after me bear in mind that there have been others who worked on their behalf to make the world a better place to live, opening doors, paving new roads, and proving that change is possible. Following your dreams is possible, and working, living together in harmony is possible, and the way forward. Martin Luther King, Barack Obama, Joe Biden and Kamala Harris, Simone Biles, Tiger Woods, Muhammad Ali, Nelson Mandela, and so many others have worked, suffered, and sometimes even died on your behalf to set the path for a better future for our society.

We will have generations going forward where more is possible. Blacks producing rock bands, rock bands working with Black songwriters and musicians (or whatever nationality they might be), a new generation of youth who understand how to protect themselves and their business when it comes to legal matters, work ethic, setting examples, and so on.

Hopefully, the sacrifices I've made breaking down barriers, taking the impact and blows endured on my journey, will open doors and set precedents for others to flourish far beyond what I've had or will have the opportunity to accomplish in my lifetime and far beyond what you may believe you are capable of.

As a matter of fact, it already has, to a certain extent. As mentioned, I went from the only man seen with a blond Mohawk to now a society that has millions of them. It's not that the goal was, "Wow, let's see how many Mohawks we can get happening in America!" Not at all. It's about self-expression. It's about the fact that I would hope them seeing the Plasmatics and myself on all those big national TV shows would make people who felt limited watch and say, "Hey, there's no reason why I can't do this, too. I've wanted to do it, but I didn't feel comfortable. I felt people might laugh at me, I thought I might be looked at, you know, in a different way, but he did it, so now it's my turn."

This happens through musicians, artists, sports figures, and others. An entire society in pop culture has finally felt free enough to go against the roots, as I've been told so many times, that I believe it's a significant contribution in moving people of color forward. You have to first lose the fear, and you need the self-confidence to move forward and fight for things that you want, whether it be a job position that's way up at the top, that you think there's no chance you'd ever get, whether it's becoming a successful singer, rock singer, rock producer. Rather than walking around saying, "You know, that's not going to work. I'll probably never get that job or become that." That's not the way to think. This is what makes the world move forward and evolve, abolishing these limitations that have been placed upon us for so many years from racism, classism, and other socially created barriers. JUST DO YOU is what I say yet again.

Here's a funny story from when I was at a bar in Florida called the Blue Martini. I look up on stage and there's a Black guy with a blond Mohawk playing his ass off on guitar, singing, running around on people's tables, a great performer. I was sitting with a good friend of mine, Malcolm Bluemel, who previously had owned Planet Rock, the premier rock radio station in England. I didn't want to say anything, but Malcolm stopped the guy and said to him, "Do you know who this guy is?" At the time I was off season, and I had shaved my Mohawk. But Malcolm persisted, "That's Jean Beauvoir."

This kid freaked out. He could not believe that playing at Blue Martini in Naples he would meet me! He basically told me that his entire thing was modeled after me, and that he'd been a fan of my *Drums Along the Mohawk* for so many years. He was shaking when we were speaking.

It felt good. Another time, the Roots and Jimmy Fallon's guitarist, Captain Kirk, who is Black, was so humbly brought into my rehearsal room one day at Gibson Guitars NYC by the director Jim Felber, who was my endorsement contact. The Captain shared with all of us that he had seen an introduction video shown to incoming students at the school he was about to attend, where I had also attended. The video highlighted me as a school success story, as he put it, to inspire others. He thanked me and told me that I was the reason he came to believe that he could succeed and become a working, successful, and esteemed guitarist in any genre.

It's an extraordinary feeling when somebody either writes or tells you that you've changed their lives. I've had people say to me, "I was in the hospital, seeing little hope, depressed, and your lyrics, your songs gave me the strength to want to pull through. I thank you Mr. Beauvoir." Others have written or said, "You were the soundtrack of my life. Your album *Drums Along the Mohawk* or others made my childhood or teenage years all they were," or "When I met my wife, this is the song we played at our wedding, it's our song till now," or "I'm Black or White or something else, and I would have never started playing music if it wasn't for seeing you."

I've experienced so many examples of this nature that it's truly made me understand that I'm doing what I was meant to do. I've always felt that my purpose in life is to educate, integrate, break down barriers and make people believe in themselves, give them hope, power, and strength to move forward in life and to strive for what it is they feel they deserve—not to settle for what other people tell them they deserve.

I was witness—along with millions of other Americans and viewers from around the world—to that horrid day, May 25, 2020, when George Floyd was killed by a racist police officer. First, I send my deepest sympathies to the Floyd family for all they've had to witness and endure because of this horrific killing of their loved one. It's hard to imagine a greater pain. It's hard to believe that with the progress that has been made, this kind of atrocity could still happen.

This was an extremely alarming wake-up call, amplified around the world, showing the widespread injustice that still exists—mainly in the US, with George Floyd being one of several victims who were brought to light. I witnessed millions of people of all races marching in the streets. Children and teenagers taking a solid stand towards righteousness and the preservation of their future. It prompted unity despite a pandemic that was and is still killing millions. Yet masses chose to put their lives on the line to say ENOUGH IS ENOUGH!

George Floyd's passing turned a page in our society, which I pray will significantly change the thinking of many who may now choose to take a different path toward compassion, understanding, and equality for our future.

Here's a statement I wrote in the heat of the moment . . .

BLACK LIVES MATTER

Black lives absolutely matter and should do so equally, and we must build on the progress that has been made thus far.

There have been and still are so many who have made a mark, a difference, in the effort to change a mind-set, which has been so deeply ingrained in our society.

Many have put their lives on the line. . . .

I can attest and speak to this from very personal experiences, all I have endured, bad and good from both sides. . . .

My life's purpose from the age of twelve has been to bring the races together, break down color barriers, change the perceptions that so many unjustly adhere to. . . .

To live as one in unity, with mutual respect. . . . My scepter has been my music, where I share all I have to say with the world. . . .

From my time with the Plasmatics and up until today, my decision to introduce the blond Mohawk as a young Black punker was to make a point. A point, which was strongly solidified when the Plasmatics erupted all over US mainstream television . . .

To support individuality, having the confidence and belief in yourself to JUST DO YOU. I've preached self-respect, self-expression, individuality, and equality for all.

Being a rock 'n' roll performer, every time I get on that stage, what I see in front of me is beautiful harmony where none of these injustices exists. I dream of a world like this, people. . . .

I've witnessed a significant change throughout my many years in my chosen profession, but it hasn't been easy, and I damn well knew it wouldn't be. . . .

I've tasted the blood, literally and also metaphorically. It's a beautiful thing. . . .

We still have a long way to go, people, and it will take some time. If everyone does their part, and most people know what that part is, I believe we can attain significant change toward a harmonious, beautifully colorful world. . . .

With all my love and sincere gratitude to all of you who have been there for me throughout the years and showed me the appreciation and respect that you have. . . .

I thank you.

With Peace and Love,

Jean Beauvoir

ACKNOWLEDGMENTS

SUSANNE, I WANT TO THANK YOU, but can't thank you enough, my beautiful wife, for the countless hours, days, and months you spent helping me with this book! Your contributions, work ethic, discipline, patience, and love throughout the process was essential and so truly appreciated. Thank you!!!

To my amazing children, Darius and Izabel, I so love you both! To my wonderful four-legged companions through the years, Sasha and Kiki, RIP, and my buddy Rocky, who have stayed up many a night patiently watching me work! Also, Bella and Jake.

To my mom and dad for giving me "Breath of Life"!

To Rolf and Gertie Hultberg and the entire Hultberg family for your kindness, love, and welcoming me into your family!

To my sister, Malou Beauvoir, and her husband, Pierre Bastid, for all your love and support . . . Thank you!

My brother, Pierre Beauvoir, and his loving family, Max Beauvoir, Babette, Estelle, and Rachel, I hope you are all together resting in peace . . . I thank you for your spiritual guidance and keeping the Voodoo light shining. . . .

Daniel Beauvoir, Serge Beauvoir, Tit Raoul Beauvoir, and Comena; Nathalie, Yves, and Nancy Brunet, your families and all of my other relatives whom I perpetually pray for, wishing you all the strength, continued tenacity, and resilience to weather the never-ending storms, earthquakes, and other challenges you've had to endure throughout the years in Haiti.

To Kara Rota and Michelle Williams for seeing, understanding, and believing in my purpose, I so appreciate all your help, guidance, and patience throughout this process. . . . I thank you both, also Benjamin Krapohl and the entire staff at Chicago Review Press, for bringing my story to the world!

To John Ostroski, thank you so much my longtime friend for all your support and organizational skills lent to this project! Keep rockin'! Ian McCurdy, thank you for reconnecting John and me! To Stephen Armstrong, for getting this ball rolling and for your contributions . . . thanks a million!

To my incredible manager, the late Gary Kurfirst, thank you for believing in me and my vision when no one else did and beyond the shadow of a doubt. . . . I wish you peace and happiness wherever you may be. . . .

To my brilliant attorneys Paul Schindler, Stu Silfen, and Ralph DePalma, and my other talented representatives for helping me stay out of harm's way!

To my genius accountant, Jerry Eisner, I thank you so much for all your help and loving support!

To my talented bandmates, musicians, and singers who have supported me on stage and off, it's been my sincere pleasure to rock with you all!

To all the talented artists and bands I've worked with throughout my career . . . I thank you for the wonderful experiences we've shared and the opportunity to create magic!

To the journalists who have supported me, been honest, and stayed the course through thick and thin . . .

To my nearest and dearest friends for being there through joy, happiness, despair, and times of need . . .

To the women I've loved and who have loved me throughout my life . . . Thank you for putting up with me!

There are far too many others I've encountered throughout my journey who have played a pivotal role in my life story. . . . It's not possible to acknowledge you all individually. . . . You know who you are! I send you my deepest gratitude from the very bottom of my heart for your contributions. . . .

To my spirits, who have watched over me, guided me, and protected me throughout my life . . .

And to all my fans for being there, year after year, decade after decade . . . You have been and remain my reason to rock!